Image, Sound & Story

Image,

THE ART OF TELLING IN FILM

Sound

CHERRY POTTER

& Story

SECKER & WARBURG London

First published 1990
by Martin Secker & Warburg Limited
Michelin House,
81 Fulham Road,
London
SW3 6RB

A CIP catalogue record for this book
is available from the British Library.

ISBN (hardback)   0 436 38032 3
     (paperback) 0 436 38034 X

Photoset by Rowland Phototypesetting Limited
Bury St Edmunds, Suffolk
Printed and bound in Great Britain
by BPCC Hazell Books
Aylesbury, Bucks., Member of BPCC Limited

For Mary and Percy

Contents

Preface   1

Part One: Film in Microcosm   3

  Introduction   5
  1 From Montage to Story: *Persona*   8
  2 What's Going On Out There In The World?:
    Touch of Evil and *The Lacemaker*   23
  3 The Interior World: *Wild Strawberries, The Conformist*
    and *Kaos*   39
  4 Metaphors and Archetypes: *For a Few Dollars More*
    and *Kaos*   67

Part Two: The Macrocosm or the Whole Story   83

  Introduction: Questions of Structure   85
  1 The Beginning: *Midnight Cowboy* and *Viridiana*   92
  2 The Development: *Midnight Cowboy* and *Viridiana*   115
  3 The Ending: *Midnight Cowboy* and *Viridiana*   135
  4 Departures from the Classic Form   151
    1 The Disruption of a Genre: *Heaven's Gate*   154
    2 The Problem of the Woman Protagonist:
      Les Rendez-vous d'Anna   160
    3 The Classic Form and Feminine Disruption: *Mirror*   165
  5 *Persona* Revisited   170

Part Three: The Creative Process and Telling Your Own Stories   189

  Introduction: The Creative Process   191
  1 The Eight Pre-conditions for Creativity   196
  2 Generating and Gathering Material   200
    1 Free-writing   201

Contents

2 Image Gathering   206

3 Developing a Sense of Place   208

4 Research   212

3 Characterization and Dialogue   215

4 The First Draft and After   228

5 'And they all lived . . .'   238

Acknowledgements   241

Index   243

Preface

This is a book about the conceptual basis of film and what consti-
tutes film language. By conceptual basis I mean what is first formed
in the mind of the writer or film-maker; thoughts, ideas, images,
sounds, dreams, memories, fantasies, stories. This rich interplay is
the origin, inspiration and fertilization, the first stage of bringing
film stories into being. It is not intended to be an academic book, or
a theoretical book. My concern is entirely with the practical process
of creativity in relation to the film experience. Much of what you
will find here is based on material I have developed during my ten
years of experience teaching film-making in Britain, Europe and
Canada to both film students and film industry practitioners.

The book is divided into three parts. The first part focuses on film
language. I have explored short sequences, or microcosms, from
seven different feature films to reveal both how the unique language of film is used and how the conceptual and creative process
of the film-maker manifests itself in individual microcosms within
the whole. The seven different microcosms have been chosen
because they each focus on a different aspect of film language and
the creative process. This section is also about raising our sensibility
to film and, through exploring the unique language of film, developing our capacity to perceive, feel and become aware of the
richness and breadth of the film experience.

The second part is devoted to storytelling. Here I have explored
whole films, or macrocosms, to see how the ideas behind the film
reveal themselves in the structural dynamics of the whole. In this
section I also consider the nature of classic narrative structure and
the implications of subverting or departing from the form, both
from the point of view of the film-maker and the audience.

The third part is an exploration of the creative process itself. How
do we get in touch with the stories we have to tell? How do ideas,

images, characters, sequences, come into being? How do we develop methods of working both with our conscious and unconscious minds? How do we get the material out of our heads and on to paper, and then shape it, develop it and structure it, finally to produce a screenplay ready for the film production process to begin?

Film is both a hybrid of all other art forms and a unique language in its own right. As such it is a universal medium and one of the most profound art forms of our times with a central role to play in twentieth-century cultural life. But it is also a medium of mass entertainment which means that a large area of the film industry is solely concerned with commercial values and the making of money.

The history of all art forms involves a degree of conflict between cultural and commercial values. Film production is the most expensive of all art forms and we are living in an era that appears to place paramount priority on commercialism. Consequently those film-makers who want to make films which can stand alongside the great works of literature, theatre, music and painting in the cultural development of humanity, experience their work as increasingly devalued and under threat, in spite of the fact that many of the greatest 'art' films, including many of the films I have explored in this book, have also made fair amounts of money. While it is undoubtedly true that artistically excellent films rarely make as much money as the legendary blockbusters, on the other hand they rarely lose as much money either. But whatever the reason, the result is that those of us concerned with the cultural role of film are increasingly beginning to feel like an endangered species.

My primary motivation for writing this book is to make some contribution towards ensuring the survival of film as an art form. Ensuring the survival of any species is rarely simply a question of finance. It means communicating, telling, teaching and so developing an understanding of the intrinsic nature of the species, in our case film, and hence what is required to give it meaning and life. Most importantly, that is what this book is about.

In examining and discussing the films in this book, I have chosen to describe what actually happens on the screen, rather than using the original screenplays which, in many cases, would not include some of the elements of the film which we are specifically interested in. Many of the screenplays have been published and are, of course, interesting in their own right.

One FILM IN MICROCOSM

Introduction

We have all been exposed to so much film drama, often of indifferent quality, on our TV sets, that we have become over-familiar with and de-sensitized to the medium. We are also in danger of thinking of film simply in terms of linear stories which function primarily at the level of superficial excitement, or what is going to happen next? When that question is answered there is little more to think about and the film is quickly forgotten. This form of the medium is like a drug and encourages a passive conformity in the viewer. But, because of its prevalence, we have learnt many bad habits from it, almost by osmosis.

To combat this we need to re-examine the very basics of film language, and consider the medium as if we have never experienced it before. This will be the first step in raising our sensibility to film.

Sensibility means the ability to perceive or feel, the capacity for responding to emotion, the capacity for responding to aesthetic stimuli, discernment, awareness, emotional or moral feeling. Developing the capacity to perceive, feel and become aware of the richness and the breadth of the language of film will both enhance our experience of viewing films and, if we also want to be a part of the film-making process, is a vital first stage in the creative process.

The best way to begin raising our sensibility to film, while at the same time learning the language of film, is to examine the film microcosm and the film moments within it.

A microcosm is a miniature representation of a larger whole, with the essence of the larger whole somehow encapsulated in the miniature version. My dictionary uses the examples of man epitomizing the universe. And it is often noted how similar the atom, with its nucleus and circling electrons, is to the solar system itself – the ultimate microcosm. There is something profound and quite magical about a microcosm because it implies the infinite.

Many feature films can be seen, in themselves, as microcosms. But the film microcosms I am referring to here are the component sequences, usually about eight to twelve of them, which make up the whole film. (One of the things which distinguishes great films from the run-of-the-mill is how the sequences also frequently function as miniature versions of the whole.) Within these sequences, we will examine the film-maker's use of image and sound, the essential ingredients of film language.

'The primary factor in film is the image, the secondary factor is the sound, the dialogue, and the tension between these two creates the third dimension.'   INGMAR BERGMAN*

By his use of 'the third dimension' here, Bergman is suggesting far more than creating something that is life-like, or an imitation of life, he is talking about how the relationship between image and sound, the two basic ingredients of film language, can combine together, like some sort of magical, alchemical transformation, to transcend our everyday mundane assumptions about space and time and create something closer to the essence of life.

And that's exciting! It suggests throwing off a heavy weight, rising up, experiencing an exhilaration which creates vitality and energy – although for much of the time, especially at the writing stage, the creative work itself can feel like a long trudge across hard terrain. The fascination with this magical aspect of the film experience is what makes us want to see films and to make films – it's this that motivates our creativity.

Note how Bergman gave image the primary importance and the sound and the dialogue secondary importance. By this he is not saying that the dialogue is not important, because of course it is. But he is saying that it doesn't lie at the heart of the magic of the film experience, it isn't intrinsic to the basic language of film.

Most of the sequences I have chosen to explore have a bare minimum of dialogue. This is to enable us to focus primarily on what and how the images and sounds are communicating to us. The relationship between the film-maker and us, via the film, is of course very complex. First, we must bear in mind that most of what

---

*Quoted by John Simon, *Ingmar Bergman Directs* (Harcourt Brace Jovanovich, 1972) p. 308

we see and hear on the celluloid has been put there as a result of a conscious or semi-conscious decision by the film-maker. But we must also remember to fully experience the film moment itself, as we do when we are members of a cinema audience, only now we must attend far more closely than usual to each and every one of our reactions. For each 'film-phrase' we must ask ourselves: what is this stimulating me to feel? And at the same time we must ask ourselves: what is this prompting me to think? And what do I think this means?

The next stage in the process is to consider what it is on film that has caused this response, or, specifically, what image and sound, separate or in combination, has caused the effect on us as audience? In this way we will find ourselves discovering the essence of the language of film.

1 From Montage to Story:
Persona

Montage in film means the juxtaposition of images that each have a separate meaning within themselves, an additional meaning when one image is added to another, and a cumulative meaning which arises from the sequence of images as a whole.

Story, in essence, suggests one or more characters and an exploration of a dramatic question or conflict.

The first film microcosm we are going to explore is the opening of Ingmar Bergman's *Persona*. In this sequence Bergman takes us from an almost completely abstract image, through a complex montage sequence, and finally arrives at the beginnings of the story he has to tell. His extraordinary use of image and sound, and the sheer range of the film experience he offers us make this an ideal microcosm to begin our journey.

Persona is about an artist, an actress, whose business is communication, and who suddenly has a breakdown and cannot or wilfully refuses to speak. On one level Bergman's subject matter is also the subject matter of this book: *Persona* is about the creative process itself. Not at a simplistic level of craft and difficulty with craft but at the level of our deep psychological relationship with the role of the artist. The artist needs to create, to express the self fully, but at the same time she has a perverse, self-destructive instinct which brutally rejects the artist within herself and consequently within others.

Because this film touches on some of our major themes, both in the areas of creative process and film language, I have chosen to treat it as a seminal work. We will return to it later in the book to look at its story structure, and to consider what the film is saying about creativity.

While we are exploring the film you will find that I note the most simple aspects of how the medium is working on our senses at the level of image, sound and meaning as well as considering the more complex material. This is because it is often from the most simple observations that the most is to be gained.

PERSONA (1966) Written and directed by Ingmar Bergman

Sequence taken from the opening

1. Two abstract shapes, a square and a phallic shape which seems to be made up of burning white-hot metal glowing in the darkness. Discordant music combined with the sound of a film projector.

– We feel an extraordinary tension between these two abstract shapes; they seem to be held static although they are, at the same time, in an elemental process of either being drawn together or of separation. The tension between the two is made excruciating by the discordant music. We try to work out what the images are as we search for our bearings.

2. We move back, the light comes up and we begin to recognize the image; an extreme close up of a film projector. It's either starting up, or breaking down, it's difficult to know which. Film is moving through the spool; 'START' flashes across the screen, then 10, 9, 8, 7.

– Relief, now we can recognize the image. But why did the film-maker choose to open with that abstraction? The question remains with us. There is a sense of excitement; the projector literally coming to life feels good. Although it may be breaking down, at least it's moving, change is taking place.

3. Cut to the film in the projector. We can see the film image lined with sprocket holes. The image is an animated cartoon, a children's story-book picture of a little girl wearing a black bathing costume. She appears to be sitting on some rocks at the seaside, washing her face, or maybe she's crying. The image is upside-down.

– A comforting reminder of the story-books we read as a child and of childhood visits to the seaside. But why is the image upside-down

9

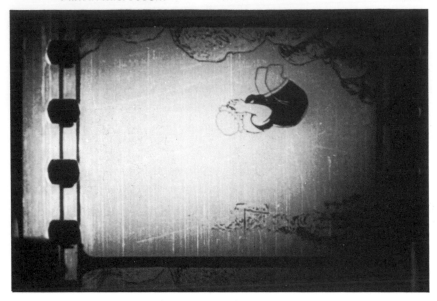

and lined with sprocket holes? Bergman seems to want to remind us that we're watching an artefact, a film.

4. Cut to some big close-ups of the projector wheels turning and then to a child's hands, fumbling and feeling each other, like babies do when they first begin to encounter life outside the womb.

– The child's hands give us a sense of wonder, awe, hope, life beginning, life reaching out.

5. The screen goes to white. In the corner of the frame a fragment from an early silent comedy appears. A skeleton pops up out of a box, frightens a man in his nightshirt, causing the man to jump into his bed and hide under the covers. We hear percussion sounds, like those that often accompany children's cartoons.

– Just as with the cartoon of the little girl, we are again back in the world of the child, feeling the pure enjoyment of watching those crazy speeded-up silent films. The film is funny because it's about such a familiar fear; a monster, in this case a skeleton, jumping out of the cupboard and frightening us as we get into bed, and a familiar reaction; hiding under the bedclothes. The sound is reassuringly in

10

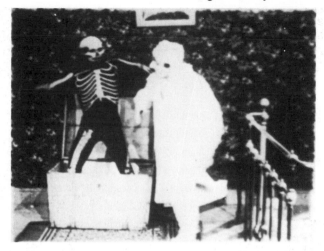

genre. But of all the early silent films Bergman could have taken a clip from why has he chosen this one? We are provoked into thinking about further meanings for his choice; a skeleton in the cupboard – a long buried secret, an event hidden away because it can not be faced, but the longer we keep it buried the greater our fear that it might jump out and attack us. Could this connect with what the film is going to be about?

6. Suddenly we are confronted with a big close-up of a spider, almost filling the frame. The spider moves sideways stealthily. The music is reminiscent of horror films.

– Those of us who are phobic about spiders will get a real shock. Even those of us who can quite happily remove a spider from our bath will shudder at this huge, fat, hairy creature. It immediately gives the feeling of evil intent. The music intensifies this feeling, making us think of predators and feel danger.

7. Close-up of a man's hands grappling with the wool of a sheep. We move over the sheep's body to find its eye, which is strangely still. Is it dead? We move back to where the man's hands were. The sheep's entrails are suddenly tumbling out of its body. The predatory music grows louder.

– So that's what the man's fumbling hands were doing – slitting the sheep's stomach open. We are shocked. The images seem to have been designed to shock. Because we only see the man's hands

11

fumbling with the animal, and there is no context for the act, the man has no individual identity, just as the animal has no identity, just one dead eye. We have been made aware of life, man and animal in intimate relation; death, innards and the sheep as a helpless victim, a reminder of the Christian saying: 'like a lamb to the slaughter'.

8. The music becomes even more discordant. We cut to another big close-up of a man's hand with a nail being hammered through the palm. The fingers recoil in pain. The hammer is sudden and jarring as it thuds on to the nail, forcing it through human flesh and bone. Thick blood congeals around the base of the nail.

– We feel repulsed by the explicit nature of this image. We, too, recoil in pain at every blow. But at the same time our intellect is very busy, the image is universally recognizable. The previous shot of the slaughtered sheep had already reminded us of Christianity, this image and sound is quite literally hammering the presence of the Christian doctrine into our skulls. Bergman is clearly concerned that we shall not just receive an intellectual idea, he wants us to feel the torture. Why? What has this got to do with the film we are about to see?

9. Cut to a peaceful woodland scene in the snow. No people, nothing moves. The discordant jarring music is replaced by the slow distant tolling of church bells.

– What relief; the hammering has stopped, the pain has gone. The woodland scene is cold and empty and in another context it might seem lonely. But given the violence of the previous image this emptiness is a relief and an escape. Even the mournful tolling of church bells in the distance is a welcome respite from the terrible slow thuds of the hammer.

10. A railing of metal spikes outside a church, and outside the railing a heap of old, dirty snow packed hard like rock.

– This image also feels desolate and lonely but the railings have been made by man, the snow has been shovelled by man and a church is a place frequented by people. We are beginning to want

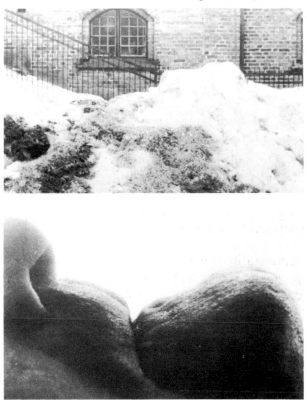

the reassurance of meeting some characters to enable us to find our bearings within a story.

11. Close-up of an old person's chin and nose.

– This image is a surprise. It's almost abstract; the craggy chin looks somehow geological, reminiscent of the rock-like packed snow we saw in the churchyard.

12. Another view of the old person's face. We can now see that it is the face of a woman and she is dead. Slow dripping water joins the sound of the distant tolling church bell.

– Only seconds ago we escaped with relief from violence and torture but we are again beginning to feel a cold chill – a feeling intensified by the dripping water and the tolling bell. We wanted hope in the form of a character and a story, but we find ourselves in what we assume to be a morgue and this character is dead.

However, there's a certain serenity in this death; it's chilling but not frightening.

13. Cut to a boy, maybe twelve years old, lying flat on his back under a white sheet on a slab, or flat bed, by a white wall. Sounds of footsteps in the distance join the dripping water.

– We're surprised to find a child in the morgue. Although, because we didn't pan from the dead old woman to find the boy, which would have confirmed that they were in the same place, we can only assume that he too is in the morgue, an assumption which is affirmed by the sound of water dripping. The new sound of footsteps is a hopeful sign of life.

14. Cut back to the old woman and her lifeless dangling hand. We can still hear dripping water and the distant footsteps.

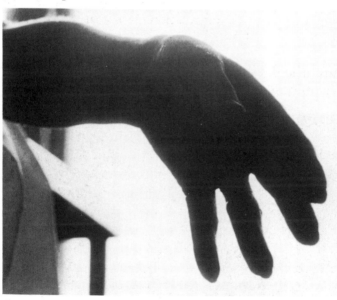

– Because we're not being confronted with, and so having to deal with a new image, but have returned to the now familiar dead old woman, we now have a moment to contemplate the montage sequence experienced so far and to make connections. The first connection that comes to mind is the variety of different ways we have experienced the human hand.

14

15. Cut to another body, this time it's an old man. His face is similar to the old woman's and his unusually plump hand rests on the sheet covering. Finally we look at his feet, which are slender and crossed at the ankles. The footsteps in the distance are getting louder, we can hear a door opening and a metal bucket clanging.

– Again we are being invited to contemplate a hand. This one, because it is plump and strangely vulnerable, seems to be a reminder of the baby's hands which we saw at the beginning of the sequence. Have we come full circle, from the spools of the projector, in their abstract form the wheels of life, from life beginning to life ending? The feet, slender and crossed, seem to be another reminder of Christ on the cross, but this time a calm reminder, the death after the violence. And whilst the sequence of images invites us to contemplate the accumulation of meaning, the sound-track is introducing us to quite a different experience. Someone must be coming, a living character, their footsteps are getting closer. The sound is giving us cause for anticipation. Is the story about to begin?

16. We return to look at the dead woman's face, but it's now strangely and uncomfortably upside-down. Suddenly a

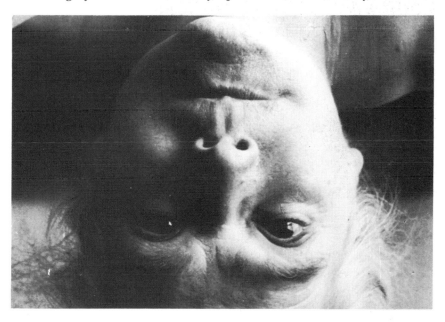

telephone is ringing, loud, near, insistent. And the dead
woman's eyes open wide, as if she has been woken up.

– The image of the upside-down dead woman's face comes as a
complete surprise. It's unnatural and discordant, as is the loud
ringing of a phone in a place of the dead. And did her eyes just
open? Has the phone, the insistence of someone wanting to communicate, jolted her back from death? Can that be possible? We
don't believe our own eyes.

17. Cut to the bed where the boy lies under his white sheet.
He pulls the sheet up over his ears to shut out the ringing
phone. His feet are revealed. The sheet is just not big enough
for him to entirely hide under. He fights with the sheet and
tries to settle. He can't. Now he's been woken up he can no
longer be dead. The telephone has stopped ringing. We can
only hear the sound of dripping water. The boy, with a look of
resignation, turns on to his stomach, hooks his spectacles
around his ears, reaches out for his book, opens it and begins
to read.

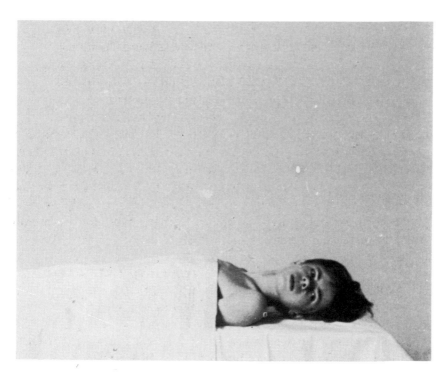

– We wanted a living character, and the sounds of footsteps and the clanging bucket led us to expect one to arrive imminently. The ringing phone acts like the final demand for a human response, although there's no sign of a phone in the room and no one apparently answers it – but then Bergman is not creating a piece of naturalistic drama. Once again we are confronted with the unexpected; our character is not the owner of the footsteps but the boy we thought was dead. Although we still appear to be in an institution of some kind, the bed is very flat, the wall very white and the water still dripping, the associations with the morgue are being rapidly forgotten.

The montage of images we have experienced so far has taught us not to expect the usual naturalistic reference points but to try to understand what we are seeing and hearing in terms of subtext. So, although we don't know who the boy is, where he is, or how he can have woken from the dead, we are immediately absorbed by his activity; his reluctant awakening and his decision to read a book. We wanted our story to begin and the boy has decided to read a story – a playful irony. Bergman knows our expectations but he's not yet ready to satisfy us.

18. Music begins, mysterious, sinister, very similar to the chords which began when we saw the spider. The music seems to take the boy's attention away from the book. He sits up on his bed and looks directly at us (at the camera). He reaches out his hand, as if attempting to reach us.

– The sound, because we have already associated it with the spider and the slaughter of the sheep, evokes the sense of an approaching predator. The boy, too, has been disturbed by the sound, it causes to him appear to be looking directly at us. (When a character looks directly at camera the effect is to make you uncomfortably aware of yourself as a member of the audience.) Is Bergman here implicating the audience with the predator?

19. Cut to a shot over the boy's shoulder. We see, from his point of view, that he's not reaching out to us, he is in fact reaching out in an attempt to touch a huge image of a woman's face. The face is ill-defined, as if seen through frosted glass. The discordant music is rising to a crescendo as the huge face moves in and out of focus. When it finally

17

re-focuses it appears to be a different woman and we slowly realize that there are two women's faces merging in and out of each other beyond the boy's reaching hand.

– The implication here is that the predator is no longer us, the audience, but the woman, although her face, huge as it is in relation to the boy, is soft and gentle, certainly not in itself threatening. What is threatening, because it's so disturbing, is the way the face seems to move in and out of focus, being first that of one woman and then that of another, and the boy's vain attempt reach out and touch a woman who is so alien and physically removed from the boy. The warmth of human contact is beyond this child's reach. This woman is beyond his touch.

20. Opening credits: simple black lettering on a white background with rapid intercutting of images: the boy, the famous picture of a Vietnamese monk burning himself in protest, the sea, the sea-shore, trees, the two women we have just seen, now together by the sea-shore, the silent film of the man being chased by the skeleton.

– This credit sequence punctuates the film; it concludes the opening montage sequence inviting us to read it as a whole, with a unity of its own and with meanings that relate to, and prepare us for, the film to follow. The predominant themes in this cold northern landscape seem to be: the wonder of life beginning, the presence of predators, the horror of violence and torture, the relief of death, the insistence of life and finally the need for human touch, especially between mother and child, and all is pervaded with the cool spirit of Protestantism, although the brief inclusion of the image of the Vietnamese monk hints at a wider spiritual and political context. At the same time as giving us the space we need to contemplate the meaning in the pre-credit montage, the credit sequence also begins to prepare us for the film to come. By including images we haven't yet seen it refers forward and sets up expectations. We realize that the two women, who we now see in a naturalistic setting, will figure prominently in the coming film. The final image, the man being chased by a skeleton, although still amusing, serves as a foreboding.

21. Cut to a simple and clinical image of a white door in a white wall.

– This image gives us a sense of place (although not strongly enough to let us get interested in the specific nature of the place); it tells us that we are in an institution. We both want and expect someone to come through the door.

22. The door opens and a nurse, Sister Alma (Bibi Andersson), crisp, young, bright, attractive, steps through the door. She stands very formally as she is greeted by the voice of her superior, a woman doctor (who remains off screen).

DOCTOR

Have you seen Mrs Vogler?

SISTER ALMA

No, not yet

DOCTOR

Then I will tell you about her and why you are to look after her.

– After the dissonance of the opening montage, to have both our expectations and our sense of place confirmed, and to be greeted by what appears to be such a bright and uncomplicated person is immensely reassuring. Although it crosses our mind that Sister Alma looks very like one of those huge out-of-focus faces the boy was trying to reach in the pre-credit sequence, we soon discount this association as we are pitched headlong into the story by the opening lines of dialogue.

'"Have you seen Mrs Vogler?", "No not yet."' Who is Mrs Vogler and why should Sister Alma see her, we immediately ask ourselves? Sister Alma clearly knows who the doctor is referring to, and, although she hasn't seen Mrs Vogler, 'not yet' suggests that she expects to shortly. Our curiosity about who Mrs Vogler is, and why she deserves to be the focus of our attention at the opening of the story, has been firmly aroused. And once more our expectations are to be confirmed; the doctor, in the very next line, tells us she is about to satisfy our curiosity.

24. The doctor tells us that Elizabeth Vogler is a famous theatre actress who stopped dead in the middle of a performance of *Electra*. At this point we cut to Elizabeth Vogler (Liv Ullmann), in the heavy mask-like make-up of Greek tragedy and the full glare of stage lighting, at the very moment when she stops speaking. Her expression oscillates between fear, uncertainty and amusement. We cut back to the innocent, open face of Sister Alma as she listens to the doctor. The doctor tells us that this incident happened three months ago and Elizabeth Vogler hasn't spoken since. Elizabeth Vogler has clearly had some kind of mental breakdown, although the doctor believes her breakdown was a conscious choice rather than the onset of a clinical mental illness. Sister Alma's task is to nurse Elizabeth Vogler back to full recovery.

– In the pre-credit montage sequence all our expectations for the setting up of a linear story were thwarted. Bergman instead, through provoking us, surprising us and shocking us, demanded that we attend to the subtext of the images he introduced us to. By opening the film in this way he has told us that we must consider this subtext if we are to fully understand what he is trying to communicate through his story. Satisfied that he has achieved that objective, he can now begin his story knowing that we will be continually probing for a deeper understanding. This also enables him to open his story in the most simple manner possible: he introduces us to Sister Alma, tells us her mission, to nurse Mrs Vogler back to health, which means getting her to speak again, and tells us enough about Mrs Vogler for us to realize that Alma's task is not going to be an easy one. In other words, Bergman tells us who his protagonist is and what her central dilemma will be, which is the dramatic question. But we are now straying into territory which I want to save for the second part of this book which is devoted specifically to the art of storytelling.

Before we conclude there are a few general points arising from this sequence which are worth noting. In narrative cinema the audience brings with them expectations of how the story should function based on all the stories they have seen and heard before.

The search for familiar reference points is an automatic part of their experience, which means that the film-maker must sense and decide how the audience's expectations relate to what he is trying to communicate. This becomes especially important if the film is departing radically from familiar narrative reference points.

Sequences of images in film, like the montage sequence we have just explored, function like sequences of words in poetry – they arouse feeling and suggest meaning according to the way they are presented and ordered, and according to the rhythm, flow and accumulation of associations. Repetition is as important as surprise. The audience needs time to absorb and reflect on what they are experiencing. Piecing together meanings which arise from separate but connected images is a gradual process. Finally, note how sound has been used in many different ways: to work in harmony with the image; to intensify or clarify a feeling or meaning; to give a sense of place; to counterpoint with the image by suggesting quite a different agenda; and to build an expectation of things to come.

2 What's Going On Out There In The World?:
Touch of Evil and *The Lacemaker*

The world is a vast and complicated place. In order to attempt to understand it we break it down into a constantly shifting mass of interlocking social, political and personal structures: continents, countries, nations, states, politicians, unions, workers, unemployed, husbands, wives, parents, children, to mention just a few. Most of us spend much of our lives caught up in a constant turmoil of conflicts and power struggles between these groups and subgroups and the individuals who are either upholding or subverting their interests as they attempt to communicate with each other to pursue their wants and needs and make their way in the world.

The positions people take, either consciously or unconsciously, in relation to the fray represent their moral stance or their life view. What they believe in will be manifest in their actions and the resulting consequences.

Making connections, seeing patterns in a section of this seething mass of humanity, exploring how characters relate to each other and rise and fall, is often a central theme of film drama, although it's sometimes only during the actual process of creating the artefact, deciding on the character to identify with and working through their dilemma, that the writer discovers precisely what it is that he or she has to say.

The first of the two film microcosms we are going to explore in this chapter is the opening of Orson Welles' *Touch of Evil*. The reason I've chosen this sequence is because Welles' use of film language and the kind of reactions he provokes from his audience are at the other end of the spectrum from *Persona*. Bergman was asking us to consider the intricacies of the interior landscape whereas Welles is directing our attention towards the exterior social and political world. His use of image and sound to piece together a few of the ingredients of a conflict taking place between subgroupings of the kind mentioned above illustrates not only the way his creative mind works but also the essence of a set of film language conventions which have since become a familiar part of the American cinema.

TOUCH OF EVIL (1958)
Written and directed by Orson Welles

Although I have broken my description down into sections, so we can consider the function and effect of each image, the entire opening sequence of *Touch of Evil* is one continuous unbroken shot and technically an extraordinary feat.

1. Black screen. As the screen gradually lightens we see an object move out of the darkness towards us. We realize that we are looking at a dark buttoned jacket around a man's midriff and the object which he holds in his hands. The object seems to be made up of a dial or timing mechanism on one side and batteries on the other. The man's fingers are carefully making an adjustment on the dial.

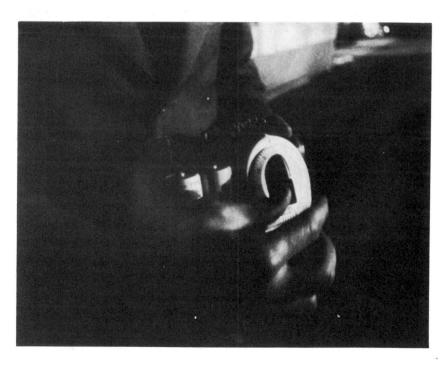

– Our first thought, as the object emerges out of the darkness, is 'what's that?' We are then given the chance to examine it while the dial is being adjusted and we slowly realize that it's a homemade bomb. We immediately become alert; something dangerous is going to happen. Our first question is quickly replaced by two more: 'who is the man?' and 'what is he going to do with the bomb?'

2. We hear the sound of a couple laughing in the distance and are swung sharply round with the bomb as the man turns towards the sound. We now move away from the bomb to find the source of the laughter and see, from the man's point of view, that it's night, we're in a badly-lit, down-at-heel town precinct and we're facing a long arched walkway where the couple, a man and a woman, are walking towards us in the middle distance. They turn and disappear from view under an arch on the side of the walkway. The man with the bomb darts stealthily across our path to enable him to see where the couple are heading.

– Notice how sound is used here to shift our attention. The distant laughter, which broke the silence of the opening image, combined with the sudden movement of the bomb, as the man swung round in reaction to the sound, gives the couple such importance that they replace the bomb as the focus of our attention. We also now have the opportunity to get an initial sense of our location, although it could be almost any town, anywhere. The couple are too far in the distance for us to get a sense of their identity and the man's movements are too fleeting for us to experience him as more than a dark, male presence.

3. The man darts back across the walkway and runs through an adjoining archway. We track along the archway wall, watching the man's shadow as it flits menacingly across an array of old peeling posters. We find him again, now in a nearly deserted parking lot beneath a skyline broken by distant, scattered buildings. He runs to a parked car, a gleaming American convertible, ducks down, opens the boot, places the bomb inside it and runs away. The music begins; at first a percussive Latin rhythm which is then overlaid with the full sound of a brass section carving out the theme as we are

25

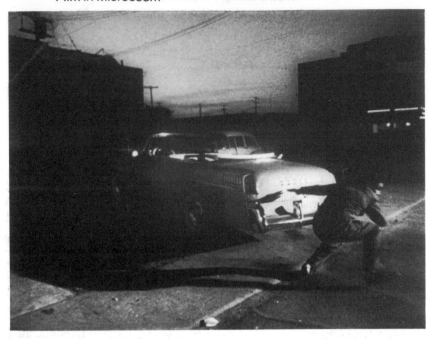

propelled up into a high shot of the gleaming convertible. The couple, a young blonde woman in an evening dress and an older man, walk into shot, get into the car and drive out of the parking lot. The opening titles begin.

– As soon as the couple disappear from view our attention is again drawn by movement to the man with the bomb. The image of his shadow flitting across the wall of peeling posters gives him a sense of menace and, by association, suggests that he is a part of a shadowy, sleazy underworld. The shiny convertible is the only sign of wealth in the vicinity. The straightforward action of placing the bomb in the boot of the convertible answers one of our questions, 'what is the man going to do with the bomb?' But we haven't been shown the man's face, or a single identifiable feature, before he runs away and so our other question, 'who is he?' remains unanswered. The music, which begins at this point, contains two distinct characteristics: first the Latin rhythm, which is reminiscent of a bomb ticking, and second the big sound of the brass section which feels in keeping with the sleazy underworld hinted at by the images. Finally, the couple, who distracted our attention from the bomb in the opening images, become fatally linked with the bomb when they get into the convertible (note how we still only see them in long-shot and so are prevented from getting to know them as individuals) and the drama is set up – we know there is a bomb in the boot of their car but they don't, the bomb is on a time switch and, as they drive out of the parking lot, a countdown to death has begun.

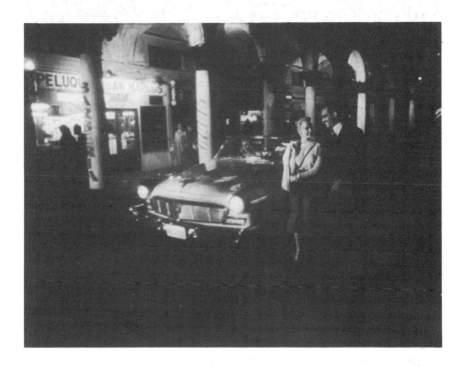

4. The convertible drives out of the parking lot, through the arched walkway and into what turns out to be a busy street outside. It is halted by a policeman while pedestrians and a flower vendor wheeling his stall cross its path. It travels further down the street where it is halted for a second time to enable more pedestians to cross. This time we move in to focus on two of the pedestrians, a new couple (Charlton Heston and Janet Leigh), as they reach the near side of the road. The man turns to glance curiously at the convertible as it passes and drives out of sight. Our attention now stays with the new couple as we watch them, talking and laughing, as

they stroll happily down the street, the man with his arm placed comfortably around the woman's shoulders.

– We are surprised by the busy normality of the street outside, so close to the scene of the crime. The image of the convertible being stopped by a policeman to let pedestrians cross seems ironic; the upholder of law and order unwittingly so close to the crime. The irony is further emphasized by the sight of the flower vendor, suggesting the innocence of a community unaware of the danger that's in their midst.

It's also worth noting how the convertible is stopped twice and it's the second time that our attention shifts to the new couple. If the car had only been stopped once we would not have had time to register the ironies mentioned above because we would still be trying to work out who the new couple are and what role they will have to play in the course of events. The reason we are giving them such significance is that they are the first characters we've met with individual identities; we can see their faces, which means we can begin to get to know them as we watch their enjoyment of each other's company as they walk along the busy street.

The moment when our focus is shifted from the convertible to the new couple is interesting, too, because the man glances curiously at the car. This glance connects him in some way to the car, although we don't yet know why – which is not unlike the way the bomb and the first couple were connected in the opening two shots. So now both couples are connected to the bomb.

5. The second couple arrive at the end of the street where there is an international border crossing. They walk past the first customs post, marked by sentry boxes and black and white car barriers, and head for the second. As they approach the customs officials, the convertible, coincidentally, draws alongside them. The couple in the car wait while the customs official questions the couple on foot.

> CUSTOMS OFFICIAL
> Are you folks American citizens?
> SUSAN
> Yes.
> CUSTOMS OFFICIAL
> Where were you born Miss?

SUSAN

Mrs. Philadelphia.

Vargas hands the Customs official two passports.

VARGAS

The name is Vargas.

The Customs official reacts to this information by calling to the man in the car, which is still waiting behind.

CUSTOMS OFFICIAL

Hey Jim, did you hear that?

MAN IN THE CAR

Sure, Mr Vargas. Out on the trail of another dope ring?

VARGAS

On the trail of a chocolate soda for my wife.

Vargas takes Susan's hand and leads her away as the Customs official reacts to the news of his marriage in surprise.

MAN IN THE CAR

(Growing impatient about the hold up) Hey, can I get through?

A second Customs official approaches as the Vargases pass by on the other side of the car.

SECOND CUSTOMS OFFICIAL

There's been a lot of talk up here about how you cracked that Grandee business. Hear you caught the big boss.

VARGAS

Only one of them, the Grandees are a big family.

Mr and Mrs Vargas walk away and the two Customs officials turn their attention to the occupants of the car.

CUSTOMS OFFICIAL

Any purchases Miss? Are you an American citizen?

WOMAN IN CAR

Hey, I've got this ticking in my head.

The convertible drives away through the raised barrier.

No really, I've got this ticking in my head.

– So, we're in a divided town, a border town, and the two couples arrive at the same place at the same time – with the bomb, of course, ticking away in the boot of the convertible.

The dialogue is mainly exposition, which means that it refers to events that have happened before the film opens: important information for our developing understanding of the story. One of the basic skills writers need to develop for this kind of drama is how

29

to weave expositional information into the dramatic action so that it doesn't stick out like a sore thumb but appears to be an intrinsic and natural part of the activity. In this case we conveniently have a Customs official on hand whose job it is to ask the questions we happen to want to know the answer to, and who happens to have heard of Mr Vargas. This is both plausible and helpful for putting over the exposition. We learn that the Vargases are newly-weds, that Mr Vargas is a well-known law-enforcer who recently cracked a drug ring and that some important members of the ring are still at large – a foreboding of things to come. Vargas and the driver of the convertible appear to be further connected by the subject of the drug racket.

Finally, as the two couples go their separate ways, we're firmly reminded of presence of the bomb in the boot because the woman in the convertible complains about the ticking in her head, although not one appears to be listening to her. This reminder feels opportune. The dialogue has contained a complicated agenda and, because we are trying to piece together a picture of these characters, the world they inhabit and what the dilemma at the heart of the story is going to be, we were in danger of forgetting about the bomb and so need to be reminded for dramatic effect.

6. We track in to find Mr and Mrs Vargas walking together on the far side of the road.

SUSAN

Mike, do you realize this is the first time we will have been together in my country?

VARGAS

Do you realize that I haven't kissed you in over an hour?

Vargas and his wife embrace. Just as their lips meet we hear the explosion. They turn and we cut to the convertible, now a mass of flames and raised momentarily in the air from the force of the explosion.

– With our reminder of the time bomb ticking away its countdown to death we move in to watch the Vargases walking happily, arm-in-arm, on the other side of the street. The danger we feel from the bomb is transferred, via the image, from the couple in the convertible to the newly-weds. We learn that they are, for the first time, about to enter the wife's country (the border is also a divide between them) and the husband responds by wanting to kiss her. We would be forgiven for interpreting 'my country' as the wife's sexuality although we know she is literally referring to America. We could also be forgiven for thinking of her sexuality as maybe a dangerous place, as we transfer the thought of the time bomb ticking away towards an explosion, on to her image.

The explosion takes place just as they embrace. The climax which we have been building towards since the opening image finally arrives with terrifying ferocity. The explosion breaks the kiss, literally separating the newly-weds. The sudden cut from the kiss to the explosion is also the first cut in the film and as such breaks the steady dramatic build-up of the continuous sequence and concludes the first part of the opening. We are now left with a crime to be solved in the form of the question, 'who placed the bomb?' and a protagonist whose job we know it is to solve crimes and who has recently broken into a drug ring leaving some important members still at large. The danger has now been transferred to Susan and Vargas' marriage.

The incident of a car bomb going off on an international border crossing is unquestionably the stuff of drama and Welles has exploited his subject to great effect. But does drama always have to be so explicitly dramatic? The stuff of drama is happening in all of our lives for much of the time, if we only choose to value it as deserving of our attention. Earlier I mentioned that, in essence, it only takes one or more characters and a conflict or dilemma to make a story. Whether it will be a 'good' story or not will depend on the individual insight of the teller and the universality of the dilemma. The microcosm we are going to explore next, which illustrates this point, is a short sequence from *The Lacemaker*, a film by Swiss film maker Claude Goretta. What is especially interesting in this sequence is how Goretta uses image and action, mainly focusing on simple gesture and body language, to show us all we need to know about a relationship between two young people. The resulting sequence is remarkable for its simplicity. The sequence is taken from two-thirds of the way into the film. As far as actual incident is concerned all you really need to know about the story so far is that Beatrice (Pomme), a shy self-effacing girl who works in a hair-dressing salon, has met and fallen in love with François, a young university student, while they were both on holiday. We have also been introduced to a rhythm, pace and atmosphere which draw our attention to those small and delicate moments between people which can have such a devastating effect on their lives. When we join the story the young couple have been living together in Paris for a number of months.

THE LACEMAKER (La Dentellière, 1977)
Written and directed by Claude Goretta

Sequence from two-thirds into the film

> 1. It is evening and we are in the living-room of a student's apartment. François is sitting with a student friend, a young woman wearing a black jumper, who is reading aloud from a book while François listens.

> YOUNG WOMAN
> This is why the phenome coincides not with a concrete phonic image but with its phonologically pertinent charac-teristics.
> FRANÇOIS
> Could you read that again please?

> François' girlfriend, Béatrice (Isabelle Hupper), wearing a simple white blouse, is at the other side of the room, ironing. As François' student friend repeats what she has just read

aloud we watch Béatrice glance briefly at the two of them
while she irons. She doesn't appear to have any
comprehension of what they are studying.

– François and his student friend are seated close together, and
although there is no hint of a physical intimacy between them their
physical proximity suggests an intellectual intimacy that excludes
Béatrice. Her exclusion is further emphasized by her position in the
room behind the ironing board, which acts like a barrier between
her and them. There's also a striking visual contrast between the
two young women; the student in her black jumper looks strong,
independent, experienced. In contrast, Béatrice, in her white
blouse, looks shy, self-effacing and innocent. As for the choice of
study matter, it's not only incomprehensible to young hairdressers,
it will also be incomprehensible to most of the audience. Goretta
has chosen an example of academic jargon far removed from
everyday life, particularly, in this case, from simple tasks like doing
the ironing. But Béatrice, judging by her innocent glance at the two
of them, doesn't have any insight into the substance, or lack of it, of
what they are discussing. All she knows is that she doesn't understand.

2. Cut to a busy Paris street, shot from above. There is a
traffic island in the middle of the street and some pedestrians
crossing. We can just make out that one of the pedestrians is
François. He sees that the second half of the road is clear and
makes a dash for it. He reaches the other side and stops to
look back. We follow his look and can just make out Béatrice,
left behind on the far side of the road. She manages to reach
the centre island and there she gets stuck behind another
sudden rush of traffic. We cut to street level and Béatrice's
point of view of François as he waits impatiently for her on
the far side of the road. We can tell by her expression and
stance that she's embarrassed and anxious about holding him
up. We then cut to Béatrice from François' point of view; she
keeps trying to get across the road but the passing cars and
lorries continually block her path. Eventually the road clears
and Béatrice runs anxiously across to join him. But François
doesn't wait to greet her, instead he turns away just before
her arrival, forcing her to run to keep up with him.

– The scene opens with a high shot which prevents us from identifying with either of the characters. The shot instead invites us to think about the different ways each of them handles the hustle and bustle of daily life and the effect this difference is having on their relationship. In other words the way they cross the road together has become a metaphor for the state of their relationship. François skilfully negotiates the dangers as he hurries on his way, anxious to arrive at his destination and irritated by Béatrice who seems to be slowing him down and holding him back. Béatrice, who normally prefers a slower pace because of her timidity in the face of the hurly-burly of modern life, is trying to rush to keep up with him, ever anxious to please him, but she's trying to force herself to move at a pace that's not naturally her own. The speed of the passing traffic increases the sense of her being in danger.

Next we join the two characters at street level. By shifting the position of the camera we leave the metaphor behind and plunge back into experiencing directly the effect the characters are having on each other, identifying with them both in their mutual dilemma because of the point of view shots. We see François' impatience with Béatrice, and, because we are seeing it from Béatrice's point of view, we know that she sees it too; she sees that he really wants to rush away from her and is waiting only out of a sense of duty and guilt. Consequently we feel her hurt. We then see Béatrice from François' point of view; inept, timid, unable to keep up with him. Now we have some insight into his dilemma too. But at the end of the scene, when Béatrice, with childlike pleasure in a difficult task fulfilled, succeeds in crossing the road, François impatiently turns away from her. We now feel her hurt at his rebuff and, because the scene ends on Béatrice, we finally make a moral judgement based on our experience of her feeling; her innocence doesn't deserve his injury.

3. It is night and we are in François' and Béatrice's bedroom. The room is gently lit by a bedside lamp. Béatrice is sitting on the bed, with her back to us, unhooking her bra strap. She takes off her bra and hangs it carefully over a chair. She stands. She's completely naked. She walks shyly over to join François, who we now see is standing, fully dressed, with his back to her, looking out of the window at the night. Béatrice silently joins him by the window. They stand side by side, with their backs to us, without moving or touching. Her

naked body looks young and vulnerable next to his fully-clothed figure. The soft lamp gently lights her skin and she looks more like an innocent offering than a sexual being. Eventually François moves his head very slightly, half glancing down at her and he moves his arm to rest his hand lightly on the back of her neck. Béatrice, taking this as a sign of acceptance, moves her own arm up and rests her hand tentatively on the small of his back. François takes his hand away from her neck and lets it drop again by his side. Béatrice looks up at him. Getting no response, she turns and walks back to the bed. Her naked body is turned fully towards us here; unselfconsciously beautiful, innocent and rejected. She sits on the bed and puts on her white nightdress. François still doesn't move from his position with his back to her by the window. Béatrice's head slumps down as she waits.

– In the street scene we saw and felt the danger that Béatrice was in. Here we see that she still hopes that what is going wrong in their relationship will prove to be a passing phase. They are in the bedroom, a place where distance is felt all the more acutely because it is the place of greatest intimacy. She undresses, goes to the window and silently offers herself to him. Self-effacing as ever she makes no demands, she simply waits, hoping he will receive her gift of herself and hoping he will give her the intimacy and reassurance she so badly needs. We know, from the two previous scenes, that there is a fundamental incompatibility between these two young people, yet, because the scene opens on Béatrice, because we go with her action, her gesture of hope, and because throughout the scene François has his back to her and us, we wait, hope and feel with Béatrice. Her innocence and vulnerability is felt all the more keenly because of her nudity in contrast to his dark clothes and stiff demeanour. By the time he moves his arm to touch her neck we so identify with her that we too can almost feel the touch and the hope it gives, shooting through her like an electric current. But, because we have a greater insight into Béatrice's predicament than she has herself (as a result of our experiencing her from François' point of view in the previous scene), we suspect that this is a false hope. Our suspicions add to the poignancy of the moment because we want to be proved wrong.

A few seconds later our suspicions are confirmed, Béatrice's hopes are dashed. The bravery that her trip to the window took has

achieved nothing. As the scene ends she is as still and silent as he is and they are both looking away from each other and from us. They appear locked into the distance between them. When Béatrice's head finally slumps down we realize she is aware of the extent of her defeat.

The danger we feel Béatrice is in, planted in our minds in the street scene, is emphasized by her almost unbearable vulnerability in this scene. The last point of hope is dashed when François takes his tentative hand away from her neck. His rejection of her feels inevitable but, given the innocence with which Béatrice has given herself so completely, leads us to ask, 'how will she cope with his rejection?'

Although in almost every way this sequence seems like the polar opposite of *Touch of Evil* the use of film language is similar. In both sequences the dramatic build-up is through image and action, not words. Both sequences are simple and direct and go straight to the heart of the matter. Both show how much can be communicated by the physical proximity of people and their gestures. In both we know more about the protagonists' predicament than they do themselves. In *Touch of Evil* only we and the mystery man who planted the bomb know it is there. We want to warn the characters in danger, but of course we can't. In *The Lacemaker* the strength of our feeling for Béatrice results from our having a greater understanding of her situation than she has herself. We want her to realize enough in time to save herself, although we know that this is beyond her capability.

Drama is as much about the predictable as it is about the unpredictable, most dramas are, after all, about familiar predicaments. Our fascination and ability to engage at a meaningful level lies not so much with the predicament itself as with the very particular nature or uniqueness of the predicament as it is portrayed. This is what causes us to see it as if for the very first time.

3 The Interior World:
Wild Strawberries, The Conformist and *Kaos*

In the previous chapter we have seen how film acts as an unseen witness, creating the illusion of showing us what we would be seeing if we were a fly on the wall, whilst at the same time inviting us to perceive the exterior world both from the subjective point of view of characters who we see inhabiting it and through the film-maker's thoughts and feelings about the characters and the world they inhabit. We are now going to move further round the film spectrum to explore dreams, memories and fantasies; areas of subjective experience which do not manifest themselves in our shared world and so would not be seen by an unseen witness.

Many of us experience an excitement when we think about these three concepts, an excitement rooted in the prospect of breaking free from the confines of so-called reality and allowing our imagination to play with our own personal and long-nurtured imagery. At the same time there is also a feeling that we might be in some kind of danger, which is partly generated by the possibility of the dark side of the experiences emerging: nightmares, traumatic memories, fearful fantasies of horror and destruction. But this feeling also arises because the experiences, whether they are dark or not, move us closer to the brink of chaos, and what feels like a mire of confusion both at the levels of content and form. The dictionary defines the word chaos as the disordered formless matter supposed to have existed before the ordered universe. Our notions of order and reality are relatively recent constructions built on shifting sands. Dreams, memories and fantasies reside in our unconscious and, by moving us closer to that formless matter, can threaten to engulf us, or, as has been the case for many artists, prove to be the source of creative inspiration.

Dreams, memories and fantasies manifest themselves in a very similar language to the language of film. Film time is compressed time: an experience that in reality may have lasted for years, weeks or hours is communicated in minutes or seconds of screen time because only the essential ingredients of the experience are selected for communication. This process of selection and editing also takes place in our imagination. So, by looking at dreams, memories and fantasies we will be further penetrating the nature of film itself.

Dreams manifest themselves like little films appearing in our sleep, when we visit our own private cinemas and usually play the lead in all the shows. Like stories, they frequently have a sense of progression, moving towards a climactic moment which sometimes causes us to wake up and take note. Although the transitions between incidents and images in dreams usually transcend every-day logic they often cause very powerful feelings and suggest meanings which, like works of art, ask to be understood via metaphoric, symbolic or associative connotations. It is here that we find the crucial insights into the state of our conscious lives, insights which illuminate the nature of our present predicament. Dreams are also about our struggle for unity; we are every element in the dream and by pointing to our centre they show us the imbalances in our equilibrium. In this sense the role of dreams is similar to the role of much story-telling, which is also about exploring imbalances and conflicts in the struggle for unity.

We usually have more control over our memories than we do our dreams; although sometimes an image, sound, smell or situation triggers the memory and we find ourselves caught up in it almost unawares. But again memory is very selective, we only remember what was significant for us at the time although some details, which in themselves may seem irrelevant to the 'story', can take on a special resonance; the pattern on the wall-paper, the child's toy left forgotten in the hall or the refractions of light in the bathroom mirror. It is often these details which generate the strongest sensations and feelings.

The boundaries between memory and invention or fantasy often become blurred in the imagination, depending on the reason why we are remembering; whether our primary desire is to reach subjective truth or whether it is to reassure our egos. Most memor-ies involve a combination of these two desires. But certain traumatic memories, which may throw our understanding of who we are into confusion or distress, become repressed by a kind of self-defence mechanism. When a repressed memory is unlocked (which is, of course, fundamental to psychoanalysis) it has a profound effect, although if processed properly this effect can take the form of a kind of exorcism. This sense of exorcism through uncovering and re-experiencing the trauma is crucial to much story-telling. It is Aristotle's 'catharsis', the cleansing which he saw as the effect of tragic drama.

But perhaps it is fantasy that provides us most directly with our emotional link to the role of story-telling. It is through our fantasies that we explore, from the safety of our own imaginations, our most secret desires. In our fantasies we can become anyone and do anything – just as when we identify with characters and suspend our disbelief in films. Desire, of course, also has its dark side, like wanting to punish, or to express all the anger we don't dare to express in real life, and even to kill. Fear fantasies also lurk just beneath the surface in most of us; fears of the future or monsters in the dark. It is these two emotions, desire and fear, which lie at the heart of most story-telling.

Finally, we must remember that our understanding of ourselves (and consequently our understanding of dreams, memories and fantasies) is, like film language, in a constant state of evolution and change.

A DREAM
WILD STRAWBERRIES (*Smultronstallet*, 1957)
Written and directed by Ingmar Bergman

Opening sequence

1. Old Professor Borg sits alone in his comfortable, old-fashioned study with his dog sleeping at his feet. As he thoughtfully smokes a cigar, we hear the following voice-over:

> PROFESSOR (*voice-over*)
> Our contact with others consists mainly of discussion when we evaluate the character and conduct of our neighbour. That is why I have refrained of my own free will from almost all so-called social life. Yes, I've kept myself to myself for most of the time. The days of my life have been filled by hard work and I'm grateful for it. First I worked to earn a living, then it developed into a love of science.

We see framed photographs of the Professor's family while he goes on to tell us about each of them.

41

My son is a doctor too. He lives in Lund. He's been married for years. There are no children of the marriage. My mother is still alive and sprightly in spite of her great age. My wife Karen has been dead for many years.

Professor Borg's housekeeper appears briefly at the door.

HOUSEKEEPER

Dinner is served Professor Borg.

PROFESSOR (*voice-over cont.*)

I am privileged to have a good housekeeper.

He stands to go to dinner but first tidies his already immaculate desk.

Perhaps I should add that I am very punctilious, a quality that has made life quite trying sometimes both for myself . . .

He walks to the door, and we see the framed photo of his son in the background.

. . . and those about me.

The Professor clicks his fingers and his dog wakes and slowly gets to its feet.

My name is Eberhard Isak Borg. I am 78 years old. Tomorrow in Lund Cathedral there'll be a ceremony; the 50th anniversary of my graduation.

The dog and his master leave the study. Fade to black. We hear music, an orchestral score, over the credits which are white on black.

– We are just a few minutes into the film and already we feel that we know Professor Borg intimately. We can also detect the area of conflict which tells us what the film is to be about. Bergman, in his usual direct and economical manner, has achieved this quite simply by having his character introduce himself to us. The effect of this introduction is not at all theatrical because although Professor Borg's words are in first-person voice-over narration they are in the past tense – while he tells us about himself we see him alone in his study unaware of our watching presence.

He tells us that he is isolated through choice (he's above normal social intercourse which he believes to be idle gossip); he has a scientific (i.e. rational) mind; he's grateful for the discipline of hard work; he's obsessively tidy and although he's aware that this has caused problems (the image connects this with his son whose photo we see in the background here), he has no intention of modifying his character to suit others, which suggests that others have tried to get him to change and failed. The few members of his family are neatly framed on his desk and although there are no grandchildren to carry on the family lineage and his wife is long dead, the Professor seems quite smugly self-satisfied.

We have to ask ourselves why Bergman has chosen to give us these particular facts from Professor Borg's long life. The theme which connects each item of information is order and control. The Professor is a man of reason, not emotion, and appears to have his life neatly pigeon-holed. But something out of the ordinary is about to happen. The very next day is the 50th anniversary of his graduation, to be held in Lund, the town where his son lives. As the credits roll we ask ourselves the question: 'how could this important anniversary affect the Professor's well ordered life?'

2. After the credits we see the Professor asleep in bed.

> PROFESSOR BORG (*voice-over*)
> In the early morning of Sunday June 1st I had an odd and most disagreeable dream. I dreamt that I was taking my morning walk but I had lost my way in a strange part of town. The streets were deserted, the houses were dilapidated.

The Professor is walking through the deserted streets in the brilliant early morning sunshine. He stops and looks up at a large clock hanging, like a shop sign, on the side of a building. The clock has no hands. Beneath the clock hangs a huge pair of spectacles with eyes painted on the lenses. One of the painted eyes seems to be bleeding. Professor Borg takes out his pocket watch and sees that it also has no hands. He puts the watch away, looks back up at the clock, takes off his hat and mops his brow anxiously. We can hear his heart beating. He moves out of the sun into the shade and leans unsteadily against the wall.

– Bergman, tells us, in the most straightforward way possible, that we are entering a dream by showing the Professor asleep and by using his voice-over to tell us that he was dreaming. The voice-over also tells us, which otherwise we couldn't know, that the Professor is taking his daily walk when he suddenly finds himself in familiar,

but at the same time foreign streets – an experience that contains opposites, that is both familiar and foreign, is something we immediately recognize from our own dreams, as we do the surreal images; the clock with no hands and the bleeding eye. So it's the Professor's own routine which has led him to this deserted place where he can neither pin down his location nor the time. His usual, rational ways of getting his bearings have gone. He's no longer in control and he's afraid. The bleeding eye contributes a sense of danger which is added to by his being deprived of all sense of time apart from the beating of his heart – he is only a heart-beat away from death.

3. The Professor walks on for a few yards, turns and walks quickly back the way he came. He stops. A man has appeared further down the street and is standing absolutely still with his back to us. The Professor walks up to him and puts his hand on the man's shoulder. The man slowly turns to the Professor who jumps in shock at the sight of his face. It is like a death mask. The man then falls to the ground. His body seems to have disintegrated beneath his clothes and a watery blood trickles from where his head should have been. Funereal bells begin to toll.

– Despite his growing fear when another person appears in this apparently deserted place the Professor wants to know who it is. But the man's solid figure, as seen from behind, turns out to be an illusion; his face (identity) is a mask of death, he is a man of no substance beneath his clothes (his outer persona) and he even lacks proper thick blood (life energy). Is the Professor meeting an image that represents his unconscious view of himself?

4. The Professor continues with his walk, his face rigid with shock. He turns the corner at the end of the street and sees a 19th-century horse-drawn hearse lurching slowly down the street towards him and there's no sign of a driver. As he watches the hearse one of its wheels gets hooked around a lamp post. The horses strain to pull the wheel free and continue on their journey. The wheel breaks off and rolls dangerously towards the Professor, just missing him. The hearse creaks horribly as the horses try to free it from where it remains caught against the lamp post. The horses suddenly break free and continue on their way dragging the three-wheeled hearse behind them. The Professor watches as the coffin slides out of the hearse and falls with a crash on to the cobbled street in front of him.

– The Victorian hearse looks more like a fairy-tale hearse than a real one which indicates that its purpose is symbolic rather than literal.

Loss of control is hurtling towards him in the form of a driver-less vehicle which carries the dead. Its journey is interrupted by a lamp post, an object which emits light, the opposite of the darkness of death. The hearse's broken wheel could have killed the Professor but it just misses him and the hearse continues on its way – death appears to have passed him by, but not quite.

> 5. The Professor looks curiously down at the coffin. The fall has dislodged its lid and the hand of a corpse hangs out as if offering itself to him. The hand suddenly grabs him and the face of the corpse appears. The corpse is the Professor, it's the Professor's dead self who, with a fearful energy, is trying to pull him into the coffin. Cut to the Professor in bed waking from his nightmare.

– The message of many dreams can be found in their climax. So what is this dream telling the Professor? The corpse inside the coffin is the Professor's own self but it's not death the Professor has to confront, not yet, we have just seen death pass him by. His self is attempting to do something even more fearful than death; to pull him into the coffin alive. This suggests that the confrontation and the fearful struggle the Professor has to face is with this aspect of his self. The dream then wakes him, as if asking him to now attend to its message.

> 6. The Professor sits up in bed, takes his pocket watch from his bedside table and checks the time. He then goes over to the window and draws the blinds. He grabs his dressing gown and hurries through the apartment. The clock strikes three. He walks into his housekeeper's bedroom. She sits up in bed shocked by his sudden appearance.
>
> HOUSEKEEPER
> Are you ill?
> PROFESSOR
> Miss Agda, please make breakfast. I'm driving down.

– The Professor reacts immediately to his dream. First he checks that the real world is still in order by looking at the time and view out of the window and, reassured that all is as it should be, he rushes to his housekeeper's room. We have a strong feeling his spontaneous and urgent behaviour is uncharacteristic, a feeling confirmed by his housekeeper's surprise at his sudden appearance

47

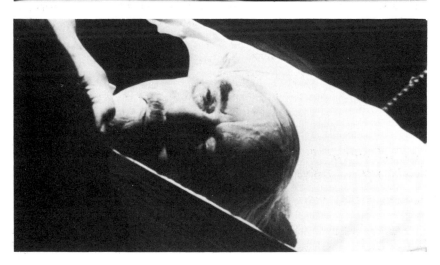

in her room and her assumption that he must be ill. But we know that he has decided to change his plans for the day as a result of his dream.

In this opening sequence Bergman has chosen to make a very clear distinction between dream and reality. He tells us that we are entering the dream, in the simplest way possible, by showing us his character asleep, and likewise he tells us when the dream is over by showing his character waking up. New screenwriters often feel that simple solutions like this are too obvious or clichéd. Of course it is important to be subtle, when the material demands it, but it is equally important to know when to be direct. In this case the climax of the sequence is the moment that the Professor confronts his self in the coffin and Bergman is concerned that we fully experience this moment because of the impact it has on his character's waking life – this is the moment that causes the Professor to change his plans for the day. If we had been uncertain about whether we were in a dream or not the power of this moment would have been greatly diminished.

It's also worth noting the relationship between the pre-credit sequence and the dream. A dream is essentially about the dreamer. Our ability to understand fully Professor's Borg's dream is dependent on our introduction to the character of the dreamer and the thematic link between his introduction of himself and the dream's insight into his self. At the end of the pre-credit sequence we wondered if the 50th anniversary celebration was going to upset the central elements governing the Professor's life: order and control. The dream takes up the theme and leads us, and Professor Borg, to its natural outcome, a sort of death in life, or to be more precise, life in a coffin – which stands as a metaphor for his present life. Anniversaries also tend to be confrontations with the self and the dramatic question we are left with at the end of the sequence is: 'what impact will this dream have on Professor Borg's 50th anniversary?'

A MEMORY
THE CONFORMIST (Il Conformista, 1970)
Written and directed by Bernardo Bertolucci

Sequence taken from the early development of the film

The film is set at the end of the 1930s. Clerici, the protagonist, is an Italian fascist now in his mid-thirties. He's been sent to France by his bosses to find and murder a left-wing university professor who was once his teacher. We join the story when Clerici and his driver are following the professor in their car with the intention of committing the murder. It is midwinter.

1. Clerici is sitting by his driver in the passenger seat of a 1930s black Citroën. They are both wearing hats and winter coats.

CLERICI
Stop. I want to get out.

The black Citroën draws to a halt. The roads are icy. The country landscape is a cold misty grey and covered with snow. Although

they are passing the elegant gates of a wealthy property there is no sign of people or even other cars in the vicinity. Clerici gets out of the car and marches ahead on foot.

CLERICI
What point is there in going? You go.

The driver opens his door and, whilst slowly following him in the car, calls to Clerici. His tone of voice is soft and persuasive, as if he's calling a petulant child.

DRIVER
Marcello.

Cut to a black car (a much earlier model than the Citroën) driving very slowly behind a boy of perhaps twelve years old. The boy is dressed in a sailor suit (of the kind worn by children at the turn of the century) and has a satchel over his shoulder. It's midsummer and the scene is set in an elegant park.

Cut back to time present. The driver is still leaning out of the open car door as he follows Clerici.

DRIVER

We must be there. We have responsibilities.

Cut to the summer park. The boy runs in front of what we can now see is a black Rolls Royce and holds his hand up like a policeman to halt the car:

BOY

Stop.

Cut to time present. Clerici walks around the front of the car to the passenger door. He bangs on the roof of the car:

CLERICI

Stop.

– The sequence opens with Clerici sitting in the passenger seat alongside the driver of the car. The two men appear to be of equal status and together on a mission but when Clerici suddenly orders the driver to stop, gets out of the car and walks in front of it, he separates himself from the driver by his odd behaviour. (In films, as in life, when a character behaves oddly the audience always wants to know why.) We know that he is having second thoughts about their mission because he says so, but the way he marches along in front of the car, especially in such miserable weather conditions, seems both petulant and childish. The driver emphasizes this in the way he responds by calling Clerici by his Christian name, Marcello, with the tone of voice of an adult trying to cajole a difficult child. It's now that we have the first cut to the summer park and the boy in the sailor suit.

Memory is usually triggered by an incident, image, sound or

smell in the present. Here there seems to be a complex network of factors causing the memory. The childish behaviour of the adult Clerici, emphasized by the driver addressing him in a tone that reminds him of his boyhood, is the strongest trigger and the actual cue into the memory. Another trigger is the visual image of the elegant gates of the wealthy country estate they happen to be passing. (Clerici himself comes from a wealthy family, a fact which plays an important part later in the sequence.) The third element is the similarity of actions and words in relation to the two cars. Clerici, in the present, walks in front of a black car which slowly follows him. The boy in the past also walks in front of a black car which follows him. The boy commands the car to halt in the manner of a master addressing his servant, as does Clerici in the present.

If we look beyond the techniques of film grammar at the content of these scenes we are also learning about some very specific aspects of Clerici's character. When the driver reminds the adult Clerici of his responsibilities, Clerici reacts by remembering himself as a child aping adult behaviour by pretending to be a policeman. We then cut to the adult Clerici stopping the car in exactly the same manner. We witness the authoritarian, controlling side of Clerici's nature and at the same time learn how these characteristics were formed in his childhood and how the child within him is still operating through the man.

2. The car stops and Clerici gets into the back seat. Inside the car we see, from Clerici's point of view, the driver's back.

DRIVER
If we don't go who'll report?
Cut to the sunny afternoon in the park. The camera tracks slowly past people standing in amongst the trees. They appear to be watching something. Sounds over of children whispering.
Cut to time present. The driver's face is out of focus and we look over his shoulder to see Clerici sitting in the back of the car looking serious and thoughtful. Sounds over of the children whispering in the summer park. A slight disturbance flickers over Clerici's face in reaction to the whispering.

– The driver has reminded him of his responsibilities and Clerici has consequently conceded to his duty and got back in the car. His attempt, in a small way, to escape something has failed. Although

in his manner he appeared like the master, or the man with the greater power, in both of these shots Clerici's image in the back of the car is dominated by the driver who is now reminding him of the higher authority they both have to report to. The image, as well as the driver's words, tells us that Clerici is no longer his own master. It could be that this time Clerici is deliberately using his memory in an attempt to either escape from, or to understand, the unpalatable nature of his present dilemma. We return to the park. This time something is going on that is causing the adults present to watch with interest, although we can't yet see what they're watching. This withholding of information is a powerful dramatic device; our curiosity is aroused but not satisfied. The dramatic build-up is further intensified by the whispering from the past that Clerici hears in the car in the present. This use of sound overlapping from one scene, time and place, into another, has the effect of taking us further into Clerici's subjective experience, (we hear the whispering with Clerici but the driver can't), and of pulling Clerici (and us as audience) back into the memory.

3. Summer afternoon in the park. A group of boys are playing in a huddle amongst the trees whispering to each other. A boy, who has perhaps been on watch, runs up to the group.

BOY
The police!

53

The group of boys quickly disbands. We can just make out a boy left lying on the ground with his trousers pulled down. The gang of boys, in their neat school clothes, tear away from the scene of the crime on their roller skates. (The lyrical theme music of the film is played while they skate away.)

The boy, who we now see is young Clerici, clambers to his feet and pulls up his trousers. A black Rolls Royce is parked nearby. On the running board, watching young Clerici, stands an elegant chauffeur, dressed in a smart military-style uniform, black boots and chauffeur's hat. The car door is open waiting for the boy.

Young Clerici picks up his satchel from a nearby park bench, ignores the chauffeur, and walks away in the direction the boys took.

The chauffeur gets in the driver's seat and slowly follows the boy. Young Clerici walks along the road tucking his shirt into his trousers. He then runs in front of the car and, pretending to be a policeman, puts his hand up and calls the car to a halt.

BOY CLERICI

Stop.

– We recognize this action of halting the car as a repeat of the fragment of memory we have already seen and realize that Clerici has now recalled the experience leading up to that moment. Again there is an intimate connection between the present and the past. The driver in the present reminds Clerici of the higher authorities they must report to and similarly a child in the past warns the gang of children in the park that the police (also higher authorities) are coming.

Although the boy, Clerici, is apparently a victim of the other children – he's the one left with his trousers down – the way this sequence has been constructed does not suggest that this incident is the emotional centre or the climax of the memory. This is partly because the scenes we have seen so far in the memory have been in long shot which psychologically places both the adult Clerici and us, the audience, in the position of curious observers rather than participants. (To experience the full emotional impact of the incident we would have needed to see the boys from young Clerici's point of view when they were accosting him, which would have given us some insight into how upset he was, or to have seen his facial expressions, which would also have told us about his feelings.) But instead we see his assailants skating away to the accompaniment of the lyrical theme music. The fluidity of movement combines with the music to evoke a feeling of sensuality rather than deep distress or trauma.

It's in this unexpectedly sensual mood that our focus is shifted from the boys to the elegant young chauffeur. The incident with young Clerici's schoolfriends has immediately been upstaged by the power of the image of the chauffeur and our consequent curiosity about what is to come. Our curiosity is further aroused when the boy ignores the chauffeur and walks away along the now deserted route that his schoolfriends took. The boy then asserts his power by making the chauffeur follow him in the car and then stopping the car when he is ready. But how much power does he really have? He is, after all, merely a young boy in the back seat with a startling-looking man in uniform driving the car.

4. We cut to young Clerici inside the car as it drives past his schoolfriend assailants. He watches them out of the back window as they skate after the car. The car soon leaves them behind and the boy turns and looks at the chauffeur curiously:

CHAUFFEUR
What's your name?

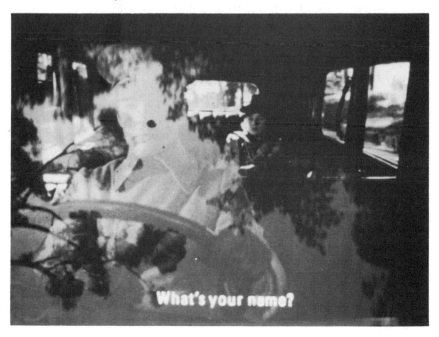

BOY CLERICI

Marcello Clerici. And yours?

Cut to the exterior of the car. It's now high above the city, cruising along an elegant driveway past palm trees and well-tended lawns.

CHAUFFEUR

Pasqualino Semirama, but call me Lino.

The car draws to a halt.

– As the car speeds past young Clerici's assailants the image tells us about his potential power, and his desire for power, because we now see his relation to them in quite a different light. He is no longer their victim, he is now the rich boy in the powerful car while they are reduced to ordinary mortals who he looks down on out of the window.

Next he turns his attention to his chauffeur who, we gather from the way they ask each other's names, is a new employee. It's worth noting here how film can create its own sense of time. Young Clerici asks the chauffeur his name very soon after they leave the gang of boys behind. We hear the chauffeur's reply over an exterior shot of the car arriving in a new location high above the city – in the split second between the question being asked and hearing the reply we have entered another world; the world of a very wealthy Italian family. The chauffeur gives his name in full but also tells the boy his nickname, which suggests a desire for an intimate rather than formal master-servant relationship, and this is our introduction to whatever is to follow in this new time and place.

The dramatic question is now: 'what is going to happen (or, given that we are in a memory, what once happened) between young Clerici and the chauffeur that is relevant to the journey the adult Clerici, a fascist assassin, is now making?

Earlier we saw how, in *Wild Strawberries*, Bergman made quite sure that we knew when we were entering the dream and when the dream had finished. We also noted how he adhered to the conventions of dream language whilst in the dream. But in life, as well as in films, the boundaries between sleep-dreams and conventional notions of reality are quite distinct. The boundaries between our experience of reality and our experience of memory are considerably less distinct. But in this sequence Bertolucci has likewise chosen to make sure his audience knows when we are in the present time, as experienced by his protagonist, and when we are entering his memory, taking great care to illuminate the very specific nature of Clerici's character by exploring each associative detail of his memory process. He has done this because, again like Bergman, the meaning he wants to communicate lies in our being able to make the connection between what happened to Clerici in the past and our understanding of the motivation for his actions in the present. The child within the man is still acting on the man. This is crucial both to what this sequence, and to what the whole film, is about.

Also, look at how, at the end of the sequence, the dramatic thrust within the memory is still energetically moving us forward. We are certainly not yet ready to leave this memory. We want to know what happens next and we feel sure it will be more more illuminating of the present-time dilemma than what we have already seen. We passed over the child being molested by his friends in the park, which for many people would in itself have been a traumatic event, relatively easily so we know that there must be another, more significant event pulling the memory forward and we want to go on to find out what it is. In this sequence Bertolucci has not only achieved a complex exploration of how memory itself works, he has also used its complexity to dramatic effect by carefully observing the urgency of the relationship between memory and present action.

A FANTASY?
KAOS (1984) Written and directed by Paolo Taviani and Vittorio Taviani

Sequence taken from the opening of the fifth story

Kaos is a film made up of five stories based on original material by Luigi Pirandello. Each of the stories is set in the area of Sicily known as Kaos which was also Pirandello's childhood home. The stories are loosely linked thematically in that together they create a portrait of a place, its inhabitants, its history, its sorrows and its magic. In this final story the protagonist, who is Pirandello himself, returns to Sicily after the death of his mother.

> 'CONVERSING WITH MOTHER' (titles white on dark blue)

1. When the film opens we hear the familiar chugging of a train for a few moments before we cut to the interior of a train

compartment. It's empty but for one smartly dressed, middle-aged man. This is Luigi Pirandello. His head rests uncomfortably on his arm on the hard wooden table in front of him. We move into a close-up of his balding head as it's rocked by the motion of the train and then down to his free arm, which is dangling lifelessly. In spite of his obvious discomfort Luigi appears to be in a deep sleep. His hat, which rests on the wooden shelf above him, is also being rocked by the motion of the train. It suddenly rocks to the edge of the shelf and falls.

We then cut to the exterior of the train as it hisses to a halt. It's entering a tiny country station which appears to be the only building in this flat empty landscape. There is a rhythmic clanging of metal as the train waits for a small group of people to climb aboard. The train begins to pull out of the now apparently deserted station when a door is flung open. Luigi jumps awkwardly out of the train and onto the platform, clutching his hat and coat in his arms. As he gains his balance his bag comes flying out of the window and lands unceremoniously at his feet.

– Long train journeys; time out from the normal routine of life, submission to the superior power of the duration of the journey; dreaming and dozing lulled by the familiar, rhythmic chugging of the wheels on the tracks. It's no accident that, after the title has faded and we are left with a dark blue screen, we hear the sound of the train for a few seconds before the image of the train compartment appears. Those few seconds, like a passing whiff, are just enough to remind us what it feels like to be a dreamy submissive traveller and to set the mood for the appearance of our sleeping protagonist.

Although he is fast asleep and we can't see his face, our interest in him is aroused, partly because there is nobody else in the compartment to distract our attention, but mainly because, with the close-ups of his balding head, his dangling hand and his hat, the film is inviting us to contemplate nothing other than this man's total submission to dead sleep.

The hat, which falls off the luggage rack, apparently of its own accord, just as the train happens to be entering the station, then reminds us of forces beyond the control of man, whether they be purely coincidental, or have that wayward quality of dreams, or even suggest a more mystical significance. The sudden movement of the hat's fall also has the effect of energizing the sequence and moving it on, preparing us for something to happen, which in this case is the arrival of the train at the man's destination.

And what a beautiful way to construct a scene of a man getting off a train! The dream-like atmosphere we've been introduced to in the opening scene is sustained. The station is a little like a station in a dream in that it's unlocated, or in the middle of nowhere. And the strange rhythmic clanking which accompanies the train as it pulls into the station adds to the feeling of otherworldliness. The distant figures have climbed onto the train and it's already departing when our man abruptly appears, as if he is being rudely disgorged by the train, with his baggage flung out of the window after him. Apart from being funny, this too has a dream-like quality about it. We know the man was fast asleep when the train entered the station (although maybe the falling hat woke him up), and we also know that he was alone in the compartment, so who is flinging his forgotten baggage out of the window after him?

2. Luigi is alone on the platform, trying to get his bearings. He picks up his bag, looks curiously after the departed train, smiles to himself and shakes his head wonderingly. He then seems to become aware of his new location and the sudden silence. He looks over the rails at the station building; broken mouldings and stucco are peeling off the

59

walls and a wayward vine is creeping over the unreadable, aged station sign. We hear a gentle, haunting music. Luigi turns his attention to the dull, flat landscape around him, as if he's still trying to understand where he is. He then looks over to the platform on other side of the rails where something attracts his attention.

We suddenly see a boy's face filling the screen. He must be eleven or twelve. He has thick dark hair and dark eyes which seem to look optimistically into the future. He is a beautiful boy, full of life, health and vitality. The haunting music swells and he raises both his arms into the air as if they are wings.

We cut back to a close-up of Luigi transfixed by this image of the boy. We then cut to the boy in long-shot. Now we can see that he's wearing a striped top and knee-length trousers and is standing on top of a small pyramid of white sand, which has been left on the station platform. He's holding his arms up in the air as if he is about to fly. But instead he allows his body to go limp, sinks onto the pyramid of sand and rolls down onto the station platform. A second boy appears, runs to the top of the sand and takes his turn rolling to the bottom.

We track slowly from the boys' game, back over the rails,

to find Luigi still standing where the train left him, with his
bag and coat in his arms, looking totally bewildered.

– When Luigi looks curiously after the departing train and smiles to
himself he seems to be asking the same question as we in the
audience are: 'Who could it be who threw his bag out of the
window?' And by the way he shakes his head wonderingly, we
know that the question will remain one of life's mysteries. It's
clearly not of consequence to our story, beyond adding to the
growing sense of our reality not being quite as well ordered,
structured and logical as perhaps it ought to be. In this mood Luigi
looks at the world he has tumbled into. The relative comfort of the
train has gone and the silence adds to our feeling his aloneness.

Then, as he looks at the ageing station building, the name
illegible, the foliage suggesting that it is somehow being reclaimed
by nature (maybe by the same forces as those that toppled the hat
off the shelf and threw the baggage out of the window?), the gentle,
haunting theme music appears on the soundtrack preparing for us
to be transported into another world. This is the moment when
Luigi's attention is attracted by something on the other side of the
tracks, and the boy magically appears.

The reason we experience the boy as magical and hypnotic is the
result of a number of different factors in combination. The first is

61

the culmination, throughout the sequence so far, of small strange moments, just unsettling enough to disturb our sense of time, place, cause and effect. The second is the image of the boy himself; he is unusually beautiful and has an optimistic innocence in his eyes that is wholly captivating. The third element is the shot itself; we cut to the boy after Luigi's attention has been attracted by him – we want to see what our character is seeing. But we don't see what he sees. Or do we?

A moment of pure film magic happens here. The logical shot which should follow, arising from our desire to see what Luigi is looking at, would be a shot of the boy from Luigi's point of view, which would be a long-shot. The boy is, after all, on the other side of the tracks. But instead of that we are given an image of the boy that Luigi could not possibly, realistically, be seeing; a big close-up of the boy's face filling the screen. Because the shots building up to this moment have been communicating Luigi's subjective experience, and the shot following the appearance of the boy is a close-up of Luigi, transfixed by the boy's image, we believe that this must also be his experience. The only way we can rationally comprehend the moment is by deciding that Luigi has imagined, or fantasized the image or that maybe it's in his memory. But the next shot shifts our point of view again. This time we view the boy from a neutral point of view (not from Luigi's) which enables us to see that the boy

is actually there, playing in what we had previously thought was an empty station. Therefore, we deduce, he can be neither a memory nor a fantasy, he must be real.

The film goes on to stress this reality, first by bringing another child into the game, and second, by panning from the boys' game, over the tracks, to where Luigi is standing watching them. In other words, if the boys and Luigi are together in the same unbroken shot, it logically follows that they must be in the same place at the same moment in history! But, in spite of this assertion, the moment we experienced earlier, when the boy magically appeared, remains so powerful we are forced, by the conflicting elements in the grammar of the film, to contemplate the multi-layered nature of Luigi's experience, and therefore of the nature of subjective experience itself. It is as if Luigi, and we the audience, are, like the station building, somehow being reclaimed by the foliage, or by time itself.

3. Luigi steps down on to the rails, crosses to the platform and, while we follow him as he walks past the station buildings towards the exit, we hear the following:

LUIGI (*voice-over*)
I had slept through the two-day journey to Sicily, my first

visit since my mother's death. Somebody had called me back. I never really understood who, but I had willingly left my house in Rome where the effort of living had lately become intolerable; my work, my children, my age. I don't want to explain the inexplicable. Still tired from sleep I wondered if I was still asleep.

Luigi stops walking, puts his foot on a station bench and fixes the buttons which have come undone on his shoe.

– The sequence up until this scene has been absorbing but also disorientating. Luigi's words now ground us in a number of simple ways and in doing so kick off the story. First we are given reasons for his disorientation; Luigi's journey has been long, he's slept for two days and he describes a mysterious feeling; he has somehow been 'called back', as if forces beyond his conscious and rational mind are operating on him. There's no suggestion that these forces are supernatural, he describes a feeling I'm sure most of us have experienced, when our actions cannot be explained in terms of our conscious will. The title of the film is *Conversing with Mother* and we now learn that he is visiting a place of huge emotional significance, his childhoold home, and that this is his first visit since his mother's death. We are also told that living for him has recently become intolerable in all the important areas of his life; his work, his children, his age – so he is not only a man who has been mysteriously 'called' back to his roots and the home of his mother but he is also a man who, because he is going through a crisis of meaning, is in great need. This information enables us to formulate the question: 'given Luigi's need will he find solace, or even a way forward, in the place where he is going?' The story has now begun.

In *Wild Strawberries* and *The Conformist* Bergman and Bertolucci both used film language to ensure that we, the audience, were quite clear about what was dream or memory and what was their protagonist's present reality. In both cases this clarity served the thematic and dramatic intentions of the sequence.

In *Wild Strawberries* Bergman's central concern was that we ask how the Professor's dream will affect his waking life, given that the Professor appears to be complacent and self-satisfied, yet the dream suggests the need for a dramatic confrontation with the self before death. It was necessary that we were able to distinguish clearly between dream and present reality because the issue was how the dream would affect his reality. In *The Conformist* Bertolucci was likewise concerned that we were able to distinguish clearly between Clerici's present preoccupation – his mission as a fascist assassin – and a specific memory from Clerici's past, because he wanted us to consider how what happened between Clerici as a boy and the chauffeur Lino is relevant to the adult Clerici's journey.

In *Kaos*, the Taviani brothers are concerned that the boundaries between present-time reality, normality, memory and fantasy are blurred. Just as the character Luigi says, 'I wondered if I was still asleep,' in other words reality for him feels like a dream. Although we are seeing Luigi in the present on a journey, just like we saw Clerici in the present on a journey, the focus and dramatic thrust of the *Kaos* sequence points towards the past. Whatever he has been 'called' for, and therefore must soon confront, lies in the past, whereas in *The Conformist* what Clerici soon has to confront lies in the present.

What is emerging here is that the way we handle dream, memory and fantasy well is always rooted in the character's experience, the dramatic question which motivates the character and, finally, in what the film-maker is trying to say. The film language, in each of these examples, serves to illuminate these three aspects with no irrelevant or extraneous information to confuse the audience. All the camera set-ups and scenes contribute to the central focus of the sequence. Even in *Kaos*, where the Taviani brothers want us to experience a complex concertinaing of time, the present being reclaimed by the past, or the past leaking into the present, they take great pains to use film language to make clear the specific moments when something strange is happening, or when something from the past leaks through to the present. Each time they break a rule of film grammar they are doing so consciously in order to contribute to what the sequence is about.

All story-telling, in our case fiction films, is rooted in the life experience of a character. Even if that character is portrayed as an animal or a creature from outer space, it is usually endowed with the human ability to experience life. And our everyday life experience is not only linear. We encounter our present through our past, our memory and our dreams. We have the capacity to imagine our distant ancestry and to fantasize a desired future. There are very few film-makers who have contributed significantly to inter-national film culture who have not entered this terrain and as new film-makers establish themselves new boundaries are broken and our perception of ourselves is once more altered.

4 Metaphors and Archetypes:
For a Few Dollars More and *Kaos*

As with dreams, memories and fantasies, metaphors and archetypes are also a part of the continuous, complex and diffuse nature of our everyday experience. They are also concepts which are fundamental to all art forms and most forms of creative endeavour. Many film writers find that the very first idea or inspiration for a new project often comes into their mind in the form of an image that is also a metaphor. The metaphor grounds the idea in a visual form and frequently acts as a guiding light throughout the writing process. In the sequence from *Kaos*, the lonely, aged station building stands as a metaphor for Luigi's state of mind, and the boy, who so magically appears with his arms held up as if he is about to fly, is an archetype of youthful optimism. But these are just two of the numerous examples of metaphors and archetypes which have occurred in the sequences we have explored so far. The purpose of this chapter is to isolate these two concepts and to look at them in greater depth.

A metaphor is a compressed similarity. In film it is an image or sound which has both a literal meaning and at the same time suggests another meaning through resemblance, implication or association with something else. The power of the metaphor derives from the relevance and compression of the comparison. In *Wild Strawberries*, for example, we are not invited to consider how interesting it is that life is like a journey, in some abstract way. The film *is* the journey. The power used by the creator to compress the comparisons into a microcism explodes into meaning. It is through metaphor that we experience depth, complexity, insight and, most importantly, unity – the way all things interpenetrate.

This process of recognition and identification clarifies and affirms what we feel our experience to be and connects us to the larger whole. This connection with something much larger than ourselves

67

and the specifics of our unique experience, through the microcosm reflecting the macrocosm, can feel like the point where art and transcendental or religious experience meet; they are both addressing similar needs that are to do with wholeness and unity.

Which brings us to the question of archetypes. 'Ah, it's a big subject' said Effie's father in Fassbinder's *Effie Briest*. He said this about everything difficult and consequently never managed to talk to his daughter about anything that mattered, and before long she was dead. 'Archetypes' is also a big subject, much bigger than seems immediately apparent in the area of fiction film story-telling. An archetype is an image which is both a metaphor and a microcosm of a myth (a myth, by definition, is an archetypal story) which has recurred, although in many different guises, throughout history and has a universal meaning. Jung, whose understanding of the human psyche is largely based on the concept of archetypes, described them as 'the instinct's perception of itself or as the self-portrait of the instinct'.* Freud also gave them a primary significance when he placed the Oedipus myth, which embodies some of our most familiar archetypes (or 'archaic remnants' as he called them) at the heart of his psychoanalytic theory. Both men agreed that the source of our archetypal images resides in the unconscious although they differed on the role archetypes have to play in our conscious lives and on the precise nature of the unconscious. The Australian Aborigines, on the other hand, would tell us that archetypes are spirits who reside in The Dreamtime and have an existence out there in the desert, the rocks, the trees and the sky, entirely independent from man; a perception of the spirit world common to many primitive cultures. The ancient Greeks would have claimed something similar for their archetypes, which they also believed had a parallel existence in the world of their Gods and Goddesses. In the more recent monotheistic religions archetypes also have an important part to play, although most of the archetypes have become woven into the fabric of story-telling which forms a bridge between man and spirit.

The first of the two microcosms we are going to explore is a sequence taken from the climax of Sergio Leone's Spaghetti Western, *For A Few Dollars More*. At the heart of most Westerns lies the archetypal confrontation between men on the frontier and what

*Quoted by Jolande Jacobi, *Complex Archetype Symbols in the Psychology of C. G. Jung*, trans. Ralph Manheim (Princeton UP, 1959) p. 36

68

they believed to be civilization. But when looking at Sergio Leone's Westerns it's worth remembering that he was an Italian film-maker and as such his insight into the Western myth, as well as being an expression of his personal concerns, has a uniquely European existential perspective.

FOR A FEW DOLLARS MORE (Per Qualche Dollari in più, 1965) Written and directed by Sergio Leone

Sequence taken from the climax of the film

Manco (Clint Eastwood) and Colonel Mortimer (Lee Van Cleef), who is the older of the two and a war veteran, are both bounty hunters in America's Wild West. They find themselves in competition because they are after the same man, Indio (Serg Volonte), a crazed murderer. The Colonel has a personal vendetta to settle with Indio. We don't yet know the precise nature of this vendetta but we do know that both men carry identical pocket watches with a photograph of the same beautiful young woman in the lid. Indio is obsessed with this photograph and (as we have recently learnt through memory flashback) many years ago whilst raping the young woman she reached for his gun and shot herself.

We join the film towards the end of the final shoot-out when Indio's murderous gang have been shot by Manco and Colonel Mortimer. Indio is left to finish the battle alone. The setting is amongst a small group of deserted whitewashed adobe houses, way out in the desert.

1. Indio suddenly emerges from one of the adobe houses and shoots the Colonel's gun clean out of his hand. He walks deliberately towards the Colonel until he reaches a suitable duelling distance. He puts his gun in his holster and takes his watch out of his breast pocket.

> INDIO
> When the chimes end pick up your gun. Try and shoot me Colonel, just try.

He flicks the watch open and the gentle tinkling chimes within begin to play a simple melody.

The Colonel glances at his gun which is lying on the ground a few feet away and looks again at Indio.

Indio takes a few steps towards the Colonel but his attention is increasingly drawn to the watch. As he listens to the simple tune the crazed killer seems to fall into a trance. The chimes are joined by the strings of an orchestra. We cut to Indio's point of view; his hand holds the open watch and the portrait of the young woman faces us. In the background is the duelling distance between Indio and the Colonel whose dark figure stands legs astride with his hands by his hips. Behind the Colonel a horse grazes beneath a tree and in the distance, beyond the desert, a mountain range stretches across the horizon.

– This image feels timeless and quite beautiful in spite of the horrifying agenda; the sequence is, after all, about killing and death. But unlike the chaotic carnage of random killing in the previous scenes, all the ceremonial elements of a ritual duel are now carefully being moved into place. Indio could easily have shot the Colonel, his mortal adversary, but instead even the crazed murderer recognizes the solemnity of the moment. He appears to submit to a higher order. He walks deliberately over to the correct distance from the Colonel and sets in motion the basic ingredients for the honourable duel, apart from the fact that his gun is in his holster and the Colonel's lies on the ground. The scene is very familiar; the force of good, the gunman who is on the side of the law, confronts the force of evil, the bad gunman or the outlaw, and the setting for the final confrontation is the wasteland on the very boundary or frontier of civilization.

Indeed Leone has pared this archetypal confrontation down to only its essential elements and most important, and totally surprisingly, he has placed at the centre, in the very heart of the scene, a pocket watch which plays a gentle melodious tune and contains a photograph of a beautiful young woman. As Indio stares at the photograph, and is transported by the chimes, a feeling which is deliberately emphasized by the addition of the orchestral strings, we see from his point of view all the essential elements in relation to each other: in the immediate foreground the image of a woman placed inside a watch, the feminine and time contained together, and, behind her, the Colonel, his mortal adversary, the horse, man's only true companion in the wasteland, the desert wastes and the distant mountain range. These images are the very opposite of domestic entrapment – here man may be alone but at least he's free. Or is he? And free from what? By placing the feminine aspect and the inexorable nature of time in the heart of the scene Leone penetrates beneath the familiar surface agenda of the duel and invites us to understand its meaning in a new light.

2. Cut to a long-shot of Indio from the Colonel's point of view; Indio's dark figure stands in front of the small group of white adobe houses.

Close-up of the Colonel watching Indio.

Close-up of Indio watching the Colonel.

Big close-up of the Colonel watching Indio.

Big close-up of Indio watching the Colonel. The chimes seem to be slowing down.

The Colonel looks down at his gun lying on the ground. His hand begins to move, as if getting ready to go for his gun.

The chimes of the watch are very slow now, the mechanism has nearly wound down. But suddenly they begin again with a renewed vigour. Both the Colonel and Indio turn their heads in surprise looking in the direction of this new sound.

We see another hand holding an open pocket watch and again the desert and mountains in the distance behind.

The Colonel puts his hand to his waistcoat pocket and pulls out a gold chain – his watch is missing. He looks at Manco, who now appears holding his watch.

A dramatic Mexican guitar is added to the soundtrack. The faces of the three men watching each other suspiciously are intercut. Indio is about to go for his gun but stops when he realizes that Manco, who is holding a pocket watch in one

71

hand and a rifle in the other, has taken control of the situation.

> MANCO
> (to the Colonel)
> Very careless of you old man.

Manco walks to the Colonel's side. He takes off his bullet belt and gives it to the Colonel.

> Try this. Now we start.

To the accompaniment of a solo trumpet Manco walks back to his position which is an equal distance between the two men, careful to keep his gun pointed at Indio, and sits on a small wall which we now see circles the duelling area. He looks from one man to the other. We cut to the dark figures of both Indio and the Colonel as they face each other, silhouetted against the desert landscape. They watch each other and wait. Manco looks down. We cut to a big close-up of his hand holding both his rifle and the pocket watch with the lid open. The image of the young woman again faces us as the chimes begin their countdown to death.

– The dramatic build-up to the final shooting and the inevitable death of one of the adversaries has begun. But, just as the chimes slow down, a new element enters the arena in the form of Manco, who appears like a God or a Fate, holding an identical pocket watch which plays an identical tune. The ritual cycle has been interrupted.

The Colonel looks at his broken watch chain and realizes that Manco has stolen his watch. Manco then refers to the Colonel as 'old man', emphasizing his own relative youth, and the aspect of father-son or teacher-pupil in their relationship, as he gives the Colonel back his gun and lends him bullets. The familiar solo trumpet, so reminiscent of the US cavalry, is also significant here. It plants the idea that order and justice, values associated with the frontier spirit, have at last arrived.

We now see that even the space where the duel is taking place, a circle created by a low wall, reminiscent of both a magic circle and a theatre arena, has a primitive ritual element. And Manco, like Indio before him, submits to the higher order of the ritual, but this time by adhering absolutely to the unwritten rules, first by making the two men equal in arms, and then by sitting an equal distance between them on the edge of the circle. Manco, the young man, the pupil, the son, is now also the adjudicator controlling the action both with his gun and, now he too is in possession of the pocket watch and so the image of the woman, with the chimes. The chimes begin the final countdown and Manco's attention, like Indio's before, is almost hypnotically attracted by their melodious sound. This time from Manco's point of view, the woman, time, the gun and the countdown to death are fatally linked.

3. The chimes slow down and finally stop. The two men draw. Indio falls to the ground but he's not quite dead, he lifts his gun in one final attempt to shoot the Colonel. He fails and his head slumps forward.

MANCO

Bravo.

The Colonel flicks his gun back into his holster and goes to check that Indio is really dead. He puts his foot on Indio's wrist, releases the watch from Indio's fist and takes it. He opens the watch and runs his thumb over the picture inside the lid. Manco walks to his side.

MANCO

There seems to be a family resemblance.

Here.

Manco hands him the other watch.

COLONEL

Naturally, between brother and sister.

– The electric moment of life just before death, which everything has been building up to, is over. The Colonel's retribution, which was apparently his motivation, has been completed. He goes on to tell Manco that the woman in the photograph, who was murdered by Indio, was his sister but somehow this information seems flat. Knowledge of the specific nature of the Colonel's relationship with the woman seems of little importance, compared to how we now see her placed in the heart of the duel. Each of the men, in turn, connect with her image in separate but almost identical ways, which unites them in relation to the feminine archetype, just as they are united in their relation to the masculine tragedy. And although the Colonel's revenge is achieved he seems relatively unmoved. Revenge has so dominated his life that he has very little identity beyond the quest. He is destined to be a traveller alone in the wasteland, searching for more ways of repeating the cycle, as is Manco, his son-figure and pupil.

The ritual has been so carefully constructed, with each image specifically placed in its relation to the others, that we are invited to probe for deeper meanings. Freud's interpretation would probably be: man fleeing his sexual fear of woman by running into the arms of Thanetos, or the death instinct. Jung might suggest that the raped and murdered woman in the photograph is the feminine archetype representing the men's anima, or the feminine part of their own psyche, and it is this that they are fleeing, just as the duel represents the eternal combat with the Shadow, the dark side of his psyche. Sartre would point to the existential quest of man, the road to freedom leading to the inevitable confrontation with death. Manco says 'Bravo' with the flat cynicism of a man who has heard it all before and has just watched yet another re-run of an old show which has many more performances to go.

If, as Jung suggests, archetypes are self-portraits of the instincts, then the duel is a self-portrait of the death instinct. The final microcosm we are going to explore could conversely be described as a self-portrait of the life instinct, although, as you will see, this is something of an over-simplification. The microcosm is the pre-credit sequence of the Taviani brothers' *Kaos*.

KAOS (1984) Written and directed by Paolo Taviani and Vittorio Taviani

Pre-credit sequence

1. Blue sky. Foliage growing on the rocks. A young peasant's dark curly head slowly rises into the frame. He has a hunter's gleam in his eye and is totally absorbed in watching something on the ground in front of him.

Cut to a nearby rock. The head of a second young peasant rises into frame to peer over the rock at what is moving on the ground in front of his companion. His face, which is ensconced in a sort of balaclava made of sheepskin, lights up when he spots his companion's prey.

Cut to a third peasant. This man is also watching but he is much older and frowns as if he doesn't know what to make of what is going on.

Cut back to the curly-haired peasant who suddenly grabs his prey and, although we can't yet see what it is, we hear the cackle of a captured bird.

CURLY-HAIRED PEASANT (*calling excitedly*)
Saro!

Saro, the peasant with the sheepskin balaclava, jumps down to the ground just in front of the captured bird. His face lights up with delight.

The captured bird, a black raven, squawks furiously as the curly-headed peasant pins it to the ground with his hand firmly planted around its neck.

The curly-haired peasant looks up at Saro and smiles gleefully.

CURLY-HAIRED PEASANT
It's a cock raven sitting on eggs.

He lifts the raven from the nest and reveals six large white eggs.
   The older peasant picks up one of the eggs, looks at it suspiciously and then puts it to his cheek.

         OLDER PEASANT
  It's warm.
         CURLY-HAIRED PEASANT
  Cock, are you hatching eggs?

– The sequence opens with the sky and the earth, the most basic dichotomy, and the peasants rise into the frame as if they're so much a part of the earth they're almost growing out of it. The animal skin Saro wears around his head still further emphasizes the primitive simplicity of these men's lives and their closeness to the land.

The peasants are so totally absorbed in what they're watching that we immediately become equally absorbed in watching them. They are alert, like animals, which gives us the feeling that they're hunting something. Their apparently innocent excitement and pleasure is catching, we feel that excitement too. What is it that's so captivating them? The older peasant frowns uneasily. What is it that causes such excitement and such an uneasy frown on the face of the older, wiser man? The more we are prevented from knowing what is going on the more our involvement and curiosity grows. (This withholding of information is an age-old dramatic device and will remain effective for as long as human beings remain curious). The build-up of drama peaks when we see the curly-haired peasant pounce on his prey, we see his pleasure, we hear a captured bird squawking, and finally the cause of such intense excitement is revealed to us; it's not just a bird but a cock raven.

The raven is, of course, simply another of God's creatures. It's also a black, scrawny creature which feeds off carrion left to rot by others, although, according to the mythology of many cultures, the raven symbolizes a foreboding of terrible calamity and doom. But our encounter with this particular raven is more complicated than that. When we first see our raven it's a captured creature squawking in terror; it is the victim and the prey of man. In spite of the apparent innocent enthusiasm of the men, and the sinister mythic associations of the raven, we find ourselves feeling sorry for the bird. Adding still further to this complexity is the information we are given that the raven is a cock, a male, and it's in the process of hatching eggs. In other words the male is behaving unnaturally by being like a nurturing female. The six eggs lie in a small vulnerable cluster in the nest. We look at them and feel awe at the mysterious beginnings of life and acutely aware of the danger to new life now their parent has been snatched from them.

So, the raven, a carrion bird normally associated with ill-omen and doom, in this case is a cock raven nurturing new life and both the father-bird and its eggs are in danger from the predator, man. But what can this combination of associations mean? What is the metaphor? We need to look at some more of the film to find out.

2. Cut to a long-shot of the scene. A huge rock is revealed on the top of a hill. Our three peasants are crouched around the raven at the foot of the rock. Nearby, three other peasants are settled around a fire.

> CURLY-HAIRED PEASANT (*calling to his companions*)
> Look at this! A cock-bird hatching eggs! Shame on you!
> What sort of cock are you?

Two of the peasants by the fire run over to see the bird. The sixth man doesn't seem interested. He stays alone by the fire.

The curly-haired peasant runs to a position near the fire and holds the raven up in the air by its feet.

> CURLY-HAIRED PEASANT
> He who hits it, gets it.

The nest containing the eggs is carried to the scene of the sport. Saro takes an egg out of the nest and hurls it at the bird.

Another young peasant has a throw. His egg smashes against the curly-haired peasant's arm.

> CURLY-HAIRED PEASANT
> Missed!

— We are now able, because of the long-shot, to place the scene in the wider context of the peasants' remote hill-top environment. This shot also enables us to see that there are not three but six peasants in the group, five who join in the fun while the sixth man chooses to separate himself from his companions by remaining alone by the fire, which singles him out for our interest. The long-shot also marks a radical change in rhythm and so begins the next stage of the drama – the setting up of the game.

Drama within scenes and sequences often moves in little arc-like shapes: the drama set up by the question, 'what is it they are watching?' peaks with the capture of the bird and is resolved when we see that the bird is a raven. But within the answer to the old question lies the germ of the new question and so as one arc peaks and is resolved the next arc begins to build. It is also worth noting that just as the dramatic build-up of the opening sequence of scenes focused our attention directly on to the metaphor, so the metaphor remains at the centre of the drama in this next build-up. We now want to know what the discovery of a cock raven hatching eggs means. The rough, simple peasants have no doubts; the bird's behaviour is unmanly and as such it deserves to be an object of fun, derision and punishment. When the egg misses the hapless bird and smashes against the peasant's arm the innocent glee on the men's faces is in sharp contrast to their destructive actions. The peasants' glee is reminiscent of how callous children in groups can be and is also a reminder of ourselves as children. The sight of an innocent creature being mocked, pilloried and stoned by the ignorant group is a familiar motif throughout human history.

3. Cut to a long-shot where we see again that only five of the peasants are joining in the sport, the sixth is still alone by the fire.

Cut back to a close-up of the curly-haired peasant holding the hapless bird up as a target. The sixth man, Salvatore, then suddenly jumps in front of him and snatches the bird from his grasp.

PEASANTS
Salvatore, what are you doing?
Salvatore calms them with his hand. He then takes a goat's bell from inside his sheepskin jacket, holds it high in the air and shakes it.

SALVATORE
Music!
We hear the clear high pitched ringing of the bell and see it silhouetted against the sky.

Salvatore then crouches down on the ground, ties the bell around the now calm raven's neck, stands, looks up to the

79

heavens and releases the bird by launching it up into the clear blue sky.

The raven flutters against the blue sky. The lyrical theme music of the film begins.

Saro and his young peasant companion watch in awe as the raven circles in the sky above them.

Salvatore watches with a kind of quiet paternal concern.

SALVATORE (*quietly*)

Go on.

We soar with the raven, higher and higher, leaving the peasants way behind as we see the world below from the raven's point of view. We soar over the steep escarpments of the barren hills, past little villages clinging to the cliff edges and circle around the ruin of an ancient Greek temple.

Opening credits.

– Now we see why the sixth peasant, Salvatore, chose to remain separate from the others. He sees something that they don't see. He feels something that they don't feel. And he acts on his feelings by saving the bird. As he calms his companion's protests with a gentle hand gesture we see the power of the man; he is like an actor, a teacher, or a prophet who has the power to hold his audience enthralled and to communicate to them something that they hadn't previously seen. When he holds the simple goat's bell up in the air, rings it and tells us this is 'music', the simple sound, against the blue sky, becomes the most pure music. And when he ties the bell around the raven's neck and launches the bird on its journey our spirits are lifted up to the heavens with the bird's flight.

Salvatore, by tying the bell around the raven's neck and giving it freedom, has put together a combination of images which gives us our much-needed insight into the significance of the metaphor. The male raven hatching eggs suggested both a foreboding of death and a nurturing of life. The opposites, destruction and creation, are united in this image, just as these equally potent forces are inextricably linked in the creative act. But, as has frequently been the case throughout history, when a work of art is not understood, it has been mocked and pilloried by the uncomprehending or ignorant. Salvatore is the only one of the peasants who understands what the discovery of a male raven hatching eggs means. When he ties the bell around the raven's neck he returns this meaning to the bird and, by creating a new metaphor for creativity, gives us the insight which enables us too to escape from ignorance and callousness and to soar up into the sky with that wonderful feeling of freedom, elation and transcendence.

As we soar with the bird the ironies of the image begin to emerge; the bell is a heavy weight around the raven's neck, could this be a last soaring before death? Is the bird, which was liberated and set free by the bell, also going to be destroyed by the bell? Life and death are as always locked together – but is this so terrible while, for the moment, we feel the intoxication and exhilaration of glorious flight? The land below is illuminated with a sense of timelessness and we see antiquity, in the form of an ancient Greek temple, presiding over the present from its position on the hill-top. The artist Salvatore's creative act has transformed our experience and given us meaning and hope.

As Bergman said, the primary factor in film is the image (the cock raven hatching eggs, masculine and feminine united), the secondary factor is the sound (the bell) . . . and the tension between these two creates the third dimension (film art). Finally, this archetypal metaphor has been about film itself.

Two

THE MACROCOSM *or* THE WHOLE STORY

Introduction:
Questions of Structure

Every art form appears to have an inner structure which is innate to the medium itself. For instance, the Ancient Greeks defined certain principles underlying the relationships between shapes within the rectangle. These basic structures can be seen in the underlying geometry of much of European fine art and architecture, and in modern movements which have stripped away the surface layers of content to present pure form. The Ancient Greeks, in particular Aristotle, also defined certain basic structures which they felt underlay dramatic narrative form, which for them, of course, was restricted to the Greek amphitheatre. Some of these basic structures can be traced through the history of western story-telling forms and the evolution of dramatic art right through to contemporary feature films.

The dynamic energy or force generated by the structures themselves would suggest that they represent something essentially human and unchanged by time. From the Ancient Greeks to the present time represents a single epoch in the history of civilization and so we are naturally adhering to a continuity of thought about ourselves, society and art. But each new artist's dynamic relationship with structure is also crucially affected by convention; the customs and practices of their period in history, which overlay these basic inner structures, but often become so accepted by popular culture that many believe them to be innate to the form itself.

The medium in our case is the feature film, which makes the question of what these basic structures are that much more complicated, because feature film is not only one of the newest art forms, it is also a hybrid: the theatre and the novel are its obvious first cousins, and photography, painting, music, sculpture (Tarkovsky

85

chose to call his book *Sculpting in Time**) and poetry are all important relations. In the following chapters we are going to focus on the classic narrative structure which film has inherited from story-telling and dramatic art, which, as I mentioned earlier, can be traced back to Aristotle. We can then move on to explore the philosophical basis of classic narrative and consider some of the implications of departing from the form from the points of view of both the audience and film-makers.

A Brief Outline of the Basic Principles

Classic narrative is basically linear. It is like a river which has a source in an inland spring. The water bubbles up from the ground and sets off on a journey, pushed forward by the energy generated at its source. It twists and turns and gains momentum according to the obstacles in its path, as if it always has one aim in view; to finally reach and unite with its destination, the sea.

Premise: The premise is the source of the river. It is the initial set of circumstances which generates the conflict and so the energy which causes the water to bubble forth and begin its journey to the sea. Some of these circumstances may have been born way back in the past life of the protagonist, or way back in the history of events which turn out to be intimately connected to the protagonist's life. The premise is when these gestating elements combine with one, or some, crucial new ingredients, and the combination, like a chemical reaction, causes the journey to begin.

Protagonist: The protagonist is the character who embodies the central conflict generated by the premise. The key attribute of a protagonist is that he or she has an overriding and conscious want or aim that is difficult to achieve.

Aim: In our river analogy the aim is to get to the sea. So, to extend the analogy a little further, the aim is like a lighthouse at the river mouth. The flashing beacon represents the vision or ideal that the protagonist is striving to reach. The story begins when the struggle to achieve the aim begins and the story ends when the aim is either finally achieved or when it is finally lost, or ceases to have its hold over the protagonist. The aim, therefore, provides the backbone for the story.

*Andrey Tarkovsky, *Sculpting in Time: Reflections on the Cinema*, trans. K. Hunter-Blair (Bodley Head, 1986)

Obstacles: The obstacles are everything that stands in the way of the protagonist achieving his or her aim. These are usually a mixture of other people and external circumstances or events which come into conflict with the aim. Obstacles can also be facets of the protagonist's own personality; unconscious needs which may prove to have a stronger hold over the protagonist than what they think they want, and character traits which thwart the protagonist's progress.

The Dramatic Question: The dramatic question arises from the conflict between the protagonist's aim and the obstacles. Providing the necessary ingredients to enable the audience to formulate the dramatic question is an essential part of the opening. From then on each sequence takes up the previous sequence's dramatic question, like a relay baton, but which, according to the course of events, is each time re-formulated into a new but closely related version of the original question posed by the opening.

Characterization and Motivation: Motivation is the character's incentive, or what causes their aim or desire. As we have just noted, the protagonists are motivated by a complex mixture of conscious wants and unconscious needs or desires. They also have highly individual personality traits, of which some hinder their progress while others provide the key to their possible fulfilment. Characterization is the totality of what a character wants and needs and their character traits, in combination with some idea of their motivation. Characterization is obviously especially important in relation to the protagonist because it's he or she who embodies the backbone of the story structure. But all of the major characters in a drama have their own aims and their own motivation, which is either in conflict or in harmony with the protagonist's aim and so provides the rich textural body of the story. Therefore equal attention needs to be paid to the characterization of all the major players.

Identification: Identification is when we experience and feel what is happening in the story from the point of view of the protagonist. Their hopes and fears become our hopes and fears.

Exposition: Exposition is the information about events that have happened before the story begins that is necessary to our full understanding of the story. In the traditional theatre exposition is usually communicated through dialogue. In film we have the additional possibilities of voice-over narration, flashbacks and memory-flashbacks to give us insight into such past events.

87

The Macrocosm or the Whole Story

The Beginning or Opening: This is the first section of the story when most, if not all, of the above ingredients have been made manifest.

Development Sequences: These are the sequences in the central body of the story which, although intricately interwoven into the flow of the story, can also, under close examination, often be seen to have a beginning, middle, ending and dramatic question of their own. Each development sequence either moves the protagonist nearer to, or further away from, his or her aim. If the development sequence takes us quite a long way from the aim, to a point where we are in danger of losing sight of it, the aim is usually re-affirmed, which puts the story back on course. The early development sequences are usually devoted to exploring the initial obstacles. In the late development sequences a momentum is usually gathering, and a sense of urgency, as we move towards the ending.

The Plant: This is when our attention is drawn to an object, a piece of information, or an incident that has little or no direct bearing on the present action but arouses our curiosity because we feel it might have an important part to play later in the story.

Dramatic Irony: This is when the audience knows something that the protagonist or major characters don't know. It has the effect of making us more aware of their vulnerability – we want to warn them, or tell them what they need to know, but, of course, we can't. In this way it increases our emotional involvement with their plight.

The Ending: This is the final part of the story when the following ingredients become manifest.

Crisis: This is an incident, near the ending of the story, which can loosely be described as the straw that breaks the camel's back, or the point of no return. It sparks off the climax, which usually follows immediately or very soon after.

Climax: The climax is effectively the end of the story. It is the inevitable outcome of the crisis. It is the incident which the entire story has, directly or indirectly, been building up to. And it always contains the final answer to the central dramatic question posed at the beginning of the story. It is in the climax that the protagonist's aim is either finally achieved or finally thwarted. In Aristotle's view, in tragedy this is the moment of catharsis, when the audience is purged or cleansed by pity or terror and so healed by the experience. (Opening and development sequences also very often have their own mini-form of crises and climaxes, but these are never so momentous that they end the story.)

Resolution: The resolution is the inevitable outcome of the final major climax. We see how the protagonist has changed (if they have survived the climax!) now that their aim has finally been disposed of. The other threads to the story are also finally wrapped up.

Theme: The theme refers to the meanings of the film or what it is about. Most of us have had the experience of leaving the cinema with friends and finding ourselves, whether we like it or not, plunged almost immediately into an intense discussion about what the film was saying. The focus of this discussion is usually the climax, the outcome of the film, and from there we work backwards. This is because, although many sub-themes may have been touched on during the course of the film, the central theme, which is of overriding importance because it is what the film's author is saying and is therefore the moral standpoint of the film, invariably comes to the surface in the climax. The climax, which is usually a highly dramatic incident, is the watershed that brings about a radical change in the protagonist, it's everything the film has been leading up to, it's the final outcome. And in films, just as in life, when a watershed incident takes place our thoughts about meaning are provoked because we want and need to understand.

Unity: 'The various incidents must be so arranged that if any one of them is differently placed or taken away the effect of wholeness will be seriously disrupted. For if the presence or absence of something makes no apparent difference, it is no real part of the whole.' Aristotle*

Aristotle's original definition, when closely examined, is difficult to better. A sense of unity is what many screenwriters and filmmakers still strive for. It means that every image, scene and sequence, whether it directly relates to the unfolding narrative or is concerned with mood, atmosphere, metaphor, or simply with telling us, in the way film does so well, about the kind of place we are in, is a carefully considered part of an organic whole. And it reminds us to think of the economy of our work, and to consider our reasons for what we want to include and what should perhaps be

*Classical Literary Criticism, Aristotle/Horace/Longinus, trans. T. S. Dorsch (Penguin, 1965) p. 43

left out because it doesn't have an intrinsic place in the overall scheme of things.

Many of the above points are mentioned in Aristotle's writings on the nature of drama. Since then numerous works about the structure of drama have been written, both about the theatre and more recently about film. Some of these works have looked at radical innovations and others have turned the form into a dogmatic formula, even going so far as to assert that the ingredients of the opening should have been dealt with by a specific page number, and by the next specified page number you should have revealed your next plot point!

Aristotle's writings are part of the beginning of a new epoch when there was a radical shift in man's view of himself, which can perhaps best be summed up as humanist. In *The Poetics* Aristotle writes that 'the unravelling of the plot should arise from the circumstances of the plot itself, and not be brought about *ex machina* . . . there should be nothing inexplicable about what happens, or if there must be it should be kept outside the tragedy.'* *Deus ex machina* literally means a god from the machine. In Aristotle's time, and throughout the preceding epoch, most people believed not only that there were hundreds of gods and goddesses acting out the most incredible and extraordinary dramas in another dimension but that these gods and goddesses and dramas had a direct effect on events in their earthly, everyday lives. The significance of Aristotle, demonstrated in the above quote, is that he shifted the responsibility for events away from the gods and firmly placed it on man himself.

Aristotle also said in *The Poetics* that '. . . in deciding whether something that has been said or done is morally good or bad, not only should we pay regard to the goodness or badness of the saying or deed itself, but we should also take into account the person by whom and to whom it was said and done, the occasion, the means, and the reason – whether for example, to bring about the greater good, or to avert a greater evil.'† In other words, if there should be nothing inexplicable about what happens, man must also bear the moral responsibility for events and this moral responsibility can only be judged in the light of all the information we need to enable us to understand 'the occasion, the means and the reason'.

* Ibid. p. 52
† Ibid. p. 71

The importance of Aristotle for understanding modern narrative conventions is that the philosophy on which he based his approach to drama has dominated western thought for the past twenty-four centuries. The philosophy is linear and rational – for everything there is a reason, if only we have all the information we need to understand it. Man is no longer a victim of forces outside of himself and beyond his control, if he is a victim of anything at all he's a victim of himself. Within the broad confines of this philosophy there are, of course, a multitude of arguments to be resolved, as the history of Western philosophy demonstrates. We will be exploring some of these conflicts when we look at departures from the classic form. But first we need to see how the classic form, outlined above, manifests itself in feature-film story-telling.

1 The Beginning:
Midnight Cowboy and *Viridiana*

If we tried to explore entire feature films in the same kind of detail we employed for the microcosms this book would become far too heavy, so I've decided to concentrate on just two films, *Midnight Cowboy* and *Viridiana*, which, although from different cultures, both conform to the classical tradition. I have broken our exploration of the two films down into their three main parts: the beginning, the development sequences, and the ending. For each part I have described only the key aspects of the developing story outlined of both films, (rather than go into the complex network of film language which we looked at in our exploration of microcosms) and I have followed each description with my observations about how the basic structure emerges from the texture of the developing films.

Both the films fall easily into three parts. In *Viridiana* the shape of each part, both in length and construction, is closer to the form's origins in the theatre, where notions of time and place were thought to be more restricted by the medium. In *Midnight Cowboy* we will see how film's natural freedom with time and place has allowed for a more episodic structure, a shorter beginning, more development sequences, and a shorter ending. Nevertheless the basic ingredients in each section are very similar to the original theatre model.

As I mentioned earlier, the danger of this kind of structural analysis is thinking of form as a formula; a set of rules which function like an empty vessel. All the screenwriter has to do is learn the formula, pour in their fresh content and, hey presto, they have a screenplay. Although this attitude to form is very prevalent in the film business it's not very conducive to producing original work. We have already taken the first step in breaking free of this formula-based approach, which is to think of the form as a philosophy of man rather than an abstract vehicle. And my intention with the following two film analyses is not to fit the films to the form but to see how the form emerges organically from the rich texture of the films, which will enable us to connect the form with its philosophical roots. Also, in this way, we will be able to get a feeling for two very different and highly personal interpretations of the form, whilst at the same time developing real understanding of the concepts of structure through experiencing how they manifest themselves in film language.

MIDNIGHT COWBOY (1969) Screenplay by Waldo Salt Directed by John Schlesinger (Based on the novel by James Leo Herlihy)

THE BEGINNING: Part One

1. Familiar sounds of a gun-fight (taken from an old Western). We then see a huge cinema screen standing against the vast and empty Texan desert landscape. But the screen is blank and the drive-in movie theatre is deserted.

2. In a cheap motel room a handsome young man, Joe (John Voight), soaps himself in the shower and sings 'Whoopie ti yi

yo, git along little dogies, you know New York will be your new home. . . .' He then enthusiastically sprays his arms and crotch with deodorant and dresses in his brand new clothes: bright red shirt, thigh-clinging pants, Stetson, and, finally, a magnificent pair of cowboy boots. This process is intercut with scenes from the scullery of a fast-food restaurant. First Ralph, an ageing black worker calls for Joe Buck, then a sweating waitress peers over a growing pile of dirty dishes and demands to know where he is, and finally the irate manager takes up the cry. Joe, as if in answer to the commotion he is causing, turns admiringly to his now fully adorned image in the mirror and says, 'You know what you can do with those dishes. And if you ain't man enough, I'll be happy to oblige.' With this proud statement, and now ready to take on the world, he kicks open the door of his seedy motel room and walks out into the sunshine.

3. We track with Joe as he walks energetically through the sprawling Texas backwater, with his brand new horse-hide suitcase swinging in his hand. The credits roll and we hear the title song '. . . . I'm going where the sun keeps shining through the pouring rain, I'm going where the weather suits my clothes . . .'

4. Joe walks proudly into the busy fast-food restaurant and tries to ask his boss for the back-pay owed him but the manager ignores his request, demands to know what he's doing in such a ridiculous get-up and tells him to get on with his work. Nobody seems bothered with Joe's departure except for the ageing black man, Ralph, his fellow dish-washer, who asks him what he's going East for:

> JOE
> There's a lot of rich women back there Ralph, begging for it, paying for it too, and the men, they're mostly tootie-fruities . . . So I'm going to cash in on some of that, right. What do I get to stay around here for? I've got places to go.
With that Joe walks back out into the street.

5. Joe passes the window of Sally's, a derelict beauty salon. He peers through the window and (in superimposition) we see a twelve-year-old boy massaging the shoulders of an

94

attractive middle-aged woman who sighs and moans with pleasure. The image suddenly disappears (as if Joe has pushed it out of his mind) and is replaced by a FOR RENT sign. Joe hurries on his way.

6. Joe jumps on the Greyhound bus bound for New York.

NOTES

1. The opening image tells us we are in contemporary South-west America which answers our first question – 'where are we?' But this image is also pure cinema; on the soundtrack we hear a Western gun-fight but the cinema screen we see is as empty and barren as the Texan desert behind – although, as the soundtrack reminds us, this was once the battle-ground of the new frontier, heartland of the American Dream.

2. Our next question is 'who?' and this question is also immediately satisfied. We meet Joe Buck in the shower and the sequence is spent getting to know him. Each new piece of filmic information gives us an additional clue as we try to work out what the basic situation is that will generate the coming film and give us an idea of what it's going to be about.

First we have Joe's song – which again contains a strange mixture

95

of the old West and a vision of the East, New York, as now being the desirable place to go.

The energy of Joe's preparations, and his brand new clothes, tell us that this is a very special day – the final burst of deodorant on his crotch even suggests that sex may be high on his agenda.

The commotion in the restaurant scullery not only shows us the nature of Joe's work but also, as we learn from his imaginary confrontation with his boss, what he's intent on escaping from.

3. We get still more insight into what Joe's escaping from when we walk with him through the sleepy suburb where his infectious optimism is further heightened by the words of the title song, which is also about making a journey to a new life.

4. When Joe arrives at the restaurant we finally learn the precise nature of his aim, and hence the situation at the root of the film. He's going East, to New York, to make his fortune as a male prostitute. We are given this crucial information in a simple and believable way – in response to a question Ralph would naturally ask at such a time. The restaurant scene also gives us further clues about the complexity of the situation. First, in spite of Joe's bravado, he doesn't have the nerve to get his back pay from his boss. And second, the naivety of his image of New York, as a city paved with rich, frustrated women and men who can't give them what they want, gives an insight into the unrealistic nature of Joe's expectations and hence into the possible obstacles and dangers ahead of him.

We now know the protagonist's aim and the first obstacle to his achieving that aim, and so the dramatic question can now be formulated: 'How will Joe Buck, given his naivety, survive as a male prostitute on the streets of New York?'

5. But we are given one final piece of information before we climb on the Greyhound bus and this is portrayed by the image of the boy massaging the woman's shoulders in Sally's Beauty Salon. The salon is derelict, which means we have entered Joe's unique interior world of either memory or fantasy and the image seems to relate directly to Joe's aim in that the young boy is somehow servicing the older woman's sexual needs. But the way the image suddenly disappears and is replaced by the immediate reality of the FOR RENT sign is almost brutal and seems to leave Joe, and us, with a sudden sense of loss. We don't yet know for sure who the boy or the woman

are but this scene suggests that the motivation for Joe's journey is not purely material, his deeper motivation relates to certain unresolved issues from his own past. In other words there are two aspects to what is motivating the aim: what the character consciously wants and what he unconsciously needs.

THE BEGINNING: Part Two

1. As the bus speeds out of the suburbs into the desert Joe tries to strike up a conversation with the driver, who totally ignores him. Snubbed and hurt Joe retreats to the back of the bus where he manages to impress two giggling teenage girls. Reassured, he gives his new boots a quick polish with his handkerchief and then turns to stare out of the window at the familiar Texan landscape. The momentousness of his departure from his home environment now seems to close in on him.

2. Dissolve from Joe's thoughtful face through to the hesitant smile of the boy we saw earlier (in Sally's beauty salon). He's now standing outside a cowboy hat shop and we hear his grandma in voice-over: 'You look real nice lover boy, real nice. Make your old grandma proud. You're the best-looking cowboy in the whole parade. You're going to be the best-looking one there.' We think these words are meant for young Joe but we now cut to the boy's point of view and see that he is watching his grandma take another cowboy, a full-grown man, into her arms, leaving Joe somehow excluded and alone. We next see grandma telling young Joe that his TV dinner's in the oven because 'old grandma's got herself a new beau'.

3. Joe's memory is interrupted by a young mother who is now on the next seat asking for some gum for her little girl. Joe takes the opportunity to proudly tell the mother that he's going to New York. She smiles politely but soon falls asleep and Joe plays peek a boo with the little girl; Joe hiding behind his cowboy hat and the little girl behind her Wonder Woman comic.

4. Joe once again drifts into his imaginary world. On the soundtrack we hear a girl whispering words of love and we see:

– Anastasia, a beautiful teenage girl, running through a field of corn towards a house.
– Joe, as one of a pack of local youths, following Anastasia down a dusty street.
– The pack of youths chase Anastasia across a desert landscape.
– Back at the house Anastasia runs into Joe's arms. They make love with Anastasia whispering to Joe that he's 'the only one' and 'the best one'.

5. Joe seems disturbed by his memories and looks to the next seat hoping to be reassured by the mother and child, but their seat is now empty and he is suddenly very alone.

6. An old man now sits in the next seat. Joe tries to make conversation by asking the old man if he knew his grandma, Sally Buck, but the old man simply shakes his head and looks away.

7. It's night and the bus speeds past lurid neon signs as we intercut with more of Joe's childhood memories: in bed with his grandma and one of her lovers; at the rodeo; as small boy in military uniform being left with his grandma by two young women; rocking on the front porch.

8. It's day and the bus is now filled with drunken servicemen. Joe hears the New York announcer on his radio and whoops with joy as he realizes they are at last entering New York City. His optimism has now fully returned.

Notes

The bus journey, taken as a whole, feels like a transition from the known to the unknown. In the first part of the opening we focused on Joe's optimism and although we realized there were dangers in the naivety of his expectations we were swept along by his confidence and energy. Now his hopes and fears, and our hopes and fears for him, are being pitted against each other in dramatic conflict, the tension growing as we near his destination.

1. The snub by the bus driver is a first reminder of how indifferent strangers can be and Joe is heading for a world where everyone will at first be strangers! This rejection is quickly counteracted by his momentary success with the giggling girls, and when he polishes his boots we are reminded of the optimism of his sexual agenda.

2. Joe is leaving his home environment, probably for the first time ever, and his thoughts and feelings turn naturally towards his home and past. We have already been given a hint that there are complexities in Joe's childhood that are motivating his present action. We now enter a more disturbing memory. We think grandma's loving words are meant for young Joe and feel a real shock when we realize that the boy is simply an onlooker, displaced and excluded by grandma's new beau.

3. The young mother and child sitting next to Joe revive our hopes by reminding us of the potential friendliness of strangers. And the game Joe plays with the little girl also serves to remind us of the childlike traits in Joe's character; cowboys, like Wonder Woman, populate the world of children's fantasy. Joe's childlike traits are endearing but they also remind us of the danger his naivety may put him in.

4. Joe's next venture into his world of memory is even more unsettling. The images of himself alone with Anastasia are beautiful but also seem idealized, memory tinted with fantasy, and when we see him as a member of the local gang of youths chasing Anastasia we feel a strong hint of danger and potential violence. Anastasia's words of love 'you're the only one', when put together

with Joe's earlier memory of being displaced by grandma's new beau, remind us of Joe's unfulfilled need, only now we learn the very specific nature of this need; to be loved and to be the only one. But the memory/fantasy sequence as a whole raises more questions than it gives answers, implying a larger agenda behind Joe's deep motivation and leaving us wanting to know more.

5. Finally, as the bus draws nearer to New York, we are increasingly filled with fears for Joe's future, fears emphasized by the disappearance of the mother and child, the indifferent old man, the lurid neon signs in the night and appearance of the drunken servicemen, each suggesting the very opposite dynamic to the optimism encountered in the motel room and the sleepy Texan streets. But, nevertheless, Joe whoops with joy as the bus enters New York City. This new, unknown world may be fearful and alien but Joe Buck will find a way, or will he?

In the beginning as a whole Joe Buck has been firmly established as the protagonist. His aim has been clearly stated, he's going to New York to become a male prostitute and this is the basic situation which is driving the action forward. We've been told enough about Joe for us to believe that he is capable of achieving his aim: he's handsome, he's got a beautiful body, he takes pride in his appearance, he's charming, he's energetic and enthusiastic, and his childhood experience seems to have prepared him for the work. The obstacles, or dangers, which threaten the fulfilment of his aim have also been clearly set up: he's naive, he has difficulty confronting authority (i.e. asking his boss for money), he has unrealistic expectations, his motivation seems to relate to some dangerously unresolved issues from his past, he's easily hurt when snubbed by strangers, he has childlike needs for reassurance, and, finally, the alienation and indifference he encounters on his way to New York will probably be ten times worse in the big city itself.

Joe's motivation has been touched on, both at the level of want and need. The motivation behind his want is his desire to start a new, and hopefully lucrative, life, and at a deeper level it looks like he may want to re-enact a sexual pattern he learnt in childhood with his grandma. His deeper needs for the security of love, to be 'the only one' and possibly to resolve a violent incident in his youth, have taken us still further into the complexity of the situation.

Finally, when the film opened, our hopes for Joe were paramount, we believed he was capable of achieving his aim, but by the end of the beginning our fears for him have definitely moved into the ascendant. The stakes against him are high but the potential in his character, manifested by his sheer enthusiasm, gives us hope that he may be able to find a way.

VIRIDIANA (1961)
Screenplay by Luis Buñuel and Julio Alejandro
Directed by Luis Buñuel

THE BEGINNING: Part One

1. The credits roll over a still shot of an ageing neo-classical building and are accompanied by Handel's 'Hallelujah Chorus'.

2. We then cut to a busy nunnery courtyard. A crocodile of neat little boys hurry past and a group of nuns are deep in conversation. Mother Superior walks up to the group and tells Viridiana that she wants to speak with her.

3. Viridiana, a strong, serious and beautiful young woman, listens while Mother Superior tells her that she's received a letter from Viridiana's uncle, asking permission for Viridiana to come and stay with him before she takes her vows. She tells Viridiana that she should go, her uncle is her only living relative and he's in poor health. But Viridiana doesn't want to go, her uncle has shown no interest in her before, she's only ever met him once in her life and can hardly remember him. Mother Superior reminds Viridiana that her uncle has paid for her education and sent her dowry to the convent, for which Viridiana should be grateful. And, as she's taking her vows in just a few days' time, she will never get the opportunity to see him again. Viridiana finally contains her anger and concedes: 'I have no desire to go outside again,' she says, 'but if you order me to . . .' Mother Superior tells Viridiana to go to her cell and get ready to leave in the morning. She walks away leaving Viridiana looking upset and angry.

Notes

1. The static image of the neo-classical facade remains on screen for so long that some people find it boring and others amusing. The building has nothing to commend it, the pillars are imitation Greek,

like so many establishment buildings dotted around Europe, and there is little to think about while the credits roll other than the visual pun on 'the pillars of the establishment'. The music, rather than transcending the building, merely provides an air of pomposity.

2. The wide shot of the courtyard tells us we are in an active nunnery. And the crocodile of little boys indicates the oppressive conformity of the convent educational system. When Mother Superior calls to Viridiana we immediately assume that we are meeting our protagonist because of the film's title. (But there is important information in the sequence which also leads us to this conclusion.)

3. Viridiana's conversation with Mother Superior clearly sets up the conflict. Viridiana's life is about to be interrupted: in just a few days she is due to take her vows but first she must leave the safety of the nunnery and go to visit her uncle, and she doesn't want to go. This conversation also contains all the necessary exposition: we learn that Viridiana can hardly remember her uncle, that he's her only living relative and that he's paid for her education and dowry but never given her any love. The inclusion of Viridiana's dowry here is interesting; it reminds us that when she takes her vows she will, in effect, be marrying Christ.

We also learn about Viridiana's character. First, we can see from her expression that she's not naturally obedient; on the contrary, she's a strong-willed woman who has to work to contain her emotions. She makes her wishes quite clear to Mother Superior and only gives in because she must be obedient to Mother Superior's orders. When she finally states that she has no wish to see the outside world again we believe her.

So, Viridiana's aim is already clear; she wants to devote her life to Christ and remain in the convent away from the outside world. But so far there are only two obstacles which look as if they might interfere with her aim; her enforced visit to her uncle and her difficulty with obedience which could be construed as a lack of true humility.

THE BEGINNING: Part Two

1. We are now on the country estate owned by Don Jaime, Viridiana's uncle. When the scene opens we see a little girl's

bare legs, opening and shutting like compasses as she plays under a large tree with her skipping rope. This dark-haired, wild-looking child is called Rita, and she's the housekeeper's daughter. Don Jaime, a kindly looking, elderly man, stands watching her. In the background a carriage arrives. Don Jaime tells Rita to run along and play, hangs her skipping rope on the tree and goes to greet Viridiana.

2. Viridiana climbs down from the carriage to be greeted by Ramona, Don Jaime's housekeeper, a tired, middle-aged woman, and by Don Jaime who walks with Viridiana towards the house. Viridiana tells her uncle, frankly, that she's only come to see him because her Mother Superior ordered her to and although she's grateful to her uncle materially she has no feelings for him. Don Jaime, crestfallen, although understanding her lack of feeling, asks if it's too late. 'Yes, it's too late,' Viridiana replies and firmly changes the subject by commenting on how he's neglected the farm. Don Jaime agrees that he's let the place go over the past twenty years but nowadays he hardly ever goes out. 'And when he does go out he makes me skip,' Rita suddenly calls to them from the branches of the tree above their heads. Viridiana laughs, lighting up when she sees the little girl. Don Jaime looks wistfully at Viridiana and comments on how like her aunt she looks.

3. It's night and Don Jaime is playing on his old, out-of-tune organ with an emotional sensuality. Viridiana is alone in her room, preparing her bed by placing her pillow at the head of the mat on the floor. She glances dismissively at her reflection in the mirror, shakes her hair loose from her cap, sits on the bed, opens her bodice buttons and finally takes off her black stockings, revealing her very beautiful legs. Don Jaime continues to play on his organ.

4. As Ramona passed Viridiana's closed door she bends down and peers through the key hole. Viridiana, now in a plain white nightdress, opens her case and takes out a wooden cross and a crown of thorns. Ramona goes to Don Jaime, who is still playing the organ, and tells him what she has seen in Viridiana's room.

5. Viridiana kneels on the mat and prays. The cross, the

crown of thorns, a small group of nails and a large hammer
have been carefully placed on a lace pillow in front of her.

Notes

1. We open on little Rita skipping. This dark-haired, wild child
seems to be the very opposite of self-possessed, blonde, Viridiana.
Although Rita is still a child, the focus on her bare legs suggests
both her potential sexuality and her vulnerability and hence a sense
of danger. We then see that Don Jaime is watching Rita skip, and
transpose this sense of danger on to the elderly man. Our curiosity
about Don Jaime, Viridiana's uncle, has already been aroused in the
first part of the beginning. We already suspect that he might
become a major obstacle for her and so our first encounter with the
man as a potential sexual threat, however tenuous the connection,
is significant.

Our attention is also deliberately drawn to the skipping rope
which Don Jaime hangs on the tree. This image feels like a plant. (A
plant is an image or action which has been deliberately placed to

arouse our curiosity because it will have a part to play later in the story.)

2. Viridiana's carriage arrives and first we are introduced to Ramona. We wonder if, as a major character in Don Jaime's household, she will become an ally or an obstacle for Viridiana.

Viridiana and Don Jaime walk towards the house and Viridiana's strong-willed frankness is again evident. When Don Jaime asks if 'it's too late' we realize that he's hoping to develop some kind of relationship with her, but she quickly rebuffs him and we suspect that their different desires may become a source of major conflict for Viridiana.

Viridiana's comment about the neglected farm and Don Jaime's strange reply about how he's let the place go for twenty years arouses our curiosity. What happened to Don Jaime twenty years ago?

Rita's sudden reappearance, saying that Don Jaime makes her skip, again puts in our mind the thought that Don Jaime may be some kind of sexual threat. At the same time Viridiana's evident pleasure at meeting the child sets up a strong affinity between them. It's this that leads Don Jaime to mention how like her aunt (his wife) Viridiana is. But there's no suggestion that Don Jaime has a wife now. What has happened to her?

3. We now see Don Jaime and Viridiana alone in their separate worlds which gives us a chance to get to know them both better. Don Jaime's emotional and sensual expression while he plays the organ gives us a further insight into his character. Meanwhile Viridiana is busy making herself at home by turning her room into a nun's cell. Although she dismisses her reflection in the mirror, the way she shakes her hair free and takes off her stockings invites us to see her potential sensuality as a woman, a potential she appears, as yet, to be unaware of, but which could well become another obstacle to achieving her aim. We then cut back to Don Jaime playing the organ and so connect her lack of awareness of her sensuality with his obvious awareness of his physical needs.

4. When Ramona spies through Viridiana's key hole we learn that she's not on Viridiana's side, she too is a threat and her report to Don Jaime tells us that she's spying on Viridiana at his request. We now realize that Viridiana is in danger from both of them.

5. Finally, when Viridiana prays in front of her homemade altar,

we see that although she's no longer in the safety of the convent, she's brought the convent with her, in the form of the key symbols of her belief. The symbols each represent Christ's suffering on the cross and the strength to withstand even the most formidable of oppositions. Thus Viridiana's aim is restated in terms of what it means for her to become a nun – which is to devote her life exclusively to Christ and everything he represents. But will she have the strength to withstand the threat posed by Don Jaime and his accomplice, Ramona?

THE BEGINNING: Part Three

Althought the protagonist, the dramatic question and the major obstacles have been set up, for the beginning to reach its natural place of completion, so we are fully aware of the complexity of what this film is to be about, we need to include the following sequence.

1. The next morning Viridiana goes to collect milk from the cowshed. She asks the man milking the cow if it's difficult. He suggests that she has a go but, when she's confronted with actually having to take hold of the cow's dangling udder, she backs away laughing. At that moment little Rita bounces in, pours her glass of milk over the cow's head, and informs the disbelieving Viridiana that she can see into her room from the terrace and was watching her last night. Viridiana tells her that spying is bad but Rita just runs away laughing.

2. Don Jaime finds Viridiana in the hen house. She's in such a good mood this morning that she offers to bake him a cake. Don Jaime says mournfully that he doesn't know what he will do when she's gone and he must be alone again. 'But you've chosen to be alone,' Viridiana reproaches him. When questioned about what she means, she tells her uncle that she's heard that he has a son. Don Jaime is clearly shocked to find that she knows about his dark secret, and how could she possibly understand the predicament he was in; the mother wanted to keep the child and he was in love with another woman, Viridiana's aunt. If he had acknowledged the child he risked losing her aunt. 'And what about the innocent child?' Viridiana retorts, critically.

3. It's night, religious music plays on the record player. Don Jaime is alone in his room, sitting in front of an open chest full

106

of wedding clothes, balancing a delicate, high-heeled shoe on his far too large, bare foot. He tosses the wedding bouquet onto the bed and takes a lace-up corset to the mirror where he fits it around his own large waist. Suddenly he hears a movement in the corridor and hurried to close the chest. Viridiana walks into the room. She's wearing her nightdress and carrying a basket. Although her eyes are open, she seems strangely unaware of Don Jaime's presence and we realize that she's sleepwalking. She crosses over to the fire and scoops some ashes into her basket. Don Jaime watches her in astonishment, especially transfixed by the sight of her bare legs. Viridiana takes the ashes to Don Jaime's bed, and deposits them on the sheets by the wedding bouquet. She then returns to her room.

4. It's Viridiana's last day and Don Jaime asks Ramona to help him with a plan to keep her from going back to the convent. Ramona readily agrees (because she feels indebted to Don Jaime for all he's done for herself and her child) and at his request fetches a small bottle from the medicine cabinet. Don Jaime goes to the window and watches Viridiana and little Rita skipping happily together in the garden below.

5. Viridiana is most upset when her uncle tells her that she walked in her sleep. 'Ashes mean penitence and death,' she says. 'Penitence for you as a nun, and death for me as an old man,' her uncle suggests. He then asks her to do him a very great favour. Viridiana, now feeling some real affection for him and also feeling guilty for her actions last night, says she will refuse him nothing.

6. It's night and Viridiana walks down the corridor to Don Jaime's room dressed in her aunt's wedding clothes. Don Jaime is overwhelmed at the sight of her, especially as earlier she had refused his request. He discloses that her aunt died on their wedding night wearing that very dress. Viridiana, although nervous and uncomfortable, is shocked and moved by this information. She tells him that she is happy to wear the dress for him. Her unexpected warmth helps Don Jaime pluck up the courage to ask her to marry him. But he has severely misjudged the situation. Viridiana is distressed that he should even contemplate such thing. Don Jaime gives

Ramona a sign and in response she stirs the contents of the bottle from the medicine cabinet into Viridiana's coffee and hands her the drink.

7. Little Rita comes into the kitchen where Moncho, an elderly servant, is sitting. She tells him she's afraid, she's had a nightmare, a big black bull came into her room.

8. Back in Don Jaime's room Viridiana has fallen into a drugged sleep. Don Jaime picks her up and carries her to her bedroom. He lays her on the bed, arranges her clothes and sits by her. Little Rita climbs the tree outside Viridiana's bedroom window. Don Jaime opens Viridiana's bodice and kisses her. But he soon becomes shocked by his actions and hurries out of the room.

9. Little Rita climbs back down the tree, only to be confronted by her mother. Ramona tells her curious daughter that she's seen nothing more than a little normal family affection and takes her back to bed.

10. The next morning Don Jaime comes into Viridiana's bedroom and tells the poor, bewildered woman that last night, while she was asleep, he made love to her, so now she won't be able to go back to the convent, she will have to stay with him for ever! Viridiana gives Don Jaime a look of such shock and anger that he backs out of the room.

11. Don Jaime realizes that his plan has backfired, she's still going to leave and he's only succeeded in making her hate him. In a panic he rushes back into her room and locks the door, effectively making her his prisoner. He desperately tells her that he lied to her, he didn't make love to her while she was sleeping, and finally pleads for her forgiveness. Viridiana doesn't know what to believe and refuses to forgive him. Don Jaime, accepting his defeat, hands her the key and she quickly leaves.

12. Don Jaime watches Viridiana's carriage as it pulls away from the house. He goes to his writing desk, takes up his pen and chuckles to himself; a gleeful chuckle as if he's just thought of a diabolical plan.

13. Viridiana waits at the bus station in the local town. Just as she's about to get on the bus she's approached by four policemen. They tell her she cannot leave, there's been a terrible accident. They take Viridiana back to Don Jaime's house. Ramona, little Rita and the servant Moncho are standing in the garden. Don Jaime's body dangles from the big tree. He's hanged himself with little Rita's skipping rope.

Notes

1. The scene in the cowshed not only gives us a sense of the daily life of the farm but also, if somewhat obliquely, tells us a little about Viridiana's ambivalent feelings towards her own sexuality. She's fascinated by the cow's udder but when confronted with actually having to take hold of the phallic-like dangling teat she's unable to go through with it. This is in sharp contrast to the way uninhibited little Rita disrespectfully tips her milk over the cow's head.

There is also another purpose for Rita's arrival. We learn that she has her own special place for spying on Viridiana's room. This is another plant and we wonder to what use the information will be put later in the film.

2. When Viridiana and Don Jaime meet we are immediately reminded of the conflict between them, and consequently of how
Don Jaime is a threat to her aim – he doesn't want her to leave and
she has no thoughts of staying. We are also given some additional
information – Don Jaime has a son who he has neglected even more
than his niece. (Given classical drama's principles of economy and
unity, such significant information would only be included if it's
going to play a part in the subsequent unfolding of the story.)

3. We are already wondering what has happened to Viridiana's
aunt and now we have the extraordinary scene of Don Jaime
dressing up in her wedding clothes. The music gives the scene the
solemnity of a religious ritual.

The sleepwalking scene which follows is even more extraordinary. (Like with a dream it enables us to see Viridiana's unconscious at work.) Viridiana's bare legs, witnessed so eagerly by
Don Jaime, again remind us of her sexual vulnerability. But when
Viridiana deposits the ashes on Don Jaime's bed, next to the
wedding bouquet, the strange coming together of these two
elements invites us to wonder about the meaning; death on the
sheets next to a posy of innocent wedding flowers, deflowering
maybe? This leads us to wonder what is in store for the virgin
Viridiana and, again, what happened to Don Jaime's marriage.

4. Don Jaime has now become a fully-fledged antagonist – he's
actively plotting against her, and has enlisted Ramona as his
accomplice. The small bottle Ramona fetches is yet another
ominous plant for the developing story.

The following image, of little Rita and Viridiana skipping
together seems to have more than a simple literal significance. Little
Rita and Viridiana are united by the skipping; they are both female
and objects of sexual desire and as yet unaware of the potency of
this power.

5. Don Jaime takes full advantage of the sleepwalking incident to
make Viridiana feel guilty (she has, after all, put ashes in his bed),
and chooses this moment to ask a favour of her. (Note how both the
favour and her reply are withheld.)

6. Now we find out what the favour was. The sight of Viridiana,
dressed in her aunt's wedding clothes, is dramatically far more
powerful than it would have been if we had heard his verbal request
in the previous scene (as usual, the image is more powerful than

words). Also we have the added dimension of surprise – so that's what the favour was! We then go on to learn how important this favour is to Don Jaime: his wife died on her wedding night. Suddenly many of the things we have been wondering about Don Jaime fall into place: the twenty years he has neglected the estate, his reclusiveness, his melancholy, his dressing up in his wife's wedding clothes – it's almost unbelievable, but he's been in mourning for twenty years! We are moved, and Viridiana is moved, but when he attempts to take advantage of her pity and asks her to marry him, we know immediately that he's seriously misjudged the situation and things are about to go badly wrong. Our anxiety for Viridiana is further increased when Don Jaime indicates to Ramona that it's time to mix Viridiana's drink – we recall the two of them plotting together earlier, and the small bottle from the medicine cabinet. Viridiana is clearly in real danger.

7. We have already begun to identify little Rita closely with Viridiana. She not only exists as a fully autonomous character but she's also come to represent a hidden, and possibly repressed, part of Viridiana's own identity. This is made especially apparent when we cut here to little Rita's fear of the big black bull in her dream. The image of a dangerous male animal seems to be an expression of Viridiana's fear and so further accentuates our feeling for Viridiana's present danger.

8. Don Jaime's plan, we now realize, is to rape Viridiana while she's unconscious. But, as we have learnt in the film so far, Don Jaime is a complex mixture of good and bad, and although he may have imagined that he could commit this crime, finally he's unable to go through with it.

9. Apart from Don Jaime, little Rita is the only person who knows the truth of what went on in the Viridiana's room that night. Will she bear witness later in the film or is she too young to know the importance of what she's seen?

10. The next morning Don Jaime is still determined to achieve his objective. He lies to Viridiana, believing that if she thinks he's made love to her she will have to stay with him. But again he's seriously misjudged the situation.

11. Don Jaime finally realizes that he's lost, his plan has only brought about Viridiana's hatred. In a last bid to salvage what he

111

can of his shattered dignity so that he might, at least, be able to live with himself, he begs her forgiveness. But at the same time he has locked the door, effectively making her his prisoner. Both Viridiana and Don Jaime are so caught up in the drama that neither of them realizes the significance of the situation they now find themselves in. Don Jaime doesn't realize that before you beg forgiveness from a prisoner you have to set them free. Viridiana doesn't connect his plea for forgiveness with the mainstay of her religious conviction. (This is understandable given what she's been through and the fact that she's his prisoner.) But what consequences might her refusal to forgive have, given her aim in life?

12. Viridiana leaves and Don Jaime has lost the battle, or has he? His diabolical chuckle, as he takes up his pen, tells us that he has had yet another idea, he has not yet given up hope.

13. Viridiana is about to step on the bus, to finally complete her escape from the nightmare visit, and, presumably, to return to the convent, when the police arrive. (Note how the drama of this moment is emphasized by the timing. If the police had arrived just minutes later they would have missed her and the course of her life would have been different.)

Finally, we discover the first part of Don Jaime's plan; his suicide. He is hanging from the branches of the tree where we first saw him, watching Rita skipping. It was then that we first noticed the motif of the skipping rope hanging on the tree and wondered about its significance. Now we know. Rita represented a kind of uninhibited, innocent sexuality which we immediately connected with danger, although for her and Viridiana, not for Don Jaime. We now realize that the danger was also to Don Jaime whose death was a direct result of his inability to contain his own sexual desires until it was too late. But this is not the end of the film, it's only the end of the beginning. What was it that Don Jaime wrote, just before his death, that inspired his diabolical chuckle? And how will it affect Viridiana and her attempts to achieve her aim?

In the beginning as a whole we see again how the protagonist is quickly identified by her aim, which has also been simply and directly stated. The major obstacle to Viridiana's aim, in the person of Don Jaime, is also immediately set up. In no time at all we are made aware of Don Jaime as a potential sexual threat and soon he is spying on Viridiana and actively plotting against her, by which time he has taken on the proportions of a major antagonist.

An antagonist is similar to a protagonist in that the antagonist also wants something very badly and will go to great lengths to achieve it. The only differences is that what the antagonist wants is in direct opposition to what the protagonist wants. Imagine how we would have perceived the film if it had opened with Don Jaime on his estate! We would have assumed that Don Jaime was the protagonist and the story was going to be about his attempts to achieve his aim – to keep Viridiana with him. So you can see how important it was to open with Viridiana, and to state quite clearly what her aim was, before we met Don Jaime, otherwise a different dramatic question would have been posed, giving the audience a different set of expectations about the focus and course of the film.

The beginning builds dramatically around Don Jaime's increasingly desperate attempts to keep Viridiana with him and finally reaches a climax when Don Jaime pretends to Viridiana that he's raped her and then, when it's too late, desperately begs her forgiveness. The beginning is finally resolved with Don Jaime's death, but not the film. Viridiana still has to achieve her aim, and Don Jaime may be dead, but his role as an obstacle has been kept very much alive – what was it that he wrote just before his suicide that caused such a diabolical chuckle?

Also there are further obstacles which are still very much alive: Ramona, who assisted Don Jaime in his plotting; Viridiana's lack of awareness, or denial, of her needs as a woman; and her own character traits, her lack of true humility and her difficulties with obedience, both so important for life as a cloistered nun. We don't yet know how her recent experience has changed her; she doesn't know for sure if her uncle raped her or not and, given her religious convictions, she may well believe that her refusal to forgive Don Jaime led directly to his suicide.

And what of Viridiana's deep motivation? We know she wants to devote her life to Christ, but why does she want this? We're told that she hasn't had much family support or affection in her life – she has no family other than Don Jaime, who supported her financially but gave her no love. In giving her life, and love, to Christ, perhaps she is seeking both a sense of meaning for her life and an ideal loved one (who cannot betray her because he is an ideal). We also know she has a rebellious streak in her, she's not naturally submissive or afraid. In fact her strength is formidable. When she first met Don

Jaime she told him she didn't have any feelings for him. But what about the feelings of anger and hurt she would naturally have as a result of his life-long neglect of her? Is her formidable strength partly a result of repressing these painful emotions by making herself invulnerable, which includes rejecting the vulnerability of her womanhood? When she reproaches Don Jaime for denying his own son she is, although unconsciously, also giving us some insight into her feelings about his equal denial of her, his only niece. This raises the question of whether she can truly give her life to Christ, which in its purest sense means giving unconditional love to all who need it, when she has so much repressed emotional conflict within herself.

Finally, what of our hopes and fears? Viridiana hasn't actively pursued her aim yet, she's been too busy defending herself from attack. Consequently we've only been able to identify with her hopes on an abstract level. Our fears for her, on the other hand, have been strongly activated. But because she is such a strong and, on the whole, emotionally cool person, we have needed her to experience a fair degree of opposition to enable us to emotionally identify with her. Whereas Don Jaime, although his actions have been in no way laudable (he was after all the antagonist), engaged our sympathy, almost more easily than Viridiana, because he was so emotionally open and vulnerable. There is a lesson here; identification has a lot to do with vulnerability, because vulnerability suggests an openness, a way in to the character's soul. Even if a character appears bad, if we can see our way through their defences we can begin to care about them. If a character is good, but totally defended, we can admire them but it's difficult to care for them, although we may find ourselves caring about their cause – but that is an intellectual rather than an emotional caring and difficult to sustain in a protagonist for the entire length of a feature film.

So, at the end of the beginning, although our fears for Viridiana have been somewhat alleviated by the death of her antagonist, there are still many obstacles she has to overcome, and Don Jaime's last card is still waiting in the wings! But Bunuel will now need to give us new insights into Viridiana's hopes to enable us to identify with her and so care about what happens to her in the rest of the film.

2 The Development

Earlier I mentioned that the central body of most feature films can usually be broken down into somewhere between eight and ten development sequences and when we explored microcosms we discovered that, amongst other things, each sequence, whether it was from the opening, development or ending of the film, had its own shape – with a beginning, a middle, an ending and a dramatic question of its own. Our aim now is to get a sense of the unity of the central body of the film, or how the parts add up to a whole, while at the same time looking for the basic dramatic principles underlying the development of the story.

MIDNIGHT COWBOY
Development Sequences

ONE: Joe's First Pick-up

Joe settles into his hotel, and then goes out into the teeming streets. There are plenty of middle-aged women on their own but how does he go about picking them up? After a few abortive attempts he finally manages to proposition a middle-aged woman, but omits to tell her the precise nature of their liaison before they go to bed. When he is dressed and ready to leave he finally asks her for payment. She's so insulted that she bursts into tears and Joe ends up lending her money for a taxi.

– Joe's stated aim in the beginning was that he was going to New York to find work as a male prostitute and this sequence is structured entirely around his attempt to achieve his aim in the most straightforward way possible. But it turns out not to be so easy as he had imagined. The streets are certainly full of women on their own, but how does he know which ones are in need of his services? How does he approach them? And how does he do the deal? Remember how, in the beginning, Joe didn't have the courage to ask his boss for back pay that was rightfully his. We see now how this character trait is becoming a real obstacle.

At the end of the sequence Joe's central aim has remained the same but the dramatic question has become more specific: 'how is Joe going to find the women, and even if he manages to get that far, given his shyness about money, how is he going to manage the financial side of his business?'

TWO: First Meeting with Ratso

Joe is sitting in a bar contemplating his difficulties when Ratso (Dustin Hoffman), a sharp young man with a crippled leg, admires Joe's 'colossal shirt'. Joe warms to him immediately and when Ratso warns him that the woman making eyes at him is in fact a man in drag Joe is impressed. He decides to tell Ratso his problems and ask for advice. Just as Ratso convinces Joe that what he needs is 'management' the transvestite approaches again, this time warning Joe that Ratso is a pickpocket. For a moment Joe doesn't know what to believe, but he soon decides to trust his new friend Ratso and leaps to his defence.

Limping and diminutive beside Joe, Ratso leads him through the

New York streets to the prospective 'manager's' apartment. On the way he kicks a taxi that he accuses of trying to run him over, tries all the telephone booths for loose change, greets bewildered strangers as if they are old friends and generally shows Joe the streetwise ropes. He asks for twenty bucks for his services and leaves Joe at the 'manager's' apartment door.

– We have immediately begun to address the dramatic question posed by the previous sequence. At first, meeting Ratso seems to Joe, and to us, like a possible solution to his problems. We agree that he does need 'management'. But another element is also at work here. We learnt from the beginning that Joe also needs to be loved, or at least cared for. At this stage in the film we don't imagine that Ratso could fulfil this deep need but at a simple level we realize that he could be a friend and confidant. As soon as we see the two of them walking together in the street we realize that Joe's good looks and brawn complement Ratso's streetwise wits and we become alerted to their potential as a team. But at the same time, Joe has chosen to ignore the warning about Ratso given by the transvestite, and we are getting increasingly worried that Ratso is going to rip Joe off. So our hopes for the potential in the relationship are pitted equally against our fears, exacerbated by our knowledge of Joe's naivety.

Whilst Joe's central aim remains the same the dramatic question becomes still more specific: 'who is Ratso's "manager" and what effect will the encounter have on Joe's prospects?'

THREE: Management?

For a while Joe doesn't realize that the so called 'manager' is in fact a Christian soul saver, not until the man throws open his bathroom door which, with its flashing neon effigy of Christ, doubles as an altar. The man tries to drag Joe down onto his knees to pray. The scene is intercut with images of young Joe being baptised and obviously hating every moment of it. Panic-stricken, Joe runs from the apartment building and in a blind fury searches the streets for Ratso.

The extent of his anger seems to generate still more memories from his troubled youth and we see violent images of both Joe and Anastasia being raped by the gang of youths we saw in the beginning. When Joe finally arrives back at the bar, where he met Ratso, the transvestite, realizing that Joe has been conned, laughs at him. Joe picks up a bottle in anger but suddenly remembers himself as a boy smashing his grandma's beauty salon. He puts the bottle down and leaves.

– Since the beginning we've felt that Joe's naivety will be one of his biggest obstacles and now it lets him down badly. The dramatic effect of our realizing, long before Joe does, that this man is not 'the manager' he hopes for, is very powerful. We watch in agony as they talk at cross purposes, and when the altar is eventually revealed, in its full neon horror with the lavatory behind, it is both funny and tragic. During Joe's rage, when he searches desperately for Ratso, we learn more about the incidents in his youth first introduced in the beginning. But now we are given a horrifying new revelation; both Joe and his girlfriend were gang-raped. Although the drama is still left unresolved: there is an unsettling sense of ambiguity about the incident because we know that Joe was also a member of the pack. When we finally see Joe as a boy smashing his grandma's beauty salon we realize, for the first time, that anger and violence are deeply embedded in his character. The potential for this inner violence to surface yet again functions in the drama as another obstacle which may threaten Joe's ability to succeed.

Joe's aim remains the same but the dramatic question now seems more general: 'given the extent of the obstacles against him, his recent failures, and our growing awareness of his deep needs, how will he survive alone in this indifferent city?'

FOUR: Lonely New York

Days and nights pass and Joe roams the streets without success. One evening he arrives back at his hotel to find he's been locked out of his room for not paying the bill and all his belongings have been taken as collateral.

Joe watches the young men washing dishes through a restaurant window. Dejected, he buys coffee and sits opposite a young mother and her child, hoping for some comfort. But this young mother seems high on dope and her child is equally weird. Joe spills ketchup all over his pants and to make matters worse tries to wipe the mess off with a coffee-stained napkin! Finally, with nowhere to sleep, he wanders the deserted late-night subway looking for forgotten coins in the slot machines. He catches sight of his reflection in a slot machine mirror and says, with obvious fear, 'You know what you've got to do now cowboy.'

118

– The theme of this sequence is indeed survival. Things go from bad to worse. He loses the roof over his head and his treasured horse-hide suitcase (which in the beginning represented his optimism for the future). He watches the men washing dishes – remembering his former self. He seeks a little comfort from the mother and child, but they're a far cry from the mother and child we remember from the bus and only serve to further alienate him. He spills ketchup on his pants and we remember how proudly he first dressed in his new clothes, so sure that the key to his success lay in his appearance. When finally, homeless and destitute in the subway, he catches sight of himself in the slot machine mirror, again we remember the beginning and contrast the depths he has now reached with his former confident exuberance.

In fact, throughout this entire sequence, the images we got to know in the beginning, which related to Joe's hopes and aspirations, are re-encountered in the new light of Joe's present circumstances. The effect is devastatingly sad. The contrasts serve to emphasize the change in Joe's fortunes and enable us to empathize with his present plight. If we were at all in danger of distancing ourselves from the protagonist at the end of the last sequence, because of his possible complicity in the horrific violence of his past, we are now, once again, fully identified with him and so care about his survival.

At the end of the sequence things are so bad that we think he might have lost sight of his aim. But the dramatic question is as specific as ever: 'what is it that Joe knows he has to do and that he is clearly so resistant to doing?'

FIVE: The Gay Pick-up

Joe joins the studs outside a gay pick-up cinema. He's soon approached by a gawky young student. They go into the cinema and Joe stares doggedly at a film about the space probe while the student makes love to him. The frightened and ambivalent expressions on Joe's face are intercut with scenes of him making love with Anastasia, but his recollections are confused between an ideal love-making and Joe lining up with a queue of youths for the gang-rape.

Joe and the student go to the men's lavatory for the pay-off but the student throws up in a basin and fearfully confesses to Joe that he doesn't have any money.

– Again the dramatic question is answered immediately; it may be difficult to hustle women in New York but it's easy to hustle men. Joe now learns what life as a prostitute can really be like, exacerbated for him by his fear of gay sex. Becoming a gay hustler is clearly not going to be the answer to his problems. At the same time we learn some more about his youth; Joe is bearing the burden of guilt for being a participant, as well as a recipient, in the gang-rape. Finally, his inability to ask for payment in advance lets him down again and he seems further from achieving his aim than he's ever been. The dramatic question is simply: 'what is Joe going to do now?'

SIX: Second Meeting with Ratso

As Joe crosses the street he's almost run over by a taxi. He kicks the taxi in defiance and we're reminded of his first meeting with Ratso. He then walks past a café and sees Ratso sitting inside. He lights up with all the joy of seeing a friend before he remembers Ratso's con and his anger is rekindled. But Ratso is now much sicker, his cough sounds terrible and he hasn't got any money either. He offers Joe his last cigarette butt and a roof over his head instead.

Ratso takes Joe to the derelict building where he lives. There's no heating or lighting and the only colour in the squalor is in the pictures of Florida oranges Ratso has stuck up on the walls. Joe immediately falls into a deep sleep and Ratso watches over him with an almost maternal concern.

We now see a series of violent images from Joe's dream. Images from the gang-rape, again with Joe both as victim and rapist, are intercut with young Joe's grandma sadistically spanking his bare bottom and with Anastasia accusing Joe of rape and of being 'the only one' who did it. We see Joe being imprisoned and finally the world tumbling around him. In his dream even his new friend Ratso is out to get him. Joe wakes in a terrified sweat and accuses Ratso of stealing his boots. Ratso manages to calm him down and to reaffirm their friendship. Joe falls asleep content.

– When Joe kicks the taxi we are both reminded of Ratso and told how Joe is being changed by the city; he's become more like Ratso. Ratso has changed too, he's sicker and even more broke. We remember the potential we saw in their relationship when they first met; now they seem to really need each other. So, when Ratso takes

Joe home with him, in spite of the appalling squalor, we are filled with a new hope.

Joe's dream takes us further into the traumas of his past. It's now clear that Joe was both a victim of rape and a rapist, but we are also given some new information. Joe's beloved grandma spanked him with such sadistic cruelty that this too was a kind of rape. And Anastasia not only accused Joe of rape, she told the police that he was 'the only one' and he was subsequently imprisoned. The images culminate with an overwhelming feeling of terrible violence and betrayal between Joe and the two most important women in his life, with Joe as both victim and instigator, which has resulted in an intense confusion, fear and an all-embracing paranoia.

But something very interesting happens next: Ratso deals quite calmly with Joe's paranoia and not only manages to calm him but also shows a familial concern for his well-being. So, although we've been taken still further into the depths of Joe's traumatic past, at the end of the sequence we feel that, emotionally at least, with Ratso, the streetwise cripple, he's in good hands.

Joe's aim, for the time being, has been forgotten. The dramatic question now is: 'how will Joe and Ratso survive together?'

SEVEN: Joe's new life with Ratso

With Joe's good looks and brawn and Ratso's wits and cunning, together they make a good team. Ratso tells Joe his dream which is

to go to Florida where he will get well and Joe will find more lonely rich widows than anywhere in the country. They decide that to get the money for the trip they need to clean Joe up and this time Ratso will act as manager. They wash his clothes, steal his hat back, clean his boots and finally he is once again standing admiringly in front of the mirror ready for action.

But their attempts to find Joe work fail. Winter sets in and they're freezing and hungry. They pawn Joe's radio, sell blood, walk the streets and watch the building next-door being demolished, but throughout this adversity their friendship and interdependence grows. One day Ratso takes Joe to the cemetery where his dad is buried and afterwards, while they're sitting in a café discussing the possibility of an after-life, an eccentric young couple appear and give Joe a party invitation.

– We see here how the central dramatic thrust of the story is reasserted and Ratso becomes a part of Joe's aim rather than an obstacle. Florida is both a place where Ratso will get well and where the beaches are paved with rich widows just waiting for a hustler like Joe to come along. Also, if we remember from the beginning, Joe's need for love underlay his desire to work as a hustler. This need is

now finding fulfilment in his friendship with Ratso and so Joe's aim now naturally extends to include Ratso's need to get well.

To get to Florida they need money and so, once again, Joe goes through the now familiar preparations for work. When he confronts his revived image in the mirror we are reminded of the optimism he felt in the beginning and once again we become hopeful for him. His attempt to get work fails again but, as we watch their friendship growing in the face of terrible adversity, we find that a big shift has taken place in our hearts; our hopes are now more focused on the success of Joe's friendship than on the success of his work endeavours. The fulfilment of his need is ultimately more important than the fulfilment of his want. Although this too is under threat: Ratso is slowly getting sicker.

Finally, when they are reduced to exploring the possibility of their dreams being fulfilled in the after-life, given that their hopes of fulfilment in this life are looking so slim, a wonderful act of God, or coincidence, takes place. Out of the blue they are invited to a party.

We end on an unrealistically hopeful note – 'will the party somehow get them to Florida?'

EIGHT: The Party and Joe's First Successful Pick-up

The party turns out to be a sixties extravaganza of eccentricity and drugs but Joe, much to his surprise, is picked up by a wealthy woman. Ratso negotiates the deal and for the first time since the film began Joe has actually got work as a stud. The only problem is that Ratso is so sick he can hardly stand. On the way out Ratso falls down an entire flight of stairs. The taxi pulls away, with Joe and the wealthy woman in the back. Joe is filled with anxiety as he looks at his friend, diminutive, sick and alone in the bitter winter snow.

Joe goes to the woman's apartment but finds, much to his humiliation, that he can't make love. The woman teases him by accusing him of being gay. This so riles Joe that he forces himself to prove her wrong. The next morning the woman is so pleased with the experience that she phones her friends to get Joe more work and Joe goes home to find Ratso and tell him that success is theirs at last.

– The party turns out to be a blessing in disguise as far as Joe's work prospects are concerned, but his anxiety for his sick friend outweighs all his excitement about finally achieving his aim. He now realizes that his need for the kind of familial love provided by his friendship is far more important to him. The dramatic question we

123

are left with now is: 'will Joe's financial success come in time to save his friend?'

In the development as a whole Joe's central aim, although receding somewhat in the middle sequences, has essentially remained the same throughout. (On the one occasion when we seemed to lose sight of it altogether the following sequence was devoted entirely to re-establishing its importance.) Each sequence has a beginning, development and end of its own, structured around the exploration of a specific dramatic question, which in each case relates directly to the preceding sequence. The ending of each sequence arrives at a different but closely related dramatic question. The sequences each focus on, and explore in depth, either the obstacles to Joe's achieving his aim, or the rebuilding of his hopes. All these obstacles, and his hopes, were raised in the beginning, either directly or obliquely – even the violence in Joe's past was hinted at in his early memories.

Almost all the motifs which appeared in the beginning are also repeated in these development sequences. But when we encounter them for a second, and even a third, time we see them in a very different light. Because the motifs represent Joe's hopes and fears this serves to accentuate and add poignancy to the changes in Joe's feelings and fortunes. Our hopes for Joe are always pitted against our fears resulting from the obstacles. But although things go from bad to worse, we never entirely lose sight of hope; when Joe reaches his lowest ebb Ratso reappears. Hope energizes the drama. The obstacles provide conflict.

Each development sequence changes Joe although his aim and his deep needs remain the same. But in the late development sequences a significant shift takes place; we are now far more aware of Joe's deep need. Consequently we now find that our hope is more centred on his finding fulfilment for this need than on achieving his aim. At the same time the chief obstacle also shifts: Ratso is getting sicker and their poverty is a real danger to his health. The success of Joe's aim has now become essential for the fulfilment of his need and, by the end of the development, a sense of real urgency is building: time for Ratso is running out.

VIRIDIANA
Development Sequences

ONE: Rita Skips, Viridiana's New Plan, and Two Lots of New Arrivals

Rita is happily skipping under the big tree when Moncho walks past, grabs her rope, tosses it away and tells her that if anything bad happens it will all be her fault because she's not respecting the dead. Rita recovers her rope and begins to skip again.

Viridiana, now wearing simple peasant clothes, is scrubbing the floor of her new room in one of the farm outhouses. She looks sadder and more withdrawn than before. Ramona comes to tell her that the mayor has sent a message saying that he's attended to her request. We are wondering what this request was when Mother Superior arrives, greets Viridiana warmly and demands to know why she hasn't been in touch. Viridiana tells her that although her uncle was a grave sinner, she feels responsible for his death. Mother Superior is horrified and demands a full confession. Viridiana calmly refuses Mother Superior, saying that she's decided not to return to the convent. She's still going to follow the path of the Lord, she adds, but she's going to do her work alone. Finally she asks for Mother Superior's forgiveness. The older nun forgives her cursorily, and leaves.

A group of beggars are gathering together in the town square:

Don Amalio, a blind man; Baldy, a cripple; Poca, a little old man; Refugio, a young pregnant woman; and Edina, a mother with two small children. Viridiana arrives, picks up Edina's little girl and leads the motley group out of the square. In the next square two more beggars are waiting for them; Don Zequiel, who looks like a patriarch in his thick white beard, and Hobbly, a cripple with a big black beard.

Meanwhile there have been some new arrivals back at the house. A handsome young man is staring at the portrait of Don Jaime. This is Jorge, Don Jaime's son, and he is accompanied by his girlfriend Lucia. 'I don't bear him any grudge,' Jorge tells Lucia, 'anyone can love and forget. But why did he remember me at the last minute? What was going on in his mind?' Jorge and Lucia go to the window to look at the estate, Jorge's new domain. Jorge puts his arm around Lucia and is about to kiss her when she notices Viridiana walking along the path below, followed by her band of beggars, who are also eagerly looking at the house and grounds.

Jorge and Lucia emerge from the house and watch with astonishment as Viridiana announces the rules to the beggars: the men and women are to sleep in separate dormitories, but they will all eat together. Jorge introduces himself to Viridiana, who says she's had a letter from the lawyer so she's been expecting him. At that moment one of the beggars, Don Zequiel, tries to pat little Rita on the head, she objects fiercely and tells him to go and sleep with the chickens. Moncho then aggressively warns the beggars not to let him catch them wandering about the place, or else! This warning very nearly causes a fight. Jorge is about to intervene but Viridiana manages to defuse the situation with a few strict words and leads the women to their quarters while the men begrudgingly follow Moncho.

– The scene with Rita skipping functions as a bridge between the end of the beginning and the beginning of the development. We have already come to associate the motif with the danger of innocent sexuality and, when Don Jaime hanged himself with the rope, with death. We now see the motif being firmly re-established which means it will also have relevance to the developing story.

In the beginning of *Viridiana* we were taken through an entire 'mini story', with its own climax and resolution – the death of the antagonist. And although there were many unresolved threads there was also a strong sense of ending. Dramatically the story now needs to be re-energized at the core, which is what this next scene does by restating the new terms of Viridiana's aim. As soon as we meet her we see that she's changed and with the arrival of Mother Superior we learn that although she's decided not to return to the convent she's kept the central part of her initial aim intact. She's still intent on devoting her life to Christ but she's decided to do this alone.

But how is Viridiana going to serve the Lord on her own, or more specifically what is her new plan? And what new obstacles will it entail?

We find out the answers in the next scene; the beggars are waiting at pre-arranged meeting points for Viridiana to arrive and take them home. Once again we see how raising our curiosity in the previous scene, by withholding the plan so we can now discover it through image and action, is more dramatically powerful.

Meanwhile, back at the house, Jorge and Lucia have also arrived. Jorge is looking at his father's portrait, which immediately connects the two men. He wonders why his father remembered him at the last minute, what was going on in his mind, and in so doing voices the dramatic question we were left with at the end of the beginning when Don Jaime wrote what, we now realize, was his will.

Jorge and Lucia look out of the window just as the beggars (whose arrival interrupts their kiss), are also eagerly looking at their new dwelling, and we soon deduce the sheer complexity of the new situation. Viridiana has carefully made her plans in the light of a letter from the lawyer, which suggests that Don Jaime has willed the property to her and Jorge equally. But how will Viridiana and Jorge get on? How will Jorge get on with the beggars? And how will Viridiana get on with the beggars who are each complicated adults in their own right? But Viridiana's rule of separate dormitories suggests that she's not planning on taking their adult needs into account. What effect will this have on the success of her new venture? Finally little Rita and Moncho's hostility and the violence which very nearly erupts as a result, gives us some insight into the dangerous feelings lurking just beneath the surface and how little it takes to ignite them. Although Viridiana manages to calm them this time, will she continue to be able to do so?

We have now learnt the nature of Viridiana's plan, and we know that her faith and strength of character are formidable, but given the above obstacles what chance does she have of success?

TWO: Two Dinners, and Jorge Visits Viridiana

In the big house Ramona eagerly serves her new master (gazing at him adoringly) whilst he argues with Lucia. Jorge complains about Viridiana being 'rotten with religion' and Lucia jealously accuses him of only being annoyed because Viridiana doesn't take any notice of him.

In the outhouse the beggars are also eating together. Their conversation is full of vulgar innuendo until Viridiana arrives and, like children, they submissively change their tone. Viridiana has brought some new beggars to join them. She sits them down and then announces to her appalled flock the good news: tomorrow they will all be given work to do. Suddenly the beggars notice sores on the arms of one of the new arrivals and realize that they have a leper in their midst. They angrily demand that he be thrown out. Viridiana firmly tells them to show the poor man compassion, bids them goodnight and tells them she expects them all to be in bed by 8 p.m. But as soon as Viridiana is out of the room Hobbly tells the leper to clear off or he will slit his belly open. As the beggar slinks away Hobbly picks up little Rita's skipping rope and ties it around his waist.

Jorge visits Viridiana in her room in the outhouse to discuss his plans for the estate. She quickly puts her wooden cross and the crown of thorns away in the drawer and tells him that she really isn't interested, he's free to do what he thinks best. But instead of leaving Jorge sits on the bed, which he discovers to his amusement has no mattress, just hard wood. He provocatively tells Viridiana that he's not married to Lucia; he doesn't need anyone's blessing to live with a woman. She conceals her embarrassment and shows him to the door. Finally alone again, Viridiana goes to the window and stares thoughtfully out at the night.

– Jorge has quickly slipped into Don Jaime's place. He's master of the estate, Ramona adores him, but like Don Jaime, his equilibrium is upset by his desire to also have power over Viridiana which does not bode well for her.

In the outhouse our fears for Viridiana are also intensified. The beggars are used to living at the rough end of society. They've learnt about the raw basics of survival and don't know how to hide beneath the bourgeois niceties of life. Like children they manipulate Viridiana by behaving one way in front of her and differently behind her back. And although she is warm towards them, and they are impressed by her goodness, the sexual innuendo and the violence are ever-present beneath the surface. We wonder how long Viridiana's method, a mixture of compassion and a strict regime, will last before a serious eruption occurs. And at the end of the scene, when Hobbly threatens to slit the leper's belly open and ties Rita's skipping rope around his waist, we see the motif with which we associate so much, now in the hands of the most violent beggar. We are shocked and our anxiety for Viridiana's safety is still further intensified.

With our fears in the ascendant we go to Viridiana's room and there we are confronted with the other key motif from the beginning, the wooden cross and the crown of thorns; symbols of Viridiana's hope, faith and strength. But this reminder is soon counteracted by Jorge, who walks into her room, uninvited, and arrogantly tells her that he is living in sin, threatening both her privacy and her faith.

In the final shot, when Viridiana looks out of the window at the night, we are well aware of the magnitude and the loneliness of the task she has set herself: 'can Viridiana, through faith, compassion and work, both change the beggars and withstand Jorge's more sophisticated attack?'

THREE: *The Beggars at Work, Jorge at Work, Viridiana and Jorge Meet*

Hobbly is painting a picture of a religious scene. He asks Viridiana to pose as the Virgin. She obliges with good humour and whilst she is posing asks Refugio when her baby is due. Refugio has no idea. Poca, the little old beggar, laughs at Refugio, saying she doesn't even know who the father is, it was dark at the time.

Meanwhile, Jorge is in the fields with his labourers. He sees a horse and trap pass by with a dog tied to the trap. He tells the owner that he's mistreating the poor dog. The owner doesn't agree. 'The less a dog eats, the better he hunts,' he says. Jorge saves the dog, by buying it, and takes it back to the fields with him. In the background another trap passes by with another dog tied to its wheels. Viridiana then walks by with Poca. Jorge shouts at Poca to clear off, turns to Viridiana and says, 'Helping just a few beggars does nothing for all the rest.' Viridiana replies that she's well aware of how little she can do. Jorge asks her if she will devote her life to working with beggars. She tells him openly that she's not sure, she's still recovering from a shock, and maybe one day she will return to the convent. At that moment the labourers in the fields

start shouting at the leper who has just appeared. Viridiana angrily jumps to the leper's defence. She goes to the leper and, there by the roadside, kindly bandages his sores. The leper is genuinely moved, nobody has ever cared for him before. Poca cynically intervenes, telling Viridiana that even the priest won't have the leper in his church. The leper puts his arm in the holy water and curses all damned women, hoping they will catch his affliction. The leper is furious with Poca but Viridiana patiently tells him to control his temper, and sends Poca back to join the other beggars at the house.

– It's Hobbly, the beggar with Rita's skipping rope tied around his waist, who is painting the religious scene. Is this a glimmer of hope? Is Viridiana changing him? But the scene is primarily devoted to thematic irony: the contrast between Viridiana posing as the Virgin Mary, the good woman, the saint, and her opposite, Refugio, the dark fallen woman.

We then go immediately to another scene devoted to thematic irony: Jorge 'saves' the mistreated dog while another trap passes by with yet another mistreated dog tied to its wheels. He then rudely treats the beggar, Poca, like a dog and tells Viridiana that helping just a few beggars does nothing for the rest.

130

The following scene, when Viridiana rescues the leper from Jorge's abusive labourers and kindly bandages his sores, is very moving; we want to defy Jorge's arrogant cynicism and to believe that her compassion can work miracles. But again our hopes are soon qualified; we learn about the extent of the leper's bitterness through Poca's story, and once again the theme of woman, cause of all ills, dangerous and damned, emerges.

Although most of this sequence has been devoted to an exploration of the complex thematic ironies underlying the story, during the discussion between Jorge and Viridiana her aim is restated. Her reply is brief. But when she admits that she's not so sure of herself and that she's recovering from a shock, she seems to be more open and vulnerable than before. She's changing. We even wonder if the woman in Viridiana is responding, just a little, to Jorge's masculine charm. This conversation is most important structurally, because by giving us the opportunity to gauge a little of how Viridiana is reacting to events, it encourages our continued identification with her dilemmas as the centre of the story.

In this way, by the end of the sequence, Viridiana's aim, although qualified, has been reaffirmed and the dramatic question, although softened a little, remains much the same as before.

FOUR: Work Continues and the Conditions are Set for the Ending

Lucia prepares for bed while Jorge examines some of Don Jaime's ornaments. She accuses Jorge of being more interested in Viridiana than her and says she's going to leave him in the morning. Jorge doesn't seem too bothered, he's more interested in his father's silver crucifix, which he's most amused to discover, as he pulls out the sharp blade, is in fact an evil-looking penknife.

Jorge's labourers are now working on the outside of the house. Jorge tells his foreman that he will be away for the night but will be returning tomorrow evening.

In the orchard, beneath the almond blossoms, Viridiana announces 'The Angelus'. The beggars kneel amongst the trees, (except for Hobbly who leans on his stick and the leper who lurks in the background), and Viridiana conducts the prayers. This is intercut with shots of the labourers working on the house – sawing, loading, hammering, building – as we hear 'Hail Mary full of grace, the Lord is with thee, blessed art thou amongst women and blessed is the fruit of thy womb, Jesus . . .'

Viridiana arrives back at the house. Jorge tells her that their

meeting in town with the lawyer is arranged for tomorrow and he is sending the car to pick her up. He then asks her to come and live in the big house with him, now that Lucia has gone. Viridiana is surprised by this news and asks why Lucia left. 'Why do men and women separate?' asks Jorge cynically. Viridiana lowers her eyes and blushes; she has no idea. On the way to her room the servant, Moncho, tells her that he's had enough of the beggars and he's leaving the estate.

Meanwhile Jorge goes with Ramona to an outbuilding. While they're looking through old house furnishings Jorge asks Ramona if she ever heard his uncle mention him. 'No,' she replies, 'but he must have loved you if he left you all this.' Jorge is sceptical about his uncle's intentions, but Ramona is again looking at him adoringly. As Jorge and Ramona make love we cut to the corner of the room where a cat suddenly pounces on a rat.

The next day the car arrives to take Viridiana into town. Little Rita has got a toothache and so she and Ramona are coming too. This means the house will be left empty. Viridiana, realizing this, asks Don Zequiel, the elderly beggar with the big white beard, to look after everything while they are away. Finally the car pulls out of the grounds leaving Don Zequiel in charge.

– Lucia's main reason for leaving Jorge is her suspicion about his designs on Viridiana. This affirms our suspicions. Her departure will undoubtedly increase Viridiana's vulnerability to Jorge, whose wholly material approach to life, and indifference to the woman he has been living with, doesn't bode well for any woman he might have a relationship with in the future, least of all a woman with Viridiana's high ideals. The inclusion of the bizarre crucifix pen-knife increases the feeling of a latent violence lurking beneath the surface of events and connects the danger with Don Jaime's legacy. (It may also prove to be another plant for later in the story.)

Both Viridiana's work and Jorge's seem to be going well. The prayer meeting in the orchard is peaceful and devout and the labourers are making good progress. But, in this apparently harmonious setting, many significant small events are occurring. Jorge's designs on Viridiana appear to be motivated more by challenge than by feeling, but the effect he has on her seems to be increasing her awareness of her naivety as a woman and hence her sense of herself as vulnerable. In contrast Jorge's very practical approach to sex is demonstrated by the way he makes love to Ramona, so soon after asking Viridiana to live with him. The cut away to the cat pouncing on the rat firmly stamps out any romantic notions inattentive members of the audience may still be nurturing about Jorge. If he does finally manage to conquer Viridiana she certainly won't discover through him an earthly love to replace her ideal love of Christ.

The rest of this sequence is devoted to setting the preconditions for the ending: Jorge is going away for the night and returning tomorrow evening, Viridiana is joining him in town tomorrow, Lucia has left, Moncho leaves, and finally little Rita gets toothache and so has to be taken to the dentist by Ramona. The result of all these coincidences is that there is no member of Don Jaime's estate left to oversee matters while they are away, and Don Zequiel, the elderly beggar with the white beard, has to be left in charge.

Viridiana's central aim, to devote her life to Christ, although changed quite radically as far as her method of achieving it is concerned, remains, in essence, consistent throughout. But because of the 'mini ending' at the end of the beginning, which led to

Viridiana's radical change of plan, the development has required a new beginning: a restating of her aim, her new method for achieving it, and a re-establishment of the obstacles. So the first sequence of the second act is similar in structure to a beginning.

Jorge has stepped into Don Jaime's shoes as a major obstacle, in that he also wants to control and seduce Viridiana, although his methods are far more subtle. And the beggars have replaced the convent as far as Viridiana's means of achieving her aim are concerned although, because she has led such a cloistered life and hasn't faced up her own repressions, her schoolmarmish methods for controlling the beggars, and for dealing with Jorge, seem wholly inadequate for dealing with her present circumstances.

The dramatic irony is that we can see how the storm clouds are gathering and how things are going from bad to worse, but Viridiana, in her naivety, can't. But each sequence also contains a glimmer of hope; maybe she will be able to survive, against all the odds. Our hope is rooted in Viridiana's strength of character and the idealism of her faith, which we are reminded of when we see the motif of the cross and the crown of thorns, and during the moments of real tenderness and love when she bandages the leper's arm and holds the harmonious prayer meeting under the almond blossom. In spite of our sneaking suspicion that these moments of hope are vain, they serve to energize the drama because they counteract the obstacles.

Three motifs from the beginning are repeated in the development; Rita skipping, the skipping rope itself, and the cross and crown of thorns. Apart from the complexity of what each of these motifs symbolizes, which provides thematic continuity, they also function dramatically in that they represent both the danger Viridiana's is in and, as far as the cross and the crown of thorns is concerned, her strength to resist.

Finally, this last development sequence sets the preconditions for a very dangerous situation. Lucia acted as a constraint on Jorge's advances to Viridiana, and Moncho acted as a constraint on the male beggars. Now Moncho and Lucia are gone Viridiana is more vulnerable than at any previous time in the film. We also have the extraordinary situation of all the responsible members of Don Jaime's estate being away at the same time and a beggar, Don Zequiel, being left in charge. Danger is definitely in the ascendant and we seem to be moving towards some kind of catastrophe, although we don't yet know what form it will take.

3 The Ending:
Midnight Cowboy and *Viridiana*

At the end of the developments of both *Midnight Cowboy* and *Viridiana* a real sense of urgency was building, creating a sense of potential danger for both our protagonists. Crisis and climax are concepts we associate with danger in our everyday lives and, as we saw in the introduction to classic structure, they are also concepts which, along with the theme and the resolution, have a crucial role to play in determining the classic ending. The question facing us now is how these concepts manifest themselves in the texture of the two films we are exploring and how a full understanding of the meaning of these four concepts sheds light on the classic structure as a whole.

MIDNIGHT COWBOY

The ending

1. At last it looks as if Joe's fortunes have turned. His night with the woman he met at the party was a success, and he's got another job lined up for the end of the week. He returns to the derelict building, clutching food and medicine, eager to tell Ratso the good news that they won't have to steal any more. But Ratso is now sicker than he's ever been. He's sweating and shivering so much he can hardly hold the mug of soup Joe makes him, let alone eat. He confesses to his friend that he can no longer walk and he's scared. Joe is momentarily annoyed with Ratso; how can he have got so ill just as Joe's on the verge of success as a hustler? He suggests getting a doctor, but Ratso thinks doctors, like the police, are dangerous. Florida, he insists is the only answer. But to get there they need more than the twenty bucks Joe earned the

135

night before and they can't wait for the job at the end of the week; Ratso might not last that long.

– Joe's annoyance with Ratso for getting so ill just as he's on the verge of getting a proper income from hustling expresses the conflict between what he has been wanting throughout the film and his devotion to Ratso. But the dramatic question we were left with at the end of the development was: 'will Joe's success as a hustler come in time to save Ratso?' This question is now restated with an even greater urgency. Ratso is so ill that they cannot even risk waiting until the end of the week for Joe's next job, they have to get to Florida as quickly as possible. There is, of course, an easier option in their present predicament and that is to fetch a doctor, which is why it becomes necessary to deal with Ratso's fear of doctors at this point (for the sake of the believability of the rest of the film). Florida, if we remember from the development, became a part of the aim – in Florida Joe will find it easier to get work as a hustler and Ratso will recover (or so they believe). At the end of the scene the stakes are higher than they have been at any point previously in the film – Joe's ability to find money is now a matter of life and death.

2. Joe goes back out onto the streets, desperately worried about his friend and determined to find the money somehow.

He phones the woman he scored with the night before, but she's left town. He's in an amusement arcade, shooting at tin cowboys whilst trying to think of a plan, when Towny, a lonely middle-aged businessman, attracted by Joe's cowboy image, approaches him. Joe's need to help his friend is greater than his fear of the gay hustle and he goes with Towny to his hotel room.

– Again the obvious solution to the problem has to be dealt with first; which is to ask the woman Joe spent the previous night with for money. So he phones her only to find that she's left town. But more importantly, it now becomes clear that Joe's deep need for a loving friendship, a need we detected in Joe way back in the beginning of the film, outweighs his desire to achieve his aim. This shift is made visually clear with the image of Joe shooting tin cowboys; the motif which has stood for Joe's pride in himself as a hustler throughout the film, now becomes a cheap amusement and an object for destruction. There's also a hint of danger here – shooting is, after all, a desperate act. The irony here is further emphasized when we discover that Towny has approached Joe because he's attracted by his cowboy image.

We've seen Joe resort to a gay hustle before (in the development), so we know that for him it's a solution only to be resorted to in the most desperate of situations.

3. While Towny phones his mother Joe practices asking him for money in the bathroom mirror: 'Listen,' he mutters urgently, 'I've got a sick boy on my hands and I've got to get him south as quick as I can.' But when Towny finishes his call he's changed his mind about the deal. In an agony of masochistic guilt, he asks Joe to leave. The scene now becomes intercut with images (from Joe's imagination) of him carrying Ratso's sick body out of the building and through the freezing streets of New York to the bus station. 'Listen,' he tells Towny through clenched teeth, 'I've got family,' and in a desperate fury he strikes him and takes the cash he needs from his wallet. But Towny has fallen by the telephone and manages to grasp hold of the receiver to call for help. Joe grabs the phone and rams the receiver brutally into Towny's already bleeding mouth.

– The opening image, of Joe practising asking for money in the bathroom mirror, serves to communicate the complexity of the conflicting emotions going on within Joe by reminding us of so many different moments in the film: the pride and optimism in the beginning, when he put on his new cowboy clothes in front of the mirror and practised giving notice to his boss; the moment when he first met Ratso, who admired his 'colossal shirt' in the bar mirror; the moment when he was desperate, alone and trying to pluck up courage for his first gay hustle in the subway mirror; the revival of hope, when his cowboy outfit was again clean and he was ready to go back on the streets with Ratso as his manager. In this scene the motif is again Joe's attempts to find courage and hope, but it's now combined with Joe's paternal words about having a sick boy on his hands which reminds us, once more, of the seriousness of Joe's present plight. So, when Towny changes his mind about the deal we know immediately that this is the crisis, the straw that breaks the camel's back.

Joe can't walk away this time, he's 'got family', as he says, and he's 'the only one' who can help Ratso. (Remember how in the beginning he wanted to be 'the only one' for Anastasia and his grandmother.) The intercut images of Joe carrying Ratso to the bus station further demonstrate how Joe's mind is fixed on his objective, he must save his 'family' whatever the cost.

And the cost is great. Most of the major obstacles have been dealt with in the development sequences but two crucial ones are left; his difficulty in asserting himself over money matters, and the deep inner violence born in his personal history. Although Joe is basically a lovable person he's been involved in some horrifying incidents in his past and when under extreme pressure he's capable of equally extreme violence. These two character traits are both crucial causal elements to the crisis and climax. The violent side of Joe's character takes him over. The climax, which is the tragic consequence of the crisis, is Joe's attack and probable murder of Towny.

4. Ratso, coughing and bathed in sweat, sits next to Joe as the bus speeds through the New York suburbs. Joe gently tucks the blanket around his friend. 'You didn't kill him, did you?' asks Ratso. 'You've got blood on your jacket.' Joe says he doesn't want to talk about it. Night falls and then a new day dawns as the bus speeds south. Joe wakes to find Ratso crying. 'I'm falling apart here,' Ratso says and confesses that

he's wet his pants. Joe makes a joke of it to cheer Ratso up and asks him what size pants he wears. Through the window we can now see the blue sky and palm trees of Florida. Joe emerges from a store near the bus stop wearing a pale yellow short sleeved shirt and inconspicuous pants. He dumps his cowboy jacket, Stetson and boots in a nearby garbage bin and heads back to the bus. As the bus continues on its way south he dresses Ratso in a brightly coloured shirt decorated with palm trees and tells his friend his new plan: 'When we get to Miami I'm going to get some kind of a job,' he says, 'because hell, I ain't no kind of a hustler. There must be an easier way of making money than that. Some kind of outdoor work? What d'you think?' He glances at his friend who, although his eyes are strangely staring, appears to be asleep. Realizing that something is wrong, Joe tries to shake his friend awake, but Ratso is dead.

– This penultimate sequence of the film is the first part of the resolution. Ratso asks Joe the question we want to know the answer to: Was it murder? Joe doesn't want to talk about it, instead he tucks the blanket around poor, shivering Ratso. He's done what he had to do, he's got Ratso on the bus to Florida, and at this moment his concern for Ratso, who is still physically deteriorating, blots out all other concerns. Also, we can imagine that Joe probably got out of that hotel room so fast he doesn't know the answer.

The long bus journey south brings to mind Joe's bus journey in the beginning of the film. Joe is once again travelling towards a new life, only this time the predominant feeling is of an era ending. The motif of his cowboy outfit, which through most of the film represented his determination to achieve his aim, is finally disposed of in a garbage bin, and Joe, wearing the inconspicuous clothes which now represent his future hopes, tells Ratso that he no longer wants to be a hustler, he's decided to get a real job. But Ratso, like the hustler era in Joe's life, is dead.

5. The bus pulls to a halt as Joe tells the driver what's happened. The driver asks Joe to close his friend's eyes and tells the curious passengers that there's nothing to worry about, just a little illness and they're only a few minutes away from Miami. The bus continues on its final leg of the journey. In response to the curious passengers who are staring at

Ratso's body, Joe protectively puts his arm around his friend's shoulders and holds him tight. The bus cruises into Miami and we watch, through the reflections of the passing buildings on the bus window, Joe's face as he holds Ratso's body in his arms. Ratso looks somehow peaceful, protected from life. Joe looks bewildered, devastated, sad, but somehow, in his fresh new clothes, stronger and more able to cope with life than we've seen him before. Fade to black.

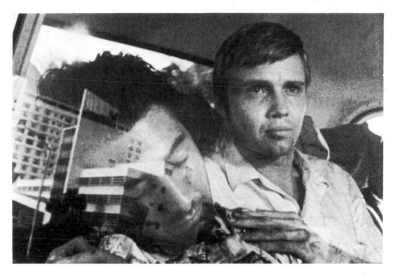

– Joe, as on his first bus journey, has to confront the indifference of strangers and, as we watch his face through the reflections of the city buildings, we realize that he is also once again arriving in an alien city environment. But he has changed since that first journey. He now has a new strength, born of his recent experience. He wants to make something of his life rather than become consumed by the criminal underworld. This is stressed by his change of clothes and by the way, in spite of his obvious fear of death, he holds his friend's body so protectively. This image also seems to tell us that he is not alone, his relationship with Ratso will remain a part of him – he's changed as a result of it, he's learnt that 'family' is the most important thing for him. Although Ratso is dead his newly found self-knowledge is a crucial to our hopes for Joe's future.

Finally, the way the reflections of the buildings pass over Ratso's body is enormously sad, speaking somehow of his death, and even of the nature of death itself, as Ratso's spirit seems to pass both into Joe's history and back into the city landscape.

So, all the major strands which were set up in the beginning and pursued through the development have now reached their natural, and perhaps inevitable, conclusion in the climax and resolution. Joe's unconscious need for love, which we detected in the beginning, is now fully conscious and has proved to have a more powerful influence on his life than his conscious aim. And in the resolution we learn that his aim, like the motif of cowboy clothes, has been finally disposed of.

But what of the theme which is, of course, the moral standpoint of the film? If we remember, from the outline of the basic principles of classic drama, the theme inevitably rises to the surface in the climax. Anybody who has seen the film will recall the full horror of Joe's attack on Towny. This horror is not wholly a result of the explicit nature of the violence itself. The reason why this particular image of violence so offends people is that, in spite of his involvement with a gang-rape earlier in his life, most of us have grown to love Joe Buck. And now this climax scene is asking us to love a character who has not only been a participant in a gang-rape but has also committed an act which probably resulted in murder. This presents us with a considerable moral dilemma.

The resolution of the film does not relieve us of this moral dilemma, instead it focuses on Ratso's death and Joe's hopes for a new life. Consequently at the end of the film we are forced to return to the scene of the crime and to ask ourselves what it means. Each of us will, of course, finally have to come to our own conclusion about such a difficult matter. But the film as a whole, by inviting us to love Joe Buck, seems to be saying that we cannot judge this kind of violence purely by the act alone, we have to take into account all the extenuating circumstances, or, to use Aristotle's words 'the occasion, the means and the reason'. We don't have to morally condone the violence but we do have to abandon simplistic notions of good and bad. And, by being asked to consider and understand the complexity of the good and bad within Joe Buck's character and the world he lives in, we also have to consider the complexity of these things within ourselves.

VIRIDIANA

THE ENDING

1. Viridiana and the occupants of the house are away and the beggars realize that they have been left to their own devices.

142

Hobbly (still wearing little Rita's skipping rope around his waist) suggests they kill a couple of lambs and make a roast and the women beggars decide to take a look inside the big house, promising Don Zequiel they won't touch anything. While the leper catches a small white dove in the orchard, and gently strokes its head, the women discover Don Jaime's exquisite table linen and muse on how wonderful it must be to eat off lace; after all, they're sure the patrons are not returning until the next day.

– At the end of the development we noticed now many small changes had taken place, resulting in our feeling that Viridiana was more vulnerable than at any time in the film now that the natural constraints on both Jorge and the beggars had been removed. But the most pressing question we were left with was: 'what is going to happen now that the beggars have been left alone on the estate?' This question is now immediately addressed. Viridiana's appointed overseer, Don Zequiel, can no more resist the temptations of the situation than can the other beggars and the plan for the next scene is set, although the image of the leper catching the little white dove and stroking its head so tenderly lends a certain childlike innocence to their escapades.

2. It is night in Don Jaime's dining room. The beggar's feast is in full swing, even the leper is present, although seated at a table on his own. 'Don't worry,' the women say, as still more wine is spilt, 'we'll clean it all up before they get back.'

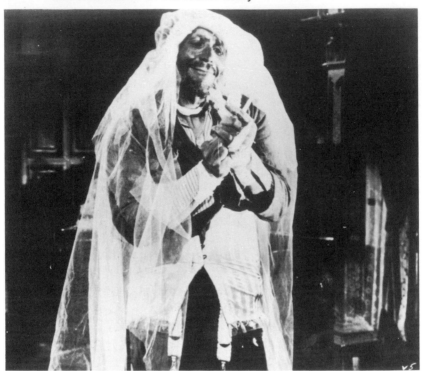

The first little furore takes place when Refugio gets angry with Edina's children for crying. The two women begin fighting but this is quickly quelled by Don Amalio who, although blind, seems to command the most respect from his fellow beggars.

Poca then announces that it's time for the photograph 'so we'll have a souvenir.' The beggars, all thirteen of them, strike up their poses behind the table with Don Amalio's commanding presence at the centre. (The image is immediately reminiscent of Leonardo Da Vinci's *The Last Supper*.) Edina goes to the front of the table, as if to take the picture, but instead lifts her skirt up to her waist (a quick flash for all the beggars to see) and cackles with glee at her joke.

The hubbub begins again. The leper now appears wearing the wedding veil and corset from Don Jaime's chest and begins a grotesque dance to the strains of the 'Hallelujah Chorus' as he pulls tufts of white dove feathers from inside his jacket and throws them, like confetti, over his comrades. One of the beggars grabs Edina and tries to make love with

144

her behind the couch. Poca tells Don Amalio, who thinks of Edina as his woman. The blind man reacts in a fury of jealousy, smashing all the glass and crockery on the table with his stick.

The beggars fall silent. They will never be able to clean up this mess. Best make a run for it while there's still time.

– From the making of the plan in the previous scene we cut, without further ado, to the feast in full swing and the first image we see is a glass of (blood) red wine spilling onto the (innocent) white lace table cloth. The women insist that they will be able to clear up the mess, but we know otherwise, and the fight between Edina and Refugio, although quickly quelled, further arouses our fears by reminding us of the ever-present violence lurking beneath the surface. This counterpoints with the next scene which functions at an almost wholly intellectual level.

The 'souvenir' photograph is both a perfect parody of the bourgeoisie's delight in taking photographs of every special occasion and of Leonardo's *The Last Supper*. [If you look at the still you will see that Don Amalio, the blind beggar, is seated in the centre, in the place of Christ. In Leonardo's painting the character who is meant to be Judas is the man seated with his hand on the table three characters to the right of Don Amalio's Christ. This man has not been seen before in the film and we don't see him again. The obvious character to put in Judas's place, as far as the story is concerned, would be Hobbly, the beggar who wears the fateful skipping rope and most threatens Viridiana's mission. But he's standing three characters to the left of Don Amalio. This suggests that Buñuel has deliberately chosen to avoid giving the tragedy an identifiable scapegoat. (We will return to this point when we discuss the theme.)]

The leper's grotesque dance instantly reminds us of Don Jaime dressing up in his dead wife's wedding clothes in the beginning of the film. What seemed bizarre then seems quite tame compared to this juxtaposition of the sacred and the profane and, as the leper showers white feathers over his comrades we realize, with a sinking feeling, that he's even killed the little white dove (of peace) we saw him earlier stroking with such affection in the almond blossom orchard.

Finally we have the crisis: Poca tells Don Amalio that 'his woman' is betraying him behind the couch, causing Don Amalio to go wild with jealousy. The crisis, as we have seen in *Midnight Cowboy*, is the point at which there is no turning back, the outcome is inevitable and unavoidable. Here most of the beggars also realize that this point has come, which is why they begin their rapid exit. (Again I will return to the implications of this scene when we discuss the theme.)

> 3. The first two beggars run out of the house just as Jorge's car pulls into the drive. Jorge, Ramona, Viridiana and Rita climb out of the car. Strains of the 'Hallelujah Chorus' can be heard from the house and the front door is standing wide open.
>
> As Jorge walks through the house more beggars anxiously pass him on their way out. Don Amalio seems to be the last, as he taps his way along the walls with his blind man's stick, stumbling, with the wedding veil caught around his feet. Jorge stares at the terrible mess in the dining room and switches off the music.

– Does this mean the height of the drama is over, and Viridiana must now face the disappointment of her failed venture and Jorge's wrath? Or could they have driven right into the eye of the storm? As Jorge walks through the house and passes Don Amalio, who, with the wedding veil caught up around his feet, has now become both the blind Christ and the jealous lover, it appears as if he's the last to leave but the tension, as Jorge switches off the 'Hallelujah Chorus', is almost unbearable. We can feel, in our dramatic bones, that a further outbreak of violence has yet to take place.

> 4. In the sudden silence Jorge hears a noise in Don Jaime's room next door. He goes to investigate and is confronted by Hobbly, who suddenly threatens him with a dagger while the leper smashes a bottle over his head. Viridiana rushes into the room just as Jorge falls to the floor. She's horrified by what she sees but before she can do anything to help Jorge, Hobbly grabs hold of her and drags her to the bed.
>
> Outside, Ramona is getting increasingly worried and decides to go to the village for help.
>
> Back in Don Jaime's room Viridiana is fighting for her life as Hobbly tries to rape her. Jorge, who has been tied up by the leper, comes to consciousness and, seeing what's going on,

146

bribes the leper to untie him by telling him that there's a lot of money hidden in the house. The leper agrees to the deal but it's too late to prevent the rape. Viridiana's hand, which was grasping hold of the skipping rope around Hobbly's waist, suddenly goes limp and she falls unconscious. The leper, encouraged by Jorge, then smashes Hobbly, over and over again, on the head with a shovel.

Outside, Ramona arrives with the police.

– It's no accident that the climax takes place in Don Jaime's bedroom, given the diabolical nature of Don Jaime's legacy to Viridiana and Jorge. And, of course, the perpetrator of the violence is Hobbly, who, at the beginning of the development, threatened to slit the leper's belly open and then tied the fatal skipping rope around his waist. He now threatens Jorge with a flick-knife (reminding us of Don Jaime's crucifix knife which so amused Jorge just days before) and his accomplice in crime is the other totally embittered beggar, the leper. (Hobbly and the leper were also the only two beggars who didn't kneel at Viridiana's prayer meeting under the almond blossoms.) This is the fateful moment when Viridiana chooses to rush into the room to find out what's going on.

The cut to Ramona waiting outside the house both gives us a moment of relief and the chance to learn that Ramona is going for the police, but how can they possibly arrive in time?

Back in Don Jaime's room the climax finally reaches its conclusion. Jorge's deal with the leper is too late to save Viridiana from rape. Her hand which clutches the skipping rope around Hobbly's waist, which has, since the beginning of the film, been associated with sexuality and death, suddenly falls limp, which tells us the rape is over. Hobbly is then battered to death while lying on top of her.

Dramatically speaking, Ramona's trip to fetch the police conveniently got her out of the way while the climax was taking place but we are also reminded of the reason why official social structures have been set up; in an attempt, if in vain, to counteract the beast in man.

5. It's another day. Moncho has returned to work in the garden and little Rita is playing happily beside him, but this time her skipping rope is gone and she plays instead with a stick.

Inside the house Jorge is talking to some workmen about house improvements while Viridiana, now wearing a floral blouse, sits on the couch with a cup of tea looking completely drained by her recent experience.

It is night and Viridiana is alone in her room in the outhouse. She takes a small hand mirror from the drawer, examines her tear-stained face and half-heartedly arranges her hair, which now falls freely onto her shoulders.

Outside in the night Moncho and little Rita are having a bonfire. Rita holds Viridiana's crown of thorns and looks at it curiously. She then pricks her finger and throws the crown onto the fire in disgust. It is soon engulfed in flames.

Inside the house rock music plays while Ramona hands Jorge a towel and kisses him playfully. (Intercut the image of the burning crown of thorns being removed from the fire with a stick.) There is a knock at the door. Jorge goes to answer and finds Viridiana standing on the doorstep. She looks lonely, vulnerable and frightened and is incapable of saying anything. Jorge smiles ironically when he realizes that at last she has sought out his company. He invites her in to play cards with himself and Ramona. The two women look at each other warily but Jorge insists that they both stay and play. 'Do you know what I thought when I first saw you?' he says, as he deals the cards, 'cousin Viridiana will end up playing cards with me.' The camera pulls back and we see that the dining room has been returned to its former order.

– The resolution begins with little Rita, who introduced both the beginning and the development of the film and who we have come to associate with the unconscious side of Viridiana. But Rita has changed, she's no longer alone in the shot, she's alongside Moncho, a protective male, and she's no longer skipping, instead she plays with a stick. And Viridiana is also no longer alone. For the first time we see her sitting quietly inside the house with Jorge and although her strength is gone and she looks like a shadow of her former self, the floral blouse and the cup of tea in her hand also make her look more like a traditional woman.

In the beginning Viridiana glanced dismissively at her reflection in the mirror. Then she wasn't interested in her feminine attributes, they had no part to play in her aim, which was to devote her life to Christ. But now, although her face is tear-stained and she's lost her former strength, she seems to be considering her potential as an attractive woman which indicates a radical change of heart.

Outside we see little Rita looking curiously at Viridiana's crown of thorns. This motif, which told us of Viridiana's strength in the beginning, and was hidden from Jorge in the development, is now finally burnt. When little Rita pricks her finger the pain causes her to throw the crown of thorns into the fire as she sucks her finger to ease the hurt. This metaphor is like a microcosm of Viridiana's entire journey.

Inside the house the 'Hallelujah Chorus', so beloved by Don Jaime, has been replaced by rock music, just as Jorge has replaced him in Ramona's affections. (The intercut image of the crown of thorns being removed from the fire suggests that the symbol still has some life left in it although we will never know who took it out of the flames.) When Viridiana knocks at the door we see a woman who has lost everything she ever cherished. She is simply a vulnerable, frightened, damaged woman in need of company and protection. And Jorge is quietly triumphant, he now has Viridiana on his terms. Finally we see the bourgeois dining room, restored to its former order; the wholly practical and materialistic man has won the battle, if not our hearts.

Viridiana's aim, to devote her life to Christ, which has been the backbone to the entire story, has failed, she has resorted to the life of any 'normal' woman. And it was the three major obstacles; Jorge (who replaced Don Jaime); the threat of violence lurking beneath the surface of the beggars; and Viridiana's naivety and innocent sexuality which, in combination, contributed to her downfall. Which brings us again to the theme.

Viridiana's inability to fully understand herself and her own inner needs has meant that she was equally unable to understand the beggars and their needs. The consequences of her treating them like children contributed to their irresponsibility on the one occasion when she treated them like adults and trusted them. But the beggars themselves have been outcasts of society for so long and, in the case of Hobbly and perhaps the leper, their bitterness and violence has become so deeply ingrained that it's possible they would have been beyond the redemption of even the most self-aware saint. (It's up to each of us to decide on the answer to this according to our own faith or lack of it.)

And what of Don Jaime and Jorge, who stepped so easily into his father's shoes? They were both middle-class men. Don Jaime was the romantic, and former idealist, who idolized woman whilst being prepared to go to desperate lengths to possess her totally (also whilst denying the other side of his character, the side that had fathered Jorge and betrayed the mother). Jorge, on the other hand, was the practical, material man, who could see little difference between human beings and animals and who naturally, according to the philosophy of the survival of the fittest, rules over woman because of the traditional patriarchal code. Maybe Buñuel and Alejandro intended Don Jaime and Jorge to represent the two aspects of man; the two alternatives facing Viridiana when she finally decided, based on the bitter experience of that fateful night, that her first love, Christ, was unable to protect her.

The complexity of these intertwining themes is apparent. The suggestion is that there are certain evils that love, in its original Christian sense, does not have the power to overcome. But this simple conclusion is tempered by the character portrait of Viridiana herself. Her motives for devoting her life to Christ are, in part, the result of the lack of love in her own life and her denial of aspects of her own psyche, in particular sexuality and a natural anger towards Don Jaime, who was her only family and who gave her so little. Sex and violence, to put it bluntly, are also the two major aspects controlling the beggars' behaviour. But because they are the very aspects that Viridiana denies in herself, she also denies them in the beggars. This is probably the reason why Buñuel chose not to seat Hobbly in Judas' seat at *The Last Supper*, because with such a complex theme he did not want to point the finger of blame and thus enable us to have an easy scapegoat. And although he has chosen to put a blind beggar in the place of Christ (who precipitates the climax, and so Viridiana's downfall, by flying into a rage of sexual jealousy) I don't think the film can be read simply at the level of an attack on Christianity. If anything is at the heart of this film it is a longing to believe that good can overcome evil. Finally, the odds are against that happening, but far from rejoicing in Viridiana's loss of faith, we share in her pain and the emptiness of her alternative life.

4 Departures from the Classic Form

The vast majority of feature films which have their origins in the western tradition, whether they are popular entertainment films or those which play a significant part in our cultural life, can be analysed (although with some very individual re-moulding) according to the basic elements of the classic form. Most frequently the re-moulding takes place in the detail of the film, at the image-sound level we explored in the first part of this book. It's in the image-sound texture of the unfolding story that the individual life view of the writer and director manifests itself, while the classic form acts as a backbone for the overall story, giving it a unity, a sense of direction and a forward motion. But what happens when the re-moulding actually amounts to a disruption, or a significant departure, from the classic form, which has of course happened in many notable cases throughout feature film history?

Although many of us may not, until now, have been so consciously aware of the basic principles underlying the form, it will have been very familiar because of our long relationship with stories, ranging from the fairy stories and adventure stories we first encountered as children right through to the feature films we now see. Indeed, our expectations of story have been so conditioned that as soon as a departure from the classic model takes place we react. Often we are not aware that such a departure has taken place, our reaction is simply a spontaneous response to our disrupted expectations. This reaction manifests itself in many different ways. We may find ourselves feeling confused, bored, alienated, angry, sad, amused by the unexpected or disturbed because we are feeling something we have never felt before. We may so dislike the experience that we decide that the film is bad; the film-maker obviously doesn't know how to put a film together. Or we may feel that something intriguing is taking place and, although it's more difficult than usual to understand our thoughts and feelings, it's worth the effort demanded because the film is taking us into territory we've never visited before.

Our need for a sense of structure is great because without structure there can be no unity. Consequently, if there is a radical departure from the classic form, the audience's passage is eased if the film provides a detectable alternative structure. Pasolini's *Theorem*, which he described as 'a little lay tract, constructed like an unresolved canon, around a religious visitation',* is a fine example of this.

The religious visitation Pasolini is referring to, if somewhat ironically, is the arrival of a young English man (Terence Stamp) into an Italian household. The household consists of father, mother, son and daughter (both teenagers) and a middle-aged maid. In the first part of the film each member of the household, in turn, forms a relationship with the new arrival and falls in love with him. The Englishman then leaves the household and we follow the reaction of each family member in turn. The son becomes an abstract artist and is reduced to pissing on his paintings in his attempt to find his true self. The mother drives round the streets seeking a replacement for her beloved in the young men who roam the streets. The daughter withdraws from the world, becoming cata-tonic. The maid returns to her village and refuses to eat anything except nettles the children bring her, which results in her becoming so light she rises into the air, as high as the church steeple. The father decides that his bourgeois life is inauthentic and, in the final scene in the film, takes off all his clothes in a crowded station concourse. We then enter his interior world and see that, although all the bystanders think he's having a nervous breakdown, in his imagination he is striding naked across a stony desert, proud and free.

Reviews of this film normally describe the young Englishman as the protagonist, but this simply reflects the loose way the term is frequently used. The Englishman doesn't fulfil any of the require-ments of a protagonist. His role is best described as a catalyst in that he remains unchanged while causing change to take place around him. He arouses the love of each household member almost by default, because of who he is, rather this being his aim and it is the uncompromising nature of this love which, after his departure,

---

*Quoted by Raymond Durgnat, *Sexual Alienation in the Cinema*, (Studio Vista 1972) p. 209.

confronts each of them with their inner selves and causes them to change.

The structure of *Theorum* would be better described as having one catalyst and five protagonists, although this stretches our definition of protagonist somewhat, because the film focuses far more on each character's change, which is rather like a chemical reaction to a catalyst, than on their pursuit of their common aim, which was to seduce the Englishman. According to the classic form there can only be more than one protagonist if they are united by the same aim. And it is the common nature of the aim, and the fact that it causes them each to change, which connects Pasolini's five characters and gives the film its structural unity. But the classic form also demands that the story reaches a climax in the fulfilment or failure of the aim, which is clearly not the case in *Theorum* – after all an 'unresolved canon' goes round and round. Sturges' *The Magnificent Seven* (based on Kurosawa's *Seven Samurai*), on the other hand, is an example of how the classic form works with more than one protagonist: although each of the seven has their own highly individual motive they are united by their single aim, which is to protect a village from bandits, and the aim is not resolved until the village is saved.

Our decision about whether films which depart from the classic structure without replacing it with a detectable and satisfactory alternative structure are either bad or taking us into new and exciting territory, depends, of course, both on the nature of the departure and on our personal predisposition. But the reaction itself is inevitable. One of the more famous cases of such a reaction was the furore caused in Cannes by the release of Antonioni's *L'Avventura*. In the beginning of the film we are led to believe that Anna, a beautiful young heiress, is the probable protagonist, although her friend Claudia's presence is also significant. But when Anna and Claudia go on a yachting trip Anna mysteriously disappears. Claudia, and Anna's fiancé, Sandro, spend the rest of the film looking for her, but their search becomes increasingly halfhearted and by the end of the film we no longer care about Anna's disappearance and the mystery is never solved. Although many people love this film for its melancholy, existential beauty, many others scream with boredom and frustration because for them the film is obscure, alienating, hermetically sealed and doesn't fulfil any of their expectations.

But, whatever your opinion of the film, one thing is not in doubt;

it's quite clear from Antonioni's other films that, although he always re-moulds at the level of image-sound, he has a perfectly adequate understanding of classic narrative form. In *L'Avventura* he deliberately disrupted his audience's expectations because he wanted to draw our attention to aspects of human experience that he felt were concealed by a goal-orientated plot. Woody Allen also disrupted audience expectations when he made *Interiors* (his homage to Bergman's *Persona*), one of his best films, but it's a serious drama and so out of line with the 'Woody Allen genre' of comedy his audience has come to love and expect of him. The price of innovation is usually a smaller audience.

There are so many examples of narrative departures from the classic form in cinema history that I've decided to focus in depth on just a few film examples, each of which shed light on a different aspect of the subject and a different set of problems to be solved.

1. THE DISRUPTION OF A GENRE

HEAVEN'S GATE (1980)
Written and directed by Michael Cimino

Heaven's Gate caused a critical storm when it first opened in America in 1980. The critics damned it absolutely saying that Cimino had had a fit of self-indulgent megalomania and the film was an unqualified disaster. In Cannes the film was subsequently slow-handclapped (although this version had been drastically cut). But a few lone voices spoke out in favour of the film claiming it to be a masterpiece. I prefer to call it a flawed masterpiece.

The film is certainly a departure from classic narrative form, which usually causes confusion in an audience on first release. It's also likely that the anger caused by the film was, in American audiences at least, a reaction to Cimino's radical portrait of American history. He based his story on a little-known incident called 'The Johnson County War'. But he made little attempt to portray the actual facts of the incident. Instead he used it as an imaginative stepping-stone to invent a story that communicated his own feelings about American history. There's nothing new in this. Shakespeare's *Macbeth* bears very little resemblance to the known facts about Macbeth's life. Aristotle commented on the uneasy relationship between art and history when he said 'poetry . . .

(referring to drama) is concerned with universal truths, history treats particular facts'.*

Heaven's Gate, because it's about the conflicts encountered by immigrants settling in the West, fits loosely into the Western genre. When we think that the film we are going to see fits into a particular genre our expectations are not only conditioned by the classic narrative form, but we also have expectations, rooted in our previous experience of the genre, about what the film's mythology should be. In the case of the Western this means that we expect a certain kind of heroism, we expect to know who is good and who is bad, and we expect the outcome of the conflict to reinforce the genre's mythology about heroism, good and bad, and the nature of the West.

By the time Cimino made *Heaven's Gate* the Western genre had already been disrupted, most notably by the Spaghetti Western. Leone's films conform absolutely to the classic narrative structure, but are distinguishable because of the way he has re-moulded, and so carved out their special identity, at the image-sound level (see pp. 69–75). Also, although the films are markedly different from American Westerns, they don't upset audience expectations of the parent genre because Leone has chosen to exaggerate a particular aspect of the Western mythology rather than to fundamentally challenge the mythology itself, which is precisely what Cimino does in *Heaven's Gate*. To exacerbate things further Cimino also departs from our expectations of classic narrative. But it's not at all easy to decide whether some of his departures from classic storytelling conventions are based on conscious, deliberate decisions, because of the originality of what he wants to say, or are simply flaws, or mistakes, which make the film unnecessarily difficult to follow.

Story Outline and Points of Departure

In the opening sequence we are introduced to two young men, Averill (Kris Kristofferson) and his friend Irvine (John Hurt), who are graduating from Harvard in 1870. We see Averill first, which suggests that he might be the protagonist but, although the two young men have the usual youthful, romantic inclinations and there is a general feeling of optimism generated by the situation, there is no mention of what either Averill or Irvine are specifically

*Classical Literary Criticism, Aristotle/Horace/Longinus, trans. T. S. Dorsch (Penguin, 1965) p. 44

aiming for. Instead of the specific narrative clues we expect from the beginning, our attention is drawn to the themes of two speeches made in the graduation ceremony. Irvine's speech, which is reactionary and complacent but clearly expresses the views of the new young generation, is in sharp contrast with that of his ageing professor, whose speech expresses a real fear for a future dominated by material values and a plea for the students to remember the importance of cultural idealism. The sequence then goes on to show how everyone is swept along by the emblematic rituals of graduation, and to establish visual motifs (which recur throughout the film) of large numbers of people moving in processions and in circles within circles, which are quite magically captivated by the cinematography. (The processions and the circle motif are reminiscent of Bondarchuk's *War and Peace*.)

We then cut to Averill dozing in a train compartment. A caption tells us that we are in Wyoming twenty years later. Long processions of newly arriving immigrants are trudging across the beautiful uncultivated landscape. An immigrant homesteader is murdered in cold blood. Irvine is at a wealthy club where the local cattle barons, threatened by the immigration from central Europe, are meeting to discuss a death list of 125 immigrants they have drawn up as part of their campaign to stop mass immigration into the country. Averill's train arrives in the town, which is packed to the brim with newly arrived immigrants. He goes to the cattle barons' club where he learns from Irvine about the death list and about its legality; it has been sanctioned by the US president. Averill angrily leaves the club.

In classic terms the beginning of the film clearly should be here, and it is, almost. The premise to the story, the drawing up of the death list, is established, as is the awful vulnerability of the immigrants and the fact that cold-blooded murders are already taking place. It's also now clear that Averill is the protagonist because he is the one most disturbed and affronted by the death list. But instead of giving us much needed information about his leading characters, Cimino has chosen to give us more emblematic scenes, contrasting the harsh and chaotic conditions encountered by the great processions of newly arriving immigrants with the old-world wealth and bigotry of the cattle barons' club.

The crucial information, that Averill is the Marshal of Sweatwater, the settlement where most of the immigrants on the death list live, is not at all clear on a first viewing. We are told nothing about how he has led his life over the past twenty years nor are we given any clues to help us understand what's motivated him to become Marshal. We're told that he's a wealthy man, so we assume that he has a wealthy family somewhere, which makes his reasons for becoming a marshal in a remote immigrant backwater even more intriguing, but we are told nothing about who, or where, his family are. We are given the important information that he turned his back on the cattle barons' club and its values some time ago, but with so little insight into his attitudes beyond that, other than a general sense of nostalgia for his student days and of defeatism in the face of present circumstances, his character remains elusive. Irvine's character remains equally elusive. We learn little about him other than that the defeatism he shares with Averill has led him to become a drunk and, although he also shares Averill's distaste for the powers that be, they now find themselves on opposing sides as Irvine is still a member of the cattle barons' club.

Some clear exposition at this stage in the story would have transformed our ability to identify with Averill's character and to fully understand what is going on. But instead, at the end of the

beginning, when we return to Sweatwater with Averill, we are still trying to get our bearings in the story.

The development sequences are mainly focused around two locations in Sweatwater: the brothel and the Heaven's Gate roller-skating rink. The rollerskating rink is also the bar and the community meeting hall and it's here that we get to know the people of Sweatwater. But again we learn little about individuals. Instead, through ritual communal events – a cock-fight, a rollerskating dance, and finally meetings about what to do about the death list – we are given remarkable, emblematic portraits of a newly formed and somewhat anarchic community; a leaderless mass of conflicting needs and desires rooted in many different cultures and languages and backgrounds. The events celebrating the joyful freedoms of their new life are in sharp contrast to their horrified reaction to what is in store for them.

Interwoven with these emblematic community sequences is the intimate, although equally anarchic, love triangle between the young brothel Madame, Ella (Isabelle Huppert), and the two men she's in love with, Averill and Nate, a local uneducated man who, in order to get on in the world, works as a gunslinger for the cattle barons. Ella's name is on the cattle baron's death list because the brothel receives stolen cattle in payment for services. Averill wants Ella to save herself by leaving the county but she won't leave unless he marries her, and he can't bring himself to make such a commitment. Nate, on the other hand, wants to marry Ella, but she can't bring herself to make that choice.

On the surface it appears that these two elements, the story of the community and the story of the love triangle, could easily weave together, according to classic narrative conventions, culminating in the arrival of the cattle barons to put their death list into practice. But Cimino has chosen to be as unconventional about the development as he was about the beginning. Although he does provide us with the occasional plot point (which is the American jargon for a re-formed dramatic question), he doesn't build his sequences around the developing plot, instead he continues to focus on the confused and anarchic aspects of the characters' lives and the ritualistic and emblematic nature of events.

In the final development sequence news comes that the cattle barons' army of mercenaries is just outside town. The people appeal to Averill, as their Marshal, for help. But Averill doesn't know what to do and gets drunk rather than supplying them with the leadership they so desperately need. This scene epitomizes how Cimino departs from the conventions the classic form applies to the protagonist. At no time in the film does Averill have a clear aim, even his attempts to persuade Ella to leave the county lack the energy of heroic action. He's endearingly romantic with her but unable to give her what she wants, even to save her life, until it's too late. And Averill's laid-back, confused, defeatist characterization is a crushing blow for those members of the audience who expect, and want, mythological behaviour from their Western genre heroes.

The climax is, of course, the inevitable massacre when the cattle barons finally arrive. The people fight because they have no choice; most of the men are on the death list anyway. Averill becomes involved in the battle despite himself and finally tries to rescue Ella and take her away to marry her, but it's too late and she is killed. We cut from Ella's death to the resolution, which is twenty years later. Averill, now elderly and listless, is on a yacht with a woman who seems equally listless. Averill stands alone on deck looking out at the dark ocean.

So, in *Heaven's Gate* the will of the protagonist to achieve his aim does not provide the dramatic energy for the story. Averill, like everyone else, is simply a part of a chain of tragic events which take their natural course. Instead of 'the occasion, the means, and the reason' being illuminated by the climax we simply experience the horror of the massacre itself and (for those in the audience who were able to enter into the spirit of the story despite its narrative departures) an overwhelming feeling for the defeat of anarchic freedom, represented by the immigrants, in the face of power and corruption, represented by the cattle barons and the government which sanctioned their actions.

The resolution; the listless, ageing Averill, apparently adrift on his rich man's yacht, is the final emblem. Rather than telling us anything specific about Averill himself, it communicates a general feeling of loss of meaning which, if we connect the scene with the opening of the film, perhaps suggests that this is the inevitable outcome for a generation who valued reactionary complacency and material acquisition above cultural idealism, an attitude which finally enabled the unscrupulous, Fascistic elements in society to take power.

In some ways, this departure from the usual emphasis on plot liberates the theme of the film and makes what could have been a familiar story treated in a familiar way all the more power-ful. But the lack of exposition and full characterization causes confusion and alienates an audience on first viewing, when we are, after all, trying to work out what on earth is going on. On the other hand, such exposition may have shifted the emphasis of the film, turning it into a story about a specific incident involving specific individuals at a specific time in history, and thus have weakened the emblematic universal quality which is obviously what Cimino was most interested in communicating.

2. The Problem of the Woman Protagonist
Les Rendez-Vous d'Anna

We have seen how the key concept in the classic model is the conflict generated by a protagonist who has an overriding desire to achieve an aim that is very difficult to achieve, which gives us the linear, forward motion towards the inevitable climax and resol-ution. Therefore an effective protagonist is a character with an actively striving will. Does this present special problems for films with women protagonists?

In *Ways of Seeing* John Berger says, 'A man's presence is depen-dent on the promise of power which he embodies. The promise of power may be moral, physical, temperamental, economic, social, sexual – but its object is always exterior to man. It suggests what he is capable of doing to you or for you. By contrast a woman's presence expresses her own attitude to herself and defines what can and cannot be done to her . . . And so she comes to consider the surveyor and the surveyed within her as the two constituent yet always distinct elements of her identity as a woman . . . in other words men act and women appear.'* If you agree with John Berger here it's not difficult to see how men, with their external object orientation, lend themselves more naturally to the traditional inter-pretation of the role of protagonist than do women.

A second problem is reflected in the emergence of two distinct female types. The first Freud described as 'the ministering Angel to the needs and comforts of man'; she is the good woman who is receptive, passive and nurturing: the wife, the mother, the nurse, the saint. The second type is the bad, or dark woman. She has a mysterious and dangerous power, is sexually active, threatening and even demonic; the witch, the whore, the hysteric or mad woman.

*John Berger, *Ways of Seeing* (BBC and Penguin, 1972) p. 45

160

Both types present limitations for the role of the woman protagonist (which can be observed by looking at woman protagonists in drama and literature over the past few hundred years). The 'good' woman protagonist can actively strive to achieve her aim just so long as her aim is to administer to the needs and comforts of a man or men, which means her aim can be either marriage or good works, without upsetting the boat. As we have seen, Viridiana strove to devote her life to Christ, but was finally broken down to the level of mortal man. And in much of nineteenth-century literature stories about woman protagonists ended with marriage, or despair, depending on whether the woman finally got, or finally lost, her man.

It appears to have been more difficult to place the second type, the 'bad' or dark woman, as the protagonist. Consequently she's more often figured as an antagonist or major obstacle to the protagonist, like Kate in *The Taming of the Shrew* (who was eventually made 'good'), Lady Macbeth or the madwoman in *Jane Eyre*. The enormous popularity of *Gone With the Wind* showed how women who behave 'badly', i.e. selfishly, can make very popular protagonists – although Scarlett certainly gets her come-uppance in the end when she finally realizes she loves Rhett, but too late; he doesn't 'give a damn'. (On the other hand, she got Tara, her childhood home, which was perhaps her greatest need and her greatest love.) The heroines of film noir (a genre characterized by ambitious women protagonists attempting to compete in a man's world) were usually punished for their selfishness or came to see the error of their ways in the end. *Mildred Pierce* is probably the most well-known and the most complex example of this phenomenon. The film is also a departure from the classic form. Strictly speaking, the male detective is the protagonist: we begin with his aim, to solve the crime, and end with his achieving his aim. Mildred, as the accused woman, is his major obstacle. But, because most of the story, told in flashbacks, is concerned with Mildred's life leading up to the crime, she becomes the protagonist as the dynamics of the drama centre on her aim and the obstacles confronting her. Her punishment also lay in her seeing the error of her ways too late, as a single mother who tried to make her way in the world without the support of a man.

In drama, literature and film, women have most often been portrayed as the object of desire, or fear, not as the desiring subject. This is partly because most of the authors have been men and also because woman doesn't fit, as easily and naturally as man, into the role of the active, striving protagonist at the heart of the classic model without certain qualifications.

Since the women's movement, it's become more acceptable for women to strive to achieve similar goals as men. (Although whether she manages to remain 'good' in the process is another matter.) These new women protagonists fit easily into the classic model not because in modern times the feminine has become less repressed, but because it's become more acceptable for women to embrace the masculine archetypes as a part of their identity and this has coincided with a period in history when women have fought hard for such freedoms. However, this doesn't address the problem of creating women protagonists who embody aspects of the feminine which appear to be in conflict with the classic model. Chantal Akerman's film *Les Rendez-vous d'Anna* is just such a film.

LES RENDEZ-VOUS D'ANNA (1978)
Written and directed by Chantal Akerman

On the surface, *Les Rendez-vous d'Anna* appears to be a simple linear narrative following the journey the protagonist, Anna, a young Belgian woman film director, makes from a small German town, where she has been attending a screening of her film, to Brussels, where her parents live and finally on to her home in Paris. But, in spite of the linearity of the journey, the structure is basically episodic in that Akerman shows no concern with building dramatic tension. Instead, she gives the seven sequences which make up the film a homogeneity which connects them thematically rather than dramatically.

In the beginning Anna has no clear want or aim; instead we focus on the overwhelming mood of loneliness and alienation which permeates the hotel, the sprawling urban landscape outside, and Anna herself, giving us a strong sense of her need, which is made explicit when, at the end of the beginning, she breaks off a casual sexual encounter with Heinrich, a German school-teacher because, as she says, 'I don't love you.'

It's Anna's need, for meaningful human contact, which connects the subsequent five 'episodes', each one focusing on an encounter she has on her journey. The first encounter is with Heinrich again, in spite of their failed love-making the night before. Heinrich talks

162

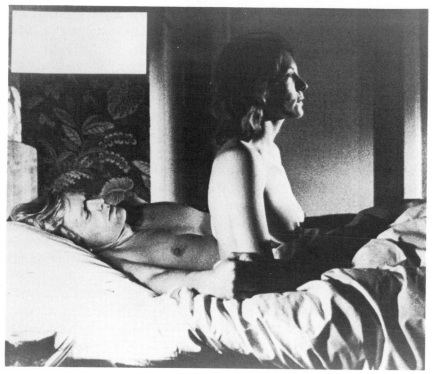

and Anna listens. His speech is a tale of losses, none of which he understands: his wife, his father, his friend and, in a sense, the loss of his country, with the war and the division of Germany.

The second encounter is with the mother of her ex-fiancé, who she meets on a station platform. The woman blames Anna for breaking off the engagement: 'Don't you want children? When your parents are dead and you have no children, who's left? For a girl to be alone is no life.' The woman then talks about her own unhappy marriage which, like Heinrich's story, is another sad tale of incomprehension and loss. By listening passively with Anna, we learn about the dilemmas she has faced in her own life and the choices she has made as a professional woman, but the alternative life scenarios offered by Heinrich and this woman's son suggest she had little chance of fulfilling her need with either of the two men.

Anna's third encounter is with a young man on the train to Paris. This man seems to be, both literally and metaphorically, a fellow traveller and, although there is also confusion and loss in his story, he wants what we think Anna wants, to meet someone 'whom I'll love and who'll love me'. This is one of the few moments of drama in the film as we find ourselves hoping that this may be a possible new life for Anna. But we are disappointed; she gets off at Brussels station leaving him alone on the train.

The fourth tale of loss comes from Anna's mother, who meets her at Brussels station and they spend the night in a hotel room together. Her mother tells Anna how her father has become so disheartened and withdrawn 'he doesn't even see me any more, he's looking inside of himself', and Anna tells her mother about her lonely life and a moment of contact and meaning she found with a lesbian lover in Italy. In spite of the distance between the lives of mother and daughter, through their mutual sadness they just about find each other and the intimacy between them is truly moving.

Anna's fifth encounter is in Paris, where she is met by her lover, a middle-aged man whose work is connected with government. But his story is also one of lost illusions: 'You can't change who you are, you get carried along. It's a case of march or die. If I was a woman I'd get pregnant and forget the rest. What is a better life? I can't even imagine it. It's not just bread for everybody, although that's a start. You know, I think things will get worse . . .' The man, almost in tears of exhaustion and despair, asks Anna to sing to him. She sings him a simple song and massages his back until he falls asleep. She then returns to her own apartment and listens to the Ansaphone; more screenings, more travelling and more rendez-vous.

According to classic narrative conventions this final encounter should be the climax, but it is a thematic rather than a dramatic climax in that it has arisen out of the culmination of the themes of each episode rather than from any dramatic build-up. The film has given us an insight into Akerman's desperately sad view of life, where the few hopes expressed have become clichés which the people she encounters cling on to in the face of their sense of loss and confusion in a northern industrial Europe of such loneliness, alienation and quiet desperation that when Anna's lover says 'I think things will get worse' the moment is chilling; worse can only be the horror of destruction. Her lover, an important and powerful man, can't even imagine a happy life any longer. His sickness seems to represent the sickness of northern Europe and Anna's simple song is the only real moment of hope in the film. We could well deduce that the only hope for Anna lies with her lesbian lover in Italy (the encounter we did not experience with her) but Anna is apparently clinging on to her need for a heterosexual relationship, maybe because she realizes that any real hope for the future lies in crossing this boundary.

Anna is a passive protagonist (a contradiction in terms according to the classic model) in that she is experiencing life rather than acting on life, although, as an independent professional woman, she is not the kind of passive object of desire familiar to so many classic stories. Her experience of life is what the film is about and Akerman has had to depart from the classic form in order to communicate the truth of such a life experience.

3. The Classic Form and Feminine Disruption: *Mirror*

Earlier I connected Aristotle's writings on drama to the beginnings of a new epoch and a shift in man's view of himself. The nature of the shift, which had slowly evolved over the centuries preceding Aristotle, involved the decline in belief in external, mythical and magical forces and the ascent of a view of the world controlled primarily by the rationality, logic and reason of man. It is only relatively recently that a few signs have begun to emerge that suggest a possible radical shift in the pendulum which leads some people to believe that we are on the verge of a new epoch.

The new science of Chaos is dramatically questioning our assumptions about linear, rational determinism with its discovery that order can breed its own kind of chaos. Some theories of psychoanalysis also challenge our ideas about rational determinism, most notably Jung's concept of a collective unconscious, which not only suggests that we have archetypal images within our innate psyche, but also throws into question our concept of ourselves as individuals and the seemingly insurmountable boundaries between us.

The new epoch Aristotle heralded marked the end of the long changeover from the matriarchy (the dominant aspect being the feminine archetype) to the patriarchy (the dominant aspect being the masculine archetype). I have qualified the concepts of matriarchy and patriarchy deliberately because it's both simplistic and dangerous to think of this shift as being a changeover of power from women to men. Edward Whitmont, a Jungian analyst and writer of the marvellous and wise *Return of the Goddess*, puts it this way: 'Maleness and femaleness are archetypal forces. They constitute different ways of relating to life, to the world and to the opposite sex. The repression of femininity, therefore, affects mankind's

165

relation to the cosmos no less than the relation of individual men and women to each other.'*

In other words he is saying that because all of us, irrespective of whether we are men or women, contain aspects of both masculine and feminine archetypes in our psyches, the 'repression of the feminine' isn't just a women's issue (which isn't to undermine its special importance for women), it raises fundamental questions for all of us about our identity and our view of life. Whitmont tells us that the 'opposition and complementariness of male and female belong among the most basic representations of the experience of dualism. They underlie the polarities of solar and lunar, light and dark, active and passive, spirit and matter, energy and substance, initiative and receptiveness, heaven and earth.'† So, this is not a question of one set of archetypes being good and the other bad, it is about acknowledging the natural law of duality and the creative energy which arises from these oppositions. It is also about the danger when either the masculine or the feminine archetype becomes so powerful it tries to exterminate the other.

Feminine archetypes, and consequently women, have been de-valued during the patriarchal epoch. Whitmont suggests that this was because of the need to separate the human ego from the encompassing consciousness of the magical, mythological world of need and instinct with its transformative, but at the same time ego threatening, dynamic of existence. By 'transformative' he means that although the descent into the underworld, or the unconscious, can be frightening and destructive, this is a crucial part of the process of change in the feminine creative cycle of growth.

Transformation, or change, is also crucial to the classic form, but the structure dictates that it can only be achieved through the climax resulting from a journey caused by the will and obedient to man's rational laws. This suggests that the Aristotelian form is a 'masculine form'. However, the aggressively striving protagonist is just one interpretation of the classic form. The protagonist who is on a quest for life and meaning is a softer interpretation, but equally valid, as we have seen in some of the film examples we have explored. In other words some film-makers, who are in touch with their feminine aspect, whether they are male or female, find work-

*Edward Whitmont, *The Return of the Goddess* (Routledge & Kegan Paul, 1983) p. 123
†Ibid. p. 128.

ing loosely within the classic structure helps to liberate their work – the masculine helps to liberate the feminine – while others have clearly found that they need to depart more radically from the classic structure in order to express themselves fully.

One of these film makers is the Russian director, Andrey Tarkovsky. His film *Mirror* seems to me to be one of the most complete disruptions of the classic form.

MIRROR (*Zerkalo*, 1974)
Written and directed by Andrey Tarkovsky

The first time I saw *Mirror*, soon after its release, I was both utterly bewitched and totally bewildered by the film. Tarkovsky's use of image and sound is amongst the most beautiful I have ever seen; it is tactile, deeply sensual and profoundly spiritual. But he doesn't lead you by the hand into 'the third dimension', he plunges you into it, and holds you captive there, defying not only the rules of film grammar and logic, but also what we have come to believe to be cosmic laws of space, time and gravity. Consequently the feeling is like falling into a magically beautiful, yet profoundly disturbing, very familiar yet totally unfamiliar place where, if you try to grasp hold of some bearings, and fix the film in terms of linear narrative development, those bearings quickly begin to feel fragile and even spurious.

It was only on the second and then repeated viewings that some of these bearings began to consolidate in my mind as crucial links feeding my need to piece together a sense of unity for the whole. For me the film then became far richer because I was not only awash with strange feelings, but intellectually the film had now begun to teach me its own way of understanding it.

Because *Mirror* has so completely disrupted the classic form – it doesn't have a traditional order of sequences that make up the story development – it is very difficult to give a summary of the film; one could only do it justice by attempting to describe the entire film and I am not going to attempt such an awesome task. But there is another crucial point of departure which I can talk about and that is the role of the protagonist. We never actually see the protagonist in *Mirror*. It is only a while after the film has begun that we begin to realize that the protagonist is not the woman we are watching on screen but a man, whose voice we hear and whose presence permeates the entire film, although we never see him. We realize

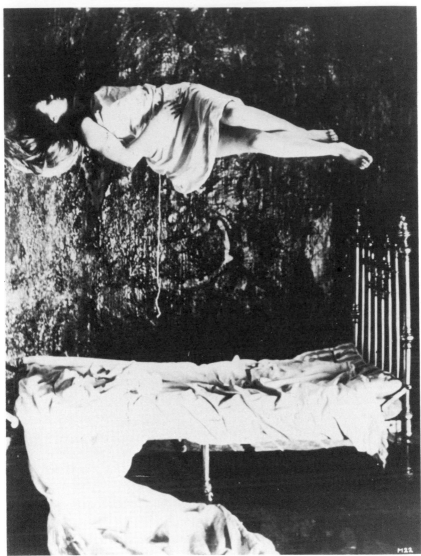

that everything in the film is exploring the subjective experience of this man whose marriage has broken up and whose life is in crisis. We never see him on screen because we have been transported into his mind, his thoughts and his memories. The woman we see so much of on screen is both his wife and his memory of his mother. The two characters are played by the same actress and, instead of trying to clarify or create order out of the confusion between

168

memory and time present, Tarkovsky seems happy for us to fully experience the confusion, to be unsure of the difference between his wife and his mother just as we are unsure of the precise borders between the past and the present.

Also the protagonist's memories are not only confined to events that actually happened to him, his experience of life includes other people's experience of life, his mother's and his wife's, his son's, his father's, his nation's, other nations'. All the boundaries that we usually use to define the self and the other, time and present reality, memory and imagination, have somehow become dissolved. Instead the film flows with disorientating ease from one experience to another and is concerned not so much with defining experience in terms of time, place and linear connection, as with reaching the essence of experience itself. This demands that we make connections between microcosmic and macrocosmic events according to our intuitive intelligence rather than according to the process of rational deduction which is our familiar mode.

This is why I feel that to understand the film we have to give ourselves over completely to 'the feminine aspect'.

5 *Persona* Revisited

In Part One we began our exploration into the nature of film language with Ingmar Bergman's *Persona*. Now we have reached the end of our exploration of film structure it feels like the right moment to revisit this film. In the process we will also find ourselves revisiting some of the major themes touched on in the book so far, ranging all the way from the image-sound basis of film language, which was our starting point, to the questions of structure we are exploring now. The film also raises the question of the creative process itself which, as I mentioned, is one of the deep underlying themes of the film and is also the subject of the last section of this book.

My final reason for returning to *Persona* at this stage in our journey is because in this film Bergman demonstrates how the classic structure, which gives the film its shape, energy and unity, can liberate, rather than stifle, the deep exploration of the feminine aspect discussed in the last chapter. The two aspects are not necessarily at war; in this film Bergman shows how they can help to define and reveal each other.

To enable us to see how this works I have chosen to use a combination of both the method we used to explore sequences in microcosm, exploring the rich detail of image and sound, and the method we used to look at structure, looking at how the dramatic threads are woven into the text and how they develop towards crisis both within the sequences and in relation to the whole film. To this end I have taken just two sequences from the film, a middle development sequence and the climax itself.

PERSONA: *A Development Sequence*

We have now reached the middle of the film. Sister Alma and Elizabeth Vogler have gone to stay in the doctor's cottage by the

170

sea. They have been getting on well although Elizabeth has still not spoken a word, apart, that is, from very late one night when Alma, flattered by Elizabeth's apparently endless ability to listen attentively, has drunk a lot of wine. In her slightly inebriated state Alma has told Elizabeth intimate details of her personal life, including secrets she has kept from her fiancé such as her seduction of a boy on the beach, her guilt at the sexual pleasure she got from making love to a complete stranger, and her subsequent abortion. In the small hours of the morning, when Alma was falling asleep with exhaustion Elizabeth whispered to Alma that she had better go to bed now, otherwise she will fall asleep at the table.

The sequence we are now going to explore begins the next day when the two women are on the beach together.

1. The weather is cold and grey. Alma and Elizabeth, both wearing anoraks, are examining shells together on the seashore.

ALMA
Elizabeth, did you speak to me last night?
Elizabeth smiles and shakes her head.

– We know that Elizabeth is lying. She did speak to Alma last night, we both heard and saw her. Elizabeth's sweet smile, as she lies, seems barefaced and cruel.

2. Cut to a long-shot of the two women walking along the bleak and rocky shoreline.

– This shot gives us the space to contemplate Elizabeth's denial as we watch the two women and wonder how it will affect their relationship.

3. Alma approaches Elizabeth and tries again.

ALMA
Did you come into my room last night?
Again Elizabeth smiles and shakes her head.

– We know Elizabeth did go into Alma's room last night. We saw her.

4. Alma walks away from Elizabeth over the harsh, bare rocks towards the grey sea. She looks very alone. She turns and looks back at Elizabeth (although, because Elizabeth is not in frame, the camera is where Elizabeth would be, the effect is of Alma looking directly at us, the audience).

– Our experience of Alma's aloneness is magnified by her bleak surroundings. The harshness of her experience of rejection by Elizabeth is intensified by the cold hard rocks and the grey empty sea. Her experience of the truth has been denied. When she turns and looks back we know she cannot accept the denial. She is the wronged innocent. And we, the audience, are in the place of the wrongdoer.

5. Cut to the cottage interior. Elizabeth, now smartly dressed, is typing a letter. She puts the letter in an envelope. Alma comes in from the rain, smiles cheerfully at Elizabeth and takes the pile of letters for posting.

– This is a change from the earlier scene. Both women appear to have forgotten about the painful moment on the beach, or to have decided to let sleeping dogs lie. Alma's smile, as she goes off to post the letters, seems especially cheerful and forgiving.

6. Alma is driving along a country lane. She keeps glancing down at the envelopes on the car seat beside her. The top one, the one we saw Elizabeth writing, has not been sealed.

– Elizabeth has not actually spoken to her since they have been together, other than the brief sentence she uttered the previous night, and that she now denies. In the envelope there will be words and what Alma most wants from Elizabeth are words of communication. Will Alma be able to resist temptation?

7. The car pulls to a halt on the lonely country lane. Alma picks up the envelope, puts on her glasses, and reads. Elizabeth's letter is to the doctor. She tells the doctor how relaxing at the beach with Alma is 'smoothing out her soul'. She goes on to say: 'Alma seems to be a tiny bit in love (with me) in a charming way. In any case it's fun studying her. Sometimes she weeps over past sins, an orgy with a boy and

an abortion afterwards. She complains that her ideas don't tally with her actions.' We can see the upset on Alma's face as she takes off her glasses and gets out of the car.

– So Alma was not able to resist temptation. Her punishment for committing the sin is in the letter itself, which does not contain what Alma expected. Rather than giving her a much wanted insight into Elizabeth it contains Elizabeth's image of herself. Everything Elizabeth has written about Alma is true; we have seen and heard it for ourself but her tone is patronizing and it's Alma's job, as the nurse, to study Elizabeth and report to the doctor, not the other way around. Finally, but of greatest significance, Elizabeth is betraying Alma's trust and confidence.

8. Alma stands absolutely still by a pond in a forest. The image seems frozen, there is no wind and the water is still. We see Alma from the far side of the pond. She looks like a powerful figure with her hands in the pockets of her black belted raincoat and in her black high-heeled boots – quite changed from the straightforward open-hearted nurse we have grown used to. And there appears to be two of her, her image is perfectly reflected in the pond.

– The world around Alma seems to have frozen while she contemplates the betrayal. This is a completely different moment from the earlier betrayal on the beach. Then the image told us she was an innocent victim, hurt, vulnerable, lonely, looking for understanding. This entire scene is one single long take of her and her reflection, (we don't cut into a close-up of the pain she is feeling which would show on her face) the camera doesn't move, the world around her seems to be frozen, she looks more like a Gestapo Commandant than a nurse, the image focuses only on her power. The dramatic question raised is how will she get revenge for her betrayal?

9. We are back in the cottage. The sun shines through the windows on to Alma who now wears a black bathing suit. She has a serious, determined expression on her face as she pours herself a glass of water, picks up her sun-hat and walks outside.

173

– Although the weather has changed we immediately see on Alma's face that her mood is consistent with the previous scene; she's still set on getting her revenge. What form will it take?

10. We watch Alma come out of the cottage door. (The whole of this scene is in long-shot and one continuous take of the front of the cottage framed by the shade of nearby trees.) Alma settles on a bench just outside the cottage door, faces the sun and closes her eyes. After a few moments, as she picks up her sun-hat, she accidentally knocks her glass on to the gravel

path. She gets up and goes inside the cottage. We wait. She returns with a dustpan and brush. She clears up the glass and takes the brush and pan inside. We watch the empty scene in front of the cottage and wait in silence. Alma reappears. This time she sits on the step by the side of the cottage door.

– The question of Alma's revenge remains with us throughout this scene. The tension Bergman created in the single take of Alma standing by the pond, and the power he invested her with in that shot, has stayed with her. She is still wearing black, although now a black bathing suit, her decisive manner remains consistent with her strong posture as she stood by the pond. This scene, like the pond scene, is also a single continuous take with the camera remaining static and Alma in the centre of the shot. The single-mindedness of the shot seems to emphasize Alma's single-mindedness. Like a cat that remains still and stares at its prey for a long time before it pounces, the tension here is building towards some kind of a climax. What will it be? We've seen Alma sipping from a glass of water and then accidentally breaking the glass. Has her unconscious already set the trap? The continual silence, apart from the occasional natural sound, serves to intensify the growing tension.

11. We see a movement through the cottage window behind Alma and immediately cut to a close-shot of Alma, her expression still serious and determined. Behind her Elizabeth, also wearing a black bathing suit, appears to be pacing up and down inside the cottage like a caged animal. Alma glances down at the gravel path in front of her. A slight tightening of the muscles on her face as we see an idea flicker into her mind.

– The sight of Elizabeth's presence seems to break the power of the long take. Just as a cat will suddenly tense all its muscles when it is about to pounce so we have jumped into a close-up of the intense concentration on Alma's face as Elizabeth paces restlessly up and down in the cottage behind her. The tension has grown. Alma looks at the gravel path and she knows what's going to happen – and so do we.

12. Elizabeth suddenly walks out of the door past Alma. We watch her bare feet on the gravel. She just misses stepping on a large shard of glass. We hold for a moment on the glass and then see Alma's eyes – she too is looking at the glass. She's waiting for Elizabeth to step on it.

– The tension is near its peak. Elizabeth has just narrowly escaped stepping on the glass, but we can tell by Alma's expression that she is still waiting for the moment. We now know for certain that this is Alma's revenge.

13. Elizabeth walks past again and again misses the glass.
Alma stands. She smiles slightly to herself and walks into the
cottage.

– Alma's smile suggests immense satisfaction. She could remove
the glass or warn Elizabeth, she has that power, but she chooses
instead to let the inevitable take its course without intervening.
And so inevitable is the coming moment that she doesn't even need
to stay and watch. Bergman has relaxed the building of tension
while he draws our attention to how the desire for revenge has
completely taken over Alma's personality.

14. Elizabeth steps on the glass and cries out with pain.

– The scene climaxes, the inevitable happens. By having Alma leave
her seat in the doorway Bergman has achieved two things. First, he
has made Alma's pleasure in taking revenge as much a part of what
the scene is about as the drama of whether or not Elizabeth will step
on the glass. And second, he has skilfully shifted Alma's physical
position in relation to Elizabeth, which, as we will see, is a very
important aspect of how we perceive their relationship in the next
scene.

15. Alma is in the cottage with her back to the door. She stubs
her cigarette in an ashtray as she listens to Elizabeth's cry. She
has a look of pride and satisfaction in a job well done. She
takes off her sun-hat, goes to the window, pulls the lace
curtain back (she holds the curtain so it appears to divide her
face) and looks steadily and uncompromisingly down at
Elizabeth.

– The reversal of their power relationship is now firmly established
by Alma's position inside the house looking down at Elizabeth. The
curtain which seems to cut across Alma's face, dividing it into two,
serves to emphasize her coldness, her hardness, her cruelty in the
face of pain, the fickleness of a divided soul.

16. Elizabeth crouches on the gravel path outside in
considerable pain as she attends to her cut foot. She looks up
at Alma with a look of vulnerability, pain and shock at Alma's
apparent lack of concern.

176

– This is the moment when Elizabeth sees that Alma knew about the glass and deliberately let her step on it. We started the sequence on the beach with the moment when Elizabeth inflicted real pain on Alma by denying what Alma knew to be true when she lied to her. At that time Elizabeth showed no concern for Alma's feelings of pain and rejection. Now, at the end of the sequence, the roles of the two women have been completely reversed. For the first time in the film we see Elizabeth's vulnerability in relation to Alma, and realize that Alma has, if she chooses, the power to change Elizabeth. (Elizabeth has already changed Alma – by rejecting her and betraying her trust in the scene on the beach she has caused Alma to seek revenge and so discover a power within herself she didn't know she had.)

17. The film appears to break down in the projector. The sound becomes distorted as if it's gone into reverse. We see quick flashes of images from the same early silent film that we saw in the opening montage: the skeleton chasing the man in his nightshirt, although now two new characters seem to have joined the chase. As before the sound is the percussion that often accompanies children's animation. The screen goes to white. We hear a man groaning in pain. The image of a hand with a nail being brutally hammered through the palm appears. This is replaced by an extreme close-up of the veins on the whites of an eye. The music is a repetition of the discordant themes in the opening montage.

– Retribution, punishment, vengeance for sin or injury, the vicious circle, all major Biblical themes. By taking us back to the opening montage Bergman is reminding us of his subtext; we must consider the relationship he is exploring between these two women, not just at a realistic level but as a metaphor. This is not to say that he is not taking great pains to be totally truthful to their characters; quite the reverse, the power of the metaphor lies in its truthfulness. In other words, the cycle of sin or injury and retribution has far-reaching consequences throughout our personal, social, spiritual and political lives and through closely examining the relationship between these two women, and by being truthful in all its complexity, we might gain some insight into the nature of this powerful cycle.

PERSONA: The Crisis and the Climax

In the intervening scenes between this and the previous sequence, the relationship between Alma and Elizabeth has developed into an intense and complex full-scale power struggle. Alma has alternately attacked Elizabeth and, shocked by her own behaviour, begged her forgiveness. Elizabeth has only spoken once; she cried out in fear when Alma threatened her with a steaming pan of boiling water. Apart from this incident she has maintained her silence with a will of iron.

The sequence we are now going to explore begins just after Alma has confronted Elizabeth about her young son. She has accused Elizabeth of having an abhorrence towards both her child and her role as mother and, after failing in her attempt to abort the unwanted foetus, totally rejected the boy since birth. Elizabeth's face registered the extreme pain she felt when confronted with this truth; the skeleton in her cupboard. During the confrontation Alma's face increasingly began to resemble that of Elizabeth's and in the climax of the scene Bergman showed us a big close-up of their two faces, Alma's and Elizabeth's, joined together as one face. This

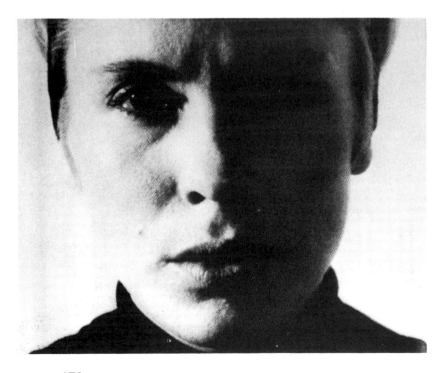

unnatural merger was ugly. Something very wrong had taken place, this wrongness stressed by the jarring, discordant music.

1. Elizabeth sits absolutely still at a desk. She's dressed all in black and a black headband gives her face a dark austerity. Her hands rest lightly on the desk in front of her. We hear a door open. Elizabeth remains motionless apart from her eyes which are immediately, defensively alert, like those of a hunted animal. In her black pullover and headband, she seems to be engulfed by the dark side of the soul. Her alert, animal-like stillness could be preparation for fight or flight.

2. Over Elizabeth's shoulder we see that Alma has come into the room and is walking towards her. Alma is wearing her nurse's uniform. She arrives at the desk, places both hands deliberately on the desk-top, bends down and stares directly into Elizabeth's eyes. The shot is lit in such a way that half of Alma's face is in darkness.

– This is the first time we've seen Alma in uniform since the hospital scenes near the beginning of the film. Then, her uniform made her

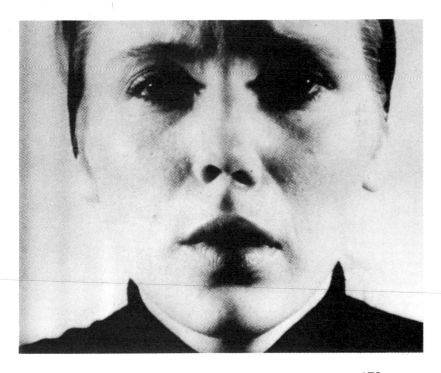

look like the ministering angel, the nurturing presence. Now the same uniform has quite a different aura. It seems to endow her with power and authority and so focuses our minds on the power relationship between them. In spite of the fact that Elizabeth is sitting behind a desk (the position we traditionally associate with the person in power), by placing her hands firmly on the desk-top and remaining standing when she stares into Elizabeth's eyes, it is Alma who seems to be in the dominant position. Her power is further emphasized by the way half of her face is in dark shadow – after all who knows what lurks in the dark shadow?

3.

    ALMA
I've learned quite a lot.
She suddenly throws a karate punch at Elizabeth's face, stopping within an inch of striking her. She slowly withdraws her fist, never taking her eyes off Elizabeth.
    ALMA
How long can I cope with it?

– 'I've learned quite a lot' . . . *from you*, Alma implies when she addresses Elizabeth. And we know she has. She has learnt how to take control, how to take power, how to frighten people, how to let half of her face remain in the dark shadow. She punches out with her fist as if to demonstrate how much she has learnt. But how long can she cope with what she has learnt? is her next question, implying that what she has learnt is a tremendous burden.

4. Elizabeth bows her head down to face the table. Alma does the same, her face crossing behind Elizabeth's. The image is now a big close-up of the profiles of their two faces, so close in the darkness that they seem to have become one profile.

    ALMA
I'll never be like you. I change all the time. Do what you like, you'll never reach me.
She sits back and stares at Elizabeth. Elizabeth returns her stare.

– When Elizabeth bows her head down she seems to be acknowledging the weight of the burden: to have to constantly maintain power in order to defend what lies behind the persona. When Alma bows her head down the two women seem united, for the moment, in the darkness. The uniting of the two, expressed by an apparent merging of their faces, happened at the end of the previous sequence. Then the halves of their two faces were joined together, fully facing us, and fully lit and the image was ugly in its unnaturalness. Here the two faces come together in the darkness and there is a moment of harmony. But the moment is all too brief – Alma's words break the illusion. She suddenly doesn't sound like Sister Alma; her words are like challenges, taunts from deep inside Elizabeth's psyche. And when they sit back and stare at each other across the table they seem absolutely equal in their confrontation.

5. Alma begins to beat her fists up and down on the table, a frustrated, rhythmic beating. We watch her fists getting more and more frantic, desperate. She suddenly stops the beating and buries her face in her apron. Elizabeth watches with cold impassivity.

– The power Alma had, which she learnt from Elizabeth, was a power based on control. Here she loses control – she freely expresses her anger, her desperation and her pain. Loss of control means loss of power. She buries her face in her apron in shame. She is now once again in the light and open and vulnerable in the face of Elizabeth's impassivity. Will nothing move Elizabeth?

6. Alma slowly brings the apron down from covering her face.

ALMA
Say defend nothing.

– She now looks soft, gentle, open – aspects which have become revealed by her expression of her anger and her pain. Vulnerability can now be accepted. It is even desirable as her words suggest, for what does vulnerable mean if not 'defend nothing'?

7. Elizabeth turns away from Alma. We see her face in the foreground; there is a sudden and real fear in her eyes. Alma is behind her persisting:

181

ALMA

Cut a light. A sort of another. Not now, No! No! . . .
warning and without times . . . unexpected . . . when it
should happen it didn't as a failure.

Alma has moved closer to Elizabeth. We can see her presence
over Elizabeth's shoulder but her figure is in total darkness. In
contrast, the pain on Elizabeth's face, as Alma tries to get her to
speak, is acute. Elizabeth's lips are moving as if she is mouthing
the words.

– Alma has suddenly taken power again, but this time not by using
what she has learnt from Elizabeth, which merely made her equal,
this time she has got in touch with a more profound power; the
power that lies in accepting one's own vulnerability; the power
expressed by 'defend nothing'. This reaches Elizabeth. We see her
fear. And then we see Alma become a dark presence behind
Elizabeth's shoulder, like the devil tempting her (like the devil
tempted Christ in the wilderness). When Elizabeth begins to mouth
Alma's words as if they are her own, the effect is as if the words
really are Elizabeth's. Alma, in her vulnerability and through
her power of empathy, has become Elizabeth. She is giving us
Elizabeth's, incoherent, fear-filled words. That is why Elizabeth is
so frightened. She is becoming revealed through another.

8.

ALMA

Yourself, where you are . . . But I ought to.

Alma says these words so sharply, like an attack, that Elizabeth
turns, as if instructed to acknowledge her. Alma's face is now
fully lit enabling us to see her accusing eyes as they meet
Elizabeth's.

– Alma's power is in the ascendant again, but this time brought
into being by her vulnerability rather than her dark aspect, consequently her face is in the light.

9.

ALMA

Say collect advises others . . . desperate perhaps.

Alma's voice is getting more desperate, more insistent, more out of control. She puts her hands over her face thus breaking the spell she had briefly cast over Elizabeth. Elizabeth is calm again and smiling slightly, she looks away.

– Alma, once again having gained power, loses it by allowing herself to go out of control.

10. We cut to a close-up of Alma's profile, her face in her hands in the semi-darkness. She moves her hands slowly away from her eyes:

> ALMA
> Takes, oh yes, but where is nearest . . . it's called what . . . no, no . . . us . . . we, no . . . I . . .

– Her voice has become more desperate, sad, alone in the wilderness, searching for something in her mind with no hope of help from outside of herself. We seem here to have been given insight into Elizabeth's private pain via Alma, who has indeed taken on her identity.

> ALMA
> Many words and then nausea . . . the incredible pain . . . the throw!

She looks across the desk as if seeing Elizabeth afresh. Elizabeth looks back at her, smiling slightly, enigmatically.

– When Alma looks at Elizabeth she realizes that she has had more than an insight into Elizabeth's mind, she has been in there.

12. Elizabeth's lips tremble and she looks down at the desktop. We see that she is looking at Alma's arm outstretched across the table, her wrist arteries facing upwards, pumped large by her clenched fingers. Alma's other hand hovers over her arm with her fingers dangling, looking strangely like the legs of a spider. The music is predatory (the same chords as those which accompanied the spider and the slitting of the sheep's stomach in the opening montage). Our attention is

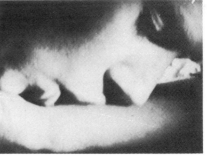

drawn to Alma's upturned wrist and then to Elizabeth's face
as she stares down at the wrist. She suddenly drops her face
down, sinks her teeth into Alma's wrist and sucks. Blood
seeps from between Elizabeth's lips onto Alma's skin.

– The image of the vampire comes to mind as soon as we connect
Elizabeth's stare with Alma's exposed wrist. The predatory sus-
pense music reminds us of the opening montage when we saw the
spider, followed by the sacrificial sheep and the crucified hand – the
latter two images bringing to mind Christian mythology and
themes of sacrifice and redemption. The visual sequence we have
now is also reminiscent of the opening montage; the fingers of the
hovering hand remind us of the spider, and the blood, seeping out
between Elizabeth's lips when pressed hard against Alma's wrist,
reminds us of the blood which seeped out around the base of the
nail when it was hammered so relentlessly into the hand.

In the previous scene we felt that Alma was somehow possessed
by Elizabeth; she was uttering Elizabeth's thoughts; now that
possession has gone a stage further; Elizabeth is sucking Alma's
blood – and not just her blood but her life blood – the arteries of the
wrist lead directly to the heart. Again something ugly, something
monstrous is taking place.

13. We cut to a shot from behind Elizabeth's head. Alma has
grasped hold of Elizabeth's head by her hair and is either
pushing Elizabeth down onto her wrist encouraging her to
suck or trying to pull Elizabeth off her.

– Alma seems to be at the same time complicit and resisting. This
suggests that she both wants Elizabeth to suck her blood, almost as
if it's a sexual act, and at the same time she cannot stand either what

184

Elizabeth is doing or the fact that she wants it. The co-existence of these incompatible opposites within her are causing a terrible build-up of tension. Something must break.

14. Suddenly Elizabeth lifts her head off Alma's wrist and Alma, in a wild frenzy, slaps her across the face over and over again. The music builds to a crescendo.

– Throughout this scene we watch Alma's face and the build-up of frenzy as she strikes Elizabeth. We never see Elizabeth being struck. This suggests that Bergman is not asking us to empathize with the pain of the receiver, in this case Elizabeth, but wanting us to look at and feel for the inflictor of pain and the pain of the inflictor. Alma's attempt to deal with the pain of her own rejection by Elizabeth has at first meant that she became like Elizabeth, in that she adopted Elizabeth's ways of wielding power in order to get her revenge; then it meant that she became one with Elizabeth, merging with her to the extent that she spoke words that came from Elizabeth's psyche, not her own; and finally, when confronted with the horror of her life blood being sucked, the contradiction of herself both wanting this at the same time as being revolted by it, has caused an eruption of uncontrollable violence.

15. The screen goes dark. In the darkness we can just make out an eye. The music has stopped.

– The silence of this moment and the stillness of the image, in contrast to the violence of the sound and images in the previous shot, serve to punctuate, to end the sequence, to give us breathing space, the space for relief and reflection. The eye we can just make out in the darkness though, suggests that the journey is not over, we still have further to go into these depths.

16. We pull back, bring up the light and reveal that the eye is Alma's. She appears to be listening outside the door of a room. She's again wearing her nurse's uniform, but this time her manner has all the calm concern we hope for from a nurse. She quietly opens the door.

– This image of Alma is so radically altered from her previous violence that we need this time to adjust to the change. The clinical white wall and door might suggest we are back in the hospital, but Bergman, given that he is not showing us an establishing shot of the place, doesn't seem too concerned with that level of realism. He is concerned that all our attention is on the deep subtext of what is going on between these two characters and to this end there is nothing, in either the image or on the soundtrack, that has not been considered for its contribution to our understanding of this subtext.

17. We cut to inside what looks like a hospital room. Elizabeth is lying in bed in her nightdress. Alma closes the door and crosses over to her bedside. We can just hear the sound of church bells tolling in the distance (again reminiscent of the opening montage). Alma gently takes Elizabeth's relaxed, sleeping body into her arms. Elizabeth's head rests on Alma's shoulder.

> ALMA
> Try to listen to me. Repeat after me.

We move into a big close-up of Elizabeth's face – gentle, relaxed, eyes closed.

ALMA
Nothing. Nothing. No nothing.
Elizabeth, as if just coming to consciousness, replies:
ELIZABETH
Nothing.
ALMA
That's it. That's right. That's the way it will be.
Elizabeth lies back down on the pillow to continue sleeping.

– This scene between the two women is in complete contrast to the one we have just seen. The strength of our experience of harmony in this scene is in direct relation to the strength of our experience of horror and discord when we witnessed the previous violence. Did they have to confront and go through that abyss to enable them to exorcise it and so find tenderness and peace on the other side?

The steps in the sequence of events in this climactic scene have, once again, a marked similarity with the opening montage. Just as earlier in this sequence we have been reminded of the violent images in the opening montage, so now the tolling bell on the soundtrack reminds us of the dead in the morgue and of the sleeping boy. In the opening montage our horror at violence was followed by the relief of escape and also by the realization that the images of a great calm that we were witnessing were images of death. The cycle has once again been acted out but this time it has significantly changed.

Alma and Elizabeth have led us to a new kind of harmony, not death. By plunging fully into the abyss they found a catharsis which, at least temporarily, has purged the elements and so enabled change.

Alma is like a mother to Elizabeth's child. Elizabeth is totally trusting of her as mother. Alma no longer confronts Elizabeth for refusing to communicate with her, she accepts Elizabeth totally for what she is. She still tries to get Elizabeth to speak but this time her attempt is not rooted in a power struggle between them; she asks Elizabeth to speak as if she is administering a healing lotion in the form of a mantra or sacred healing word. And Elizabeth, without struggle, accepts the mantra and speaks the word. Here Alma's love is unconditional and she is given to in return. Alma is no longer the innocent nurse we first met. Through the journey of the film she has learnt the wisdom of the ages.

Three

THE CREATIVE PROCESS *and* TELLING YOUR OWN STORIES

Introduction

In the film industry the writer is often treated as a technician or craftsperson, whose job it is to produce what the market wants. This attitude is positively damaging to new writers who need to develop their talent and gain a sense of meaning and personal fulfilment from the creative process itself. It's also the reason why many of the world's best writers choose to write novels or to work in the theatre, rather than film, because the worlds of literature and the theatre show a proper regard for the creative process and value writers accordingly.

The irony here is that many of our best film producers turn to adaptations from the novel or the theatre for their material, claiming that there aren't enough good screenwriters who can produce original material with depth and complexity. Sadly, they presume that the problem lies with the writers rather than recognizing that it is the film industry's insensitivity to the needs of writers that has either driven them out of the profession or turned them into industrial hacks. Few artists have ever functioned at their best when their primary motive has been to give the market what it wants.

There is an important distinction to be made here between giving the market what it wants and communicating with your audience. Most artists throughout history have desperately wanted to communicate with an audience, and preferably with as large an audience as possible. And communication is a two-way process; it means knowing enough about your audience to enable them to feel and understand what it is you are trying to communicate as well as becoming, through the creative process itself, fully aware of what it is you are trying to say. Of course the artist achieves great pleasure from the knowledge that he or she has reached an audience. But once he begins to think of the audience as the market, a new and cynical element enters into the process. The audience is now your buyer and your artefact is your product for sale. The emphasis shifts from genuine communication to the commercial viability of the product. This shift downgrades both the artist and the audience. The artist places what he thinks the audience wants and will buy on a higher level than communicating his own truth and the audience is downgraded to the level of consumers who can't tell the difference between pastiche and the real thing.

All the films I have written about in this book have, to a greater or lesser extent, peeled away the outer layers of life in order to reveal what lies buried beneath the surface. Even if the process of finding these truths has meant the writer digging through layers of suffering and difficulty, the journey is felt to be desirable and worthwhile because truth, in itself, provides a sense of meaning and consequently of value. In *The Uses of Enchantment* Bruno Bettelheim notes that 'our greatest need and our most difficult achievement is to find meaning in our lives'.* This is what artists do and this is what many audiences want to share.

All the film-makers I have mentioned in this book have an obsessive interest in discovering and exposing their own truth. They know what they want to say; they have strong individual voices (they are not making pastiches of other people's films); they have confronted their own material, which means they have grappled with their own images and stories with vitality and energy rather than accepting their material at face value, and they have valued their stories. They have loved and nurtured them into existence – which enables an audience to care about them too.

The enjoyment of play and discovery, the ability to confront whilst at the same time loving and nurturing your work, and the determination or will to follow the process through to completion, are the essential requirements for any creative endeavour. But many of us have not been taught to place a priority on self-discovery in our lives and our schooling was often dominated by rules, rote learning and rewards for conformity. As a result we have learnt to censor publicly, repress, or deny parts of ourselves which don't conform to the acceptable norm and often this public self-denial extends to include a private self-denial. We simply don't admit that there are whole areas of our experience and thought that are worthy of our attention and would also, if valued enough, be

*Bruno Bettelheim, *The Uses of Enchantment* (Thames & Hudson, 1976) p. 3

worthy of sharing with others. These aren't only areas of pain and difficulty, many of us have equally been taught to undervalue moments of real fun and joy. It's considered egotistic to express our feelings about the world we live in too emphatically and subjectively. It's more socially acceptable to be cool, sophisticated, objective, cynical, ironical; in other words to keep our true feelings to ourselves and to remain hidden. This doesn't only protect us from social disapproval, it also protects us from one of our greatest fears: rejection. But as a result, when it comes to artistic self-expression, many of us feel crippled by a sense of embarrassment, an acute lack of confidence and even shame about exposing feelings, ideas and images that have a special meaning for us.

In my profession I meet many aspiring writers, some of them have even got as far as buying a word processor to prove it. But something is stopping them. They have lots of ideas but haven't got the time to write. They are living in the wrong house or the wrong country. They can't write because of their job, their family commitments, their financial problems. They have an idea they began five years ago but haven't managed to complete it. They once wrote a script but became discouraged after the first rejection. They know they are really writers at heart but are still waiting for inspiration. When they've got the right idea they will take the world by storm. It's easy to think up numerous reasons to explain why you are not writing, as all professional writers know, but they also know that these rarely have anything to do with the truth of why you are not writing.

Becoming a writer is finally a decision you make about yourself and your attitude to life. You have to decide that you, as an individual, are prepared to be open, which means to be vulnerable, to take risks, to say what you have to say and to live with your fear of rejection and to trust your own instincts and intuitions. Making such a decision is the single most important factor in any creative person's life. Beyond that there is, of course, much you can learn to assist yourself on your journey. Developing your sensitivity to film and a thorough understanding of film language, structure and the craft skills involved is obviously a major part of this journey and what the first two sections of this book have been about.

But writing, whatever the medium you are writing for, is essentially a personal, not an academic, activity and the factor which hinders many new writers in their progress is, as I said earlier, their lack of awareness of methods and techniques which can assist in liberating their own imagination. After all, great films are not great because of the idea but because of the realization of the idea. When you attend to the process the product looks after itself.

You will probably have realized by now that the creative process involves two very different parts of yourself: the unconscious and the conscious. The unconscious is where your imagination and originality reside, and the conscious is the home of your intellect, your developing craft skills and your inner critic.

It will also have become clear to you by now that when developing yourself as a screenwriter it is of equal importance to train both of these aspects of yourself. The unconscious many produce wonderful, imaginative and original material, but without the process of sifting and crafting and shaping, the material will remain largely esoteric and unusable. Conversely, the conscious may have a through grasp of structure, complex intellectual ideas about the nature of film and know all the tricks of the trade, but unless your unconscious is feeding it original, imaginative material the conscious will produce work that is merely soulless imitations of what has gone before.

So the question facing us now is how you can fully train and utilize both your unconscious and your conscious selves, so they both become a natural and harmonious part of your working process rather than, as is so often the case, threatening each other's existence.

Process literally means a series of actions which produce growth, development and change. And attending to the process means accepting that the creative cycle, like any form of growth, has its own stages and rhythms. These stages involve periods of inactivity and gestation, as well as periods of activity and making things happen. It also means acknowledging the interconnected dual nature of process; on the one hand we have to attend to a sequence of activities with a natural order and on the other hand we ourselves are living organisms with our own rhythms and cycles which need attending to. In other words we are not just talking about getting to know the process as if it's a separate entity, like a plant that we are growing in our garden; we are at the same time getting to know ourselves and our individual relationship with the process.

In the following chapters we first look at the pre-conditions for creativity itself and the early stages of generating and gathering material. I also suggest some methods for working with both your unconscious and your conscious mind and ways of bringing into being ideas, images, characters and sequences. We then move on to the role story-telling plays in all our lives and to look at some methods for getting in touch with the stories you have to tell, including developing a writing discipline, writing the first draft screenplay, the question of evaluation and the giving and receiving of feedback. Finally, because the screenplay isn't an end in itself, like a novel or a poem, it's the first stage in the highly complex process of film-making we briefly consider the role of the screen-play in relation to the overall objective, the completed film.

1 The Eight Pre-conditions for Creativity

The first question we have to ask ourselves is whether we are in a creative state of being to start with. And if not what changes can we make practically, in our lives and our ways of thinking, to bring about a creative state of being? Silvano Arieti, in his book *Creativity: The Magic Synthesis,** suggests that there are eight key pre-conditions for creativity. Although his research relates to all forms of creativity in the arts and sciences, as a starting point for us I have decided to borrow his eight headings and consider what each of them means to the specifics of writing for film.

1. *Aloneness*

Although most creative people need intense and fertile periods of contact, it is equally important to enjoy being alone and have the space for contemplation and time with your own thoughts.

2. *Inactivity*

Time off for doing nothing except thinking and feeling about things. This isn't as easy as it sounds. We have been brought up to believe that if we are not involved in an obvious activity, whether it is one of the many mechanical tasks that fill our lives or actual productive work, we are being lazy, for which we feel guilty. Conversely there are times when it can be really beneficial to engage in seemingly mindless mechanical activity. These are times when you need to stop consciously thinking about things and allow the unconscious its period of gestation. It's often during these periods that answers to difficult problems rise to the surface.

---

*Silvano Arieti, *Creativity: The Magic Synthesis* (Basic Books, 1976) p. 373

3. Daydreaming

This is a kind of fantasy thinking that involves a fair degree of inwardness and introspection as well as immersing yourself in your imagination. It also relates directly to the roles that dream, memory, fantasy, metaphor and archetype have to play in film which we explored in Part One.

4. Free-thinking

This means allowing the mind to wander in any direction it chooses to go in with no constraints. It is not the same as free-association, which is a psychoanalytical process for generating material specifically about yourself. In free-thinking your thoughts may be wholly imaginative or intellectual, concerned with philosophical, political, or spiritual matters, or they may be about people you know, people in the news, overheard conversations etc.

5. Being in a State of Readiness for Recognizing Similarities

This is about making connections between apparently disparate and random thoughts. Arieti uses the examples of Kekule who 'identified himself in a dream as a snake swallowing its tail, and saw an analogy to the benzene molecule as a ring rather than a chain of carbon atoms', and of Bell 'who compared the human ear to a machine (which became the telephone)'.*

Similarity is, of course, the essence of metaphor, again an area we looked at in some depth in the first part of this book. 'Being in a state of readiness' seems to be the key here. It's a natural part of the process to consciously invent metaphors but we also need to be receptive to those which are already a part of our life, in our memory and our daily encounters. For screenwriters and film-makers this activity is a way of seeing and thinking about seeing.

6. Gullibility

Gullibility is usually assumed to be a weakness because it literally means to be easily taken in or tricked. Foolish people are gullible people. But if we look at it another way it also suggests an openness and innocence, a willingness to explore everything, to become attuned to what seems to you, in the moment, to be truths, and the ability to rule out the negative effect of untimely criticism and the suspension of untimely judgement. The important word here is

* Ibid. p. 376

untimely, there is, of course, a time for making discerning and critical judgements, but remember, we are talking about the pre-conditions for creativity here. If the judge in you is allowed too strong a hand too early in the process you will simply feel stifled and as a result become blocked.

7. The Remembrance and Inner Replaying of Past Traumatic Conflicts

This one is the most controversial of the eight pre-conditions because if we understand trauma in the Freudian sense, by assuming that it refers to a single incident, usually experienced in childhood, which is the root cause of subsequent neuroses, it would suggest that the 'replaying of past traumas' means that we should be recreating the incident in a literal, autobiographical form. This could be a positive hindrance, rather than assisting our creative process, so we need to think about its broader meanings.

We have already noted, in the section on dramatic structure, that conflict and the need for resolution are the central elements of dramatic energy; it is what motivates the protagonist and moves him or her forward. So it is not surprising that conflict, and the drive towards resolution, now also arises in relation to what is motivating our own creative energy and moving us forward. The importance of this concept is that it acknowledges that we all have, and will continue to have, key conflicts in our lives and that there is not only an intimate link between our motivation to create and these un-resolved conflicts, but they also draw us towards our particular creative explorations, or what stories it is important for us to tell. Numerous films, as far apart as Bergman's *Fanny and Alexander*, Terence Davis' *Distant Voices, Still Lives* and Sylvester Stallone's *Rocky* have been rooted in their author's personal history, as was *That'll be the Day*, written by Ray Connolly, one of David Puttnam's first productions, which remains amongst his best films. In Puttnam's biography *Fast Fade* we learn that the film, which is about a school dropout trying to make his way in the world, is a result of a remarkable writer/producer collaboration when 'both men shaped key characters from their own younger images and events in the story were largely autobiographical'.*

Indeed the telling of an autobiographical or semi-autobiographical story can have an important part to play in help-

---

* Andrew Yule, *Fast Fade* (Delacorte Press, 1989)

ing you find and liberate your creative voice and so enabling you to move on to new pastures at a later stage. If you feel this is the case it would be foolish to fight against it simply because of some puritan notion that personal conflicts should be hidden away like dirty linen. Many a good film would not have been made if this were true.

Even the 'new pastures' I referred to earlier are linked to our own conflicts. We may find ourselves wanting to tell the story of a character who lived in another period of history or in another country, but it is our understanding and awareness of our own conflicts which both draws us to the story and enables us to tell it with real empathy. Also, conflicts which are important to us, or what Arieti calls our 'psychological leitmotives', tend to recur during daydreaming and free-thinking, which means that if we learn to listen to our unconscious it naturally provides us with the source of our creative impetus.

8. Discipline, or The Will to Put what has been Discovered into Action

This is obviously essential. But for the writer, who for much of the time works alone, it's really a question of self-discipline as there is usually nobody to tell you to get on with it except yourself. And without the discipline to get down to the work at hand the other seven pre conditions become redundant. In some cases, because the fear of getting on with the work can be great, the self-discipline needs to be quite brutal. You can't stand shivering on the edge of the swimming pool forever, worrying about whether you've forgotten how to swim or not, there comes a time when you have to simply push yourself in. The first hours, days, or even weeks might be painful, but the flow of work will not come through thinking too much, it will only come through doing because getting what is inside of you outside, and on to paper, generates its own energy and momentum, and finally it's the activity itself which sustains you.

2 Generating and Gathering Material

If you were developing yourself as an athlete you wouldn't enter for a race straight away, you would first undergo a period of training involving routine, discipline and exercises. This is similar to the process of developing yourself as a writer; our equivalent to the race being the first draft screenplay. This early stage of the process makes all the difference when you are just beginning to get to know yourself as a writer, but many well-established, professional writers also see this as an important stage in the work-in-progress of each new project, especially in regard to generating and gathering fresh material. Only recently, a writer friend told me that he had just spent six months gathering his material and only expected to spend a few weeks actually writing the first draft, but he wasn't yet ready to begin because the shape of the whole still hadn't quite fallen into place and he hadn't yet 'found his metaphor'.

The following are some suggestions for ways of generating and gathering material. These are exercises that I have used both in developing myself as a writer and in the work I have done with my screenwriting students over the years. You may find that some of the methods are more suited to your particular temperament than others, but beware, we are full of prejudices about when and how we work best and sometimes these prejudices, if they remain unquestioned, can be real hindrances rather than the assets we've always assumed them to be.

First try letting go of all the assumptions you normally make about yourself and starting afresh. Tell yourself you know nothing about what working method is best for you; you don't know whether you like to begin work in long-hand or straight on to a typewriter or word-processor, you don't know whether you work best in the early morning or the middle of the night, you don't know whether your best quality is thinking in images but you can't write dialogue, or whether you're good at writing imagery and dialogue but as far as your intellect is concerned you need to read the entire contents of your local library before you are fit to put pen to paper. It's amazing how tenaciously people will cling on to these fixed notions about themselves, notions very often originating way back in their history in reaction to a few judgemental words from a thoughtless parent, teacher or professor.

Now think of yourself as a stranger you've just met. You are so intrigued with this person you want to know every aspect of them intimately. You want to know your deep inner life, your history and background, what makes you laugh, what makes you cry, your philosophy, your spiritual pursuits, the kind of other characters who populate both your inner and outer worlds, your ideas about the nature of life, your ideas about other people's ideas about life, what makes you angry, what excites you intellectually, what brings you to despair, what turns you on. This stranger is also something of an actor and a magician: he or she isn't restricted to telling you about the characters that populate your life and imagination, the stranger can speak like these characters, think like them, feel their feelings and know their aspirations, in short the stranger can perform the most extraordinary feats of metamorphosis if given half a chance.

These exercises are about giving yourself that chance by approaching yourself with an attitude of fresh discovery, finding out what you can and want to say and so getting to know the writer in you.

1. FREE-WRITING

This is a technique known to novelists as a way of getting in touch with their creative flow, but for some reason it's virtually unheard of in the screenwriting community. This is perhaps because novelists are aware of the important role their unconscious has to play in informing their writing, whereas many screenwriters tend to assume their work is more conscious and craft based, which is certainly true, but applies more to the later stages of the process.

Free-writing is essentially a method for discovering who the writer in you is and what the writer in you wants to say. You don't have to sit for hours torturing yourself by trying to force great ideas out of thin air. What you want to write about is already deep inside you. The question is how to get in touch with this material and how to get it on to paper.

The Free-writing Method

When you are asleep you give yourself over to your unconscious; you are literally in the dream-time. Very soon after you wake your conscious takes over and all your usual preoccupations and inhibitions come flooding in. So the first stage in the process is to get as close to your unconscious as possible and to find out what's going on in your imagination before your super-ego, or inner critic, has woken up and begun to take control.

Stage One, Early Morning Writing

1. Choose a specific day in the near future and make an appointment with yourself for what will be a sort of pre-breakfast meeting. Make this appointment for an hour before you normally wake up and set a time limit for the encounter of exactly one hour. Once you've decided on the date and the time of the appointment you must treat it as sacrosanct, nothing barring the most severe crisis will persuade you to break it.

2. When you go to bed the night before the appointment make yourself a thermos flask of tea or coffee (or whatever you normally drink first thing in the morning) and set the alarm for the appointed time.

3. When the alarm goes off force yourself into action immediately. Either go straight to your writing desk, or (if you sleep alone and find it works better for you) pick up the pen and paper you have ready by your bed, and start writing.

4. Begin writing straight away and don't stop. You may at first find yourself writing about how cross and tired you are because your sleep has been interrupted or you may have woken during a dream and find yourself writing down the dream. Never mind what it is, write it down, even if you feel that what you are writing is repetitive nonsense – what matters is that you are pushing that pen across the page and not sitting in blank inactivity. You will soon tire of writing nonsense and more specific thoughts will occur to you, a memory might suddenly appear, or a fragment of a story, or a place just asking to be described, and then maybe some characters who are acting out some kind of drama in that place. Whatever it is, whether it seems ordinary or quite fantastic, don't censor or criticize it,

simply explore it through writing, going wherever it wants to take you.

It doesn't matter if you find yourself writing in prose. During free-writing it can be unnecessarily restricting to attempt to stick strictly to screenplay form, but do remember that your ultimate goal is to be a screenwriter, not a novelist or short story writer, so encourage your mind to work as if you are describing a film you are watching in your imagination by noting down all the details, the images and sounds, observations about characters and actions, everything and anything that helps bring your writing to life on the page and that would also be manifest on film.

You may find that you spend most of the hour exploring one specific thing, or that you alight on two or three apparently unconnected fragments, or that your writing remains fairly abstract, wandering around an internal domain of feelings and present or past dilemmas. Don't worry, there is no single right or wrong way to do this exercise. And at this early stage be open to everything as you have no idea what will prove to be useful to you later.

5. When your hour is up *stop writing*. Head what you have done with the date, appointment time and the length of the session and put the work away in a folder. Then either go back to sleep for another hour or begin your day as you normally would.

6. *Don't* read through what you've written, however tempted you may be. Instead schedule in your diary three or four such appointments a week for the next two weeks.

Stage Two, Appointments with Yourself at Other Times

Once you have tried a few early morning writing sessions, begin to make appointments with yourself at different times of day or night: mid-morning, late afternoon, mid-evening, just before bed, etc. Once again make these appointments in advance, give the appointment a time limit, anything from half an hour to an hour (but not longer, you want to work at you optimum energy level, not drain yourself) and each time remember to treat the appointment as sacrosanct. And most important, when the appointment begins *write, and write anything that comes into your head*.

Although it is important to begin to associate your writing table as the place where your creative flow functions well, for some of these sessions you can also start to experiment with place: meet yourself on a park bench for half an hour, or in a café, or the reading room of a library. But wherever you are be sure to put all your energy into the encounter with yourself and write for the specified time, whatever comes into your head.

State Three, Your First Read Through and Process Sessions

I suggest you put aside a weekend for this task, two weeks after you first began the exercise, and schedule two sessions over the weekend.

Session One: Read Through

Read through all you've written (hopefully about ten or twelve sessions of writing). Remember, don't censor or criticize for writing style or content, that is not what this exercise is about. Your purpose is to discover what is going on deep inside your writer's mind, not to judge yourself. And this first read through can be an extraordinarily rewarding experience, partly because you have forgotten much of what you have written, especially the early morning writing which tends, like dreams, to slip back into the unconscious, but also because you will find there is a marked difference between the kind of work you are used to producing and the writing confronting you now. You might at first find this difference very strange and confusing and not be at all sure how to react to it. But remember to be open to it, enjoy it and value it for what it is.

Now read it all through again, but this time take a coloured pen and give the sections which seem to have a thematic unity a title or heading in large capital letters – this is so you can glance at the section from a distance of five or six feet and know what it's about, which will be important for your second session. Now put all the material away and forget about it until the next day.

Session Two: Process

Clear a large space on the floor of your workroom. Lay all the sections of writing out on the floor so you can see the headings clearly from a distance. (If a single writing session has broken down into a number of different headings simply take a pair of scissors and cut it up.) Your floor will now be covered with piles of paper. Find a place to sit where you can see all the headings and spend a while meditating on what you have in front of you.

You will soon begin to see that certain patterns and specific preoccupations are emerging and some 'umbrella headings' will suggest themselves as you begin to want to define the patterns and similarities. There will be some obvious headings like the disgruntled 'I don't know what I'm doing or why I want to writer', and 'dreams'. There will probably be a whole variety memories: 'childhood', 'adolescence', 'relationships', etc., and a whole variety of incidents, both memories and imaginary, which may be connected by theme or place. Whatever these new headings are, write them down on separate sheets of paper as they occur to you, lay them out on the floor and re-position the sections of writing under the new headings.

You will now find that you have a strange and endlessly moveable jigsaw in front of you. Some pieces of writing will want to be positioned under more than one heading. Some pieces will seem more important to you than others. Some headings will intrigue you more than others. You may want to position those which are most of interest nearest you and those of little or no interest on the periphery etc.

So simply play with the various permutations for a while. Then begin a period of selection. Put on one side the pieces that are of least interest to you, that you really wouldn't mind throwing away. Place by them the pieces that are of second least interest to you and so on until all you have remaining on the floor are those pieces, maybe four or five, which intrigue you most. You don't have to consciously know why they are apparently insisting, of their own accord, that they remain in the arena. All you need to know is that you still want them on the floor in the most important position. Sometimes you might discard something and then find that you feel unhappy without it, in which case bring it back, even if it doesn't fit under any of your existing headings, give it a heading of its own and place it on the floor in a position that feels right to you in relation to the other pieces which remain in the arena.

Finally, put the whole lot away in two separate folders, one for those of lesser interest, and the other for those of most interest to you. But don't throw anything away. You may find that a piece of writing you at first wanted to discard takes on a special importance later.

Stage Four: More Free-writing
Schedule another two weeks of writing appointments, both in the early morning and taking into account what proved to be the optimum times for you during the day or night. Approach these free-writing sessions in the same way as you approached the earlier sessions. You may feel that you want to focus on some of the

s or characters that have already begun to emerge,
nscious decide. If it wants to develop some of the
will, or it may want to bring some completely new
rena; if so it's important to be receptive to this.
t forcing your work or pushing it in a specific
n you will be in danger of losing some of the
spontaneity.

If you now find that you suddenly want to spend an hour writing that hasn't been scheduled, go with it. But apply the same discipline as the scheduled sessions, writing whatever comes into your head for a maximum session length of one hour. Your unconscious will by now be learning that it's being taken into account and you will find the flow of your work will be that much easier.

This period of free-writing and fortnightly read-throughs and selections may go on for four, six, eight, weeks depending on what you find emerging on your workroom floor. The material itself will eventually tell you when you are ready to develop it into a screen-play outline and move into the craft period of working. There will almost certainly be many possible stories in your folders, but one story will be rising to the surface as the story you want to explore now. (It may well be that you will return to some of the other material at a later stage.) You will recognize the moment of transition because the key elements of a story will finally be in your arena. You will be able to see the rough shape, know who the main characters are, and most important, the conflict will be clear. Until this moment arises you will want to return to the unconscious work, because something is still missing.

2. IMAGE GATHERING

'The primary factor in film is the image . . .' was the opening of the Bergman quote I used in my introduction to this book and much of Part One was devoted to an exploration of how image is fundamental to film language. The purpose of this exercise is to help raise your awareness of your personal relationship with images so that they become a natural part of your working process. It is similar to free-writing in that it is another way of getting in touch with your imagination and the stories you will find there.

The exercise is primarily for those of you who, because you've come from a literary or academic background, may feel insecure when it comes to working spontaneously with images. (Although, if you are from a visual or fine art background, you may find it a helpful way of overcoming any insecurity you may have about expressing yourself verbally by incorporating your love of images into the scripting process.)

The method is very simple. Your objective is to gather images to which you feel personally drawn, in order to write a short film script. Set aside a few hours a day for a week as the time when you gather images. Start by looking at images that you have already gathered – in that they are in your home; pictures, old photographs, mementos, newspaper cuttings, postcards, pictures in books – and select just six images. Remember that your only criterion for the selection is whether the image absorbs you in such a way that you want to gather it. Next go to a different place each day: specific places that have a personal meaning for you, places that intrigue you visually, places that make you want to watch what's going on, and places designed to stimulate visually like museums and art galleries. For these trips you may want to take a drawing pad or camera, but don't get sidetracked into trying to make perfect images, remember you are simply gathering records of the images for a larger purpose.

The stages in the process now become similar to those in the free-writing method. You begin by placing your images in a chaotic mass all over your floor. You then address each image by asking: 'How important is it to me?' and 'Why is it important to me?', (bearing in mind that you are thinking in terms of film and finding your own identity in relation to film). You then make your initial selections and groupings.

After a few weeks of gathering and processing material in this way you will find that your relationship with your chosen images will have developed considerably. In your imagination they will be suggesting ideas for characters, relationships between characters, metaphors, archetypes, locations, film moments, scenes and sequences. Some images may also be demanding to be in written form. Don't resist. Simply write the image or scene down and include it with the rest of your material. The final step is to arrange the material in what will be a moveable linear sequence. You can then work with the juxtaposition of images, the sequence order, decide whether you want to add or subtract images, and consider the whole in terms of beginning, middle and end. This is your basis for writing what will probably be a short film.

3. DEVELOPING A SENSE OF PLACE

In film, as the microcosm sequences we explored earlier show, place is not merely the location of the unfolding story, it is integral to the expression of ideas and emotions. This is what distinguishes film from theatre and most television and this is why it is especially important for screenwriters and film-makers to develop a sense of place.

Many film-makers form intense and passionate relationships with specific places. The Taviani brothers' love of the simple and often harsh rural landscapes in their native Italy has been fundamental to their development as film-makers. Leone was equally enamoured with the mythic elements of the frontier desert landscape, although this was a place which existed in his imagination and the world of stories rather than having had an actual part to play in his personal history. Wim Wenders, through exploring the landscapes of his own life and times in films like *Kings of the Road*, *Alice in the Cities and Wings of Desire*, has developed a now familiar iconography of the northern European and north American industrial and urban wastelands, expressing the sadness and alienation he feels about modern man. For each of these film-makers the story and the place are indivisible from each other.

The same is true for Wenders' contemporary Werner Herzog, only Herzog's quest for metaphor, through identification with a place, has led him far away from his European roots in search of places which express the conflicts and needs of the more primitive aspects of our psyche. Herzog's two South American films, *Aguirre, Wrath of God* and *Fitzcarraldo* are fine examples of this. The following extract from the screenplay of *Aguirre* (which is about a group of Conquistadores searching for El Dorado in the Amazon jungle) gives some insight into how Herzog's creativity was inspired and fuelled by his relationship with the place. It also shows how for him the script is far more than merely a blueprint or schematic plan. He needs to express himself emotionally and poetically in the script just as he does in the finished film.

> Slowly the canoe penetrates into the dusk of the jungle. The oars dip quietly, and the long slender canoe proceeds slowly among the huge tree trunks. Lianas are dangling down touching the boat. Far away a jaguar roars. Leaves the size of wagon wheels are floating on the water with turned up edges,

208

huge water lilies amongst them. Brooding dusk in the woodland. All around, the staring flowers, the ardor of orchids. The men in the canoe are very quiet. Monkeys begin to chatter above them, single leaves are fluttering down and start to float. The men are crouching in terror and only row lightly. The water stretches out through the jungle endlessly.*

But Herzog did not begin making films in exotic jungles, he began in his native Germany, although some of the places he shows in his German films, such as *The Enigma of Kaspar Hauser*, appear equally strange through Herzog's eyes.

The purpose of the following exercise is to help you develop an individual sense of place in such a way that, irrespective of whether you finally want to work from places you know or whether you prefer to invent places in your imagination, it will become a natural part of your use of film language and an intrinsic part of the stories you have to tell.

The Sense-of-Place Method

In the world of fine art there is a well-known story about how the Eskimos make sculpture. The story is basically this: the Eskimo takes a lump of stone, sits in front of it and waits. When asked what he is doing he replies that he is waiting for the stone to speak to him, to send him feelings, to tell him what it wants to become. A while later the Eskimo begins to make some marks on the stone. Then he waits again. And so on until finally the stone has been transformed into a work of art, a sculpture. This is the basis of the sense-of-place method, only your objective is to write a single film sequence, not make a piece of sculpture.

Stage One, Finding the Place

Your choice of place matters less than what happens to you in the place. This is because the stance you take in the place will be meditative, the principle being that any stone will speak to you if you are receptive enough.

I do, however, have a few guidelines for your choice. Try to find a place that is away from a populated area. You want to be alone there, not find yourself watching lots of people. And look for a place which has a distinctive landmark: a disused gravel pit, a derelict factory or mine, a railway tunnel or level crossing, deserted

Werner Herzog Screenplays (Tanam Press, 1980) p. 85

buildings, abandoned vehicles, a cave, a small wood, a pond or lake, a ruin. When you have found your place decide on the boundaries of the territory, say a hundred yards across.

Stage Two, Spending Time in the Place

Try to choose a time to do this exercise when you can go to the place for a few hours every day for a week.

Go there with no preconceptions, no ideas that you might want to work on. Instead *empty your mind*, move about the place slowly and quietly, look and listen and become a part of the place. Don't impose anything on the place, just allow it to speak to you. After a while you will probably find yourself drawn to specific spots in the location. You will find spots where you like to sit and specific images that you like to look at. You will begin to notice sounds. You will begin to make choices between the images and sounds that interest you and hold your attention and those that don't particularly affect you. You will begin to make connections between specific images and between images and sounds. The place, or aspects of the place, will begin to suggest a sense of meaning, mood, atmosphere, and maybe metaphor. Characters may begin to appear in your imagination and events that might have or could have taken place there that connect with the feelings you find growing inside you. In your imagination the place might become a part of another country or another time in history, past, or future (remember film is based on illusion: a small wood, a pond, a quarry or a sand-pit can give the illusion of being anywhere in the world at any time).

After spending a few hours in the place go home and spend a short time, maybe just half an hour, making notes about your experience. These notes will at first appear like chaotic or confused notations of images, feelings, incidents, possible relationships or encounters, or even sometimes appear as little drawings of images you've been looking at. But be careful not to force these notes to go beyond a simple record of what you actually experienced in the place itself. In other words don't start thinking up narratives to fit the place. Many of us, because of the speedy lives we live, have forgotten how to be open and receptive to a place. So it is important simply to record your experiences at this early stage in the process and not to anxiously force stories to come before they are ready.

Try to visit the place at different times, dawn, midday, evening, and if the weather varies a great deal so much the better. The experience you have there at dawn may well be quite different from how it affects you in the middle of the day or at dusk, and the grey, gloomy day or the rainstorm will almost certainly affect your imagination quite differently from a hot sunny day. And this is all a part of your exploration.

After four or five visits to the place you will probably find that your notes are naturally beginning to focus themselves. Specific images, thoughts and ideas will have begun to recur and may have already developed in some way or other. Some characters and a situation may have appeared in your imagination, or several different scenarios may be evolving. If you have more than one idea now is the time to choose just one to focus on. (Remember you are only focusing on an idea for a five to ten-minute sequence not an entire feature film.)

Stage Three, Preparing for the First Draft

This session should last for a few hours and take place in your writing room. Ask of the material you are focusing on who is or are the main characters and what is happening to them. Give them names and spend the time free-writing in prose about them. Where have they come from? Where are they going? What do they want? What's going on in them now? How do they feel in the place they are in? Write down anything that occurs to you that helps you get to know them better.

Stage Four, Writing the First Draft Film Sequence

Again this should be done in your writing room and take no more than a couple of hours. You have your idea, you know your characters, you know the location intimately, simply write the sequence paying special attention to how you are using film language to communicate what is happening.

Although the description of this exercise may sound a little mystical the basic idea is similar to the early morning free-writing. In the early morning exercise your unconscious flows to the surface because you are still close to the dream-time and your conscious censor and critic is warded off by the uninterrupted flow of your writing. Being in a place and 'listening to it' is another way of encouraging your unconscious to flow to the surface, but this time with the associative process being guided by the specific atmospheres, images and sounds you are encountering in 'your place'.

The Creative Process and Telling Your Own Stories

By asking you to empty your mind and to 'listen to' the place I am not suggesting that you have to negate who you are for the place to speak to you, but rather that *the place speaks to who you are*. When you are most receptive to the space around you, you will at the same time be most receptive to what is deepest within you. This is because, as we saw earlier, the unconscious prefers to manifest itself through stories, metaphors and archetypes than to speak directly to you. Also, paradoxically, the deeper you go into your unconscious, although you may feel as if you are getting closer to the specifics of who you are, you are also getting closer to the archetypes – which is very important if you want to touch that place in other people, your audience, which is universal.

4. RESEARCH

Your subject matter or source material does not always have to be inspired by images and incidents lying dormant in your own unconscious. Most writers, at some time in their lives, feel a positive need to get out of themselves and immerse themselves in characters and situations which at first they may know little about, whether these be characters from an historical incident or something read about in the newspapers.

But the maxim, *write what you care about and know about*, applies just as much if you are working from research as it does if you are writing about something rooted in your personal or community experience. After all, what is it that draws you to one historical character or incident rather than another, or causes one newspaper story to fascinate you more than all the others? It has to be a special sense of contact, which means there is something about the material which connects with your own experience, even if this connection at first seems oblique.

The prospect of going on a journey of discovery outwards is exciting. It gives the secret detective, explorer and archaeologist within us a chance to stretch their legs. It's fun burrowing around in libraries, newspaper archives, museums, making contact with strangers, visiting places that have played a special part in your subject's life, gathering together the pieces of the jigsaw, piecing together the clues as your story takes shape.

In a sense this process of gathering is not unlike the process of generating material in free-writing. It's just that you are collecting your images, scenes, important incidents, character portraits,

212

places, etc., from out and about in the world, rather than excavating them from your own unconscious. And there will come a time, just as with the free-writing process, when the floor of your writing room is covered with the material you have gathered and you will be shaping and ordering and making choices about what to include and what to leave out.

There are obviously a number of different approaches to research. Some writers prefer to know the rough shape of the story they want to tell before they begin, then they know precisely what they're looking for when they go on their gathering expeditions. Other writers prefer to begin with an image or incident (which is usually a metaphor), or the bare bones of the character who has inspired them, and find the shape of the story they want to tell only when it begins to emerge from the material gathered.

But every method has its dangers. The danger of the second method is that you can over-research, or simply get bogged down in so much material that you begin to feel overwhelmed by it. The danger of the first is the risk of going into a research period with a kind of tunnel-vision, looking only for facts which will fit your preconceived story-line – this leads to superficial films. The genuine quest after truth means a spirit of enquiry and to attempt to disprove hypotheses as well as to try out theories. The rewards of this method lie in the surprises as you discover and piece together the complex network of interconnected hidden ingredients which make up the story. Surprise and discovery are, of course, the two major elements which enrich the texture of all story-telling forms. Also you will find that material about the unique nature of characters is as important and revealing as the incidents which make up the plot-line and invaluable if you want your audience to become emotionally involved with your story.

Costa-Gavras's film *Missing* investigates the 'disappearance' of a young American when the junta seized power in Chile. *Missing* is a fine example of a true story that goes way beyond an accurate record of events to communicate what those events actually felt like for the characters who were caught up in them. The film does this though the remarkable characterization of its two protagonists, the father and wife of the young American. It's through their quest for the truth that we encounter the horror and carnage inflicted by the junta and the highly controversial political question of American complicity. But it's the complexity of their characterization, their relationship with each other and the way their shared experience changes them, that make the reality of the coup and the political issues, not merely available to us, but meaningful. The lesson here is that characters are not just cyphers to serve a story, they're there to live and it is through their living that the story lives.

So, although it may at first appear as if you are going on a journey outwards, if you are really to bring the story alive you have to take the material gathered inside of you, and then bring it out again with the same kind of insight you would bring to bear if you were writing from your personal experience. This is why your choice of source material is so important. It is not just a matter of choosing a character or incident that you think would make a good story that would sell, it's a matter of choosing a character or incident that intrigues you in such a way that you want and need to tell it. And your need to tell someone else's story is usually rooted in exactly the same place as your need to tell your own stories. That root is located in the heart of the conflict, which relates to our seventh pre-condition for creativity – the remembering and inner re-playing of past traumatic events. Even if the life and times of your chosen character seems a thousand miles away from your own, and their conflict is of such dramatic proportions that your own life experience seems insignificant in comparison, your identification and empathy with their conflict is, nevertheless, your way in and your motivation for telling. It is also the key to the shape and direction, not of their story (there's no such thing as an objective story), but of the story you have to tell about them.

3 Characterization and Dialogue

Characterization and story are interdependent. Characterization is all the information, both visual and verbal, which communicates to an audience the totality of who a character is and what he or she wants and needs and, especially in the case of the protagonist, it is these wants and needs which determine the backbone or structure of the story.

In films the most important visual information about characters tends to be communicated through their actions, what they do. All actions give us some insight into the nature of a character and who they are, whether these actions are highly dramatic, like placing a bomb in the boot of a car, or very minimal, like looking out of a window when someone is speaking to them. Characterization is also communicated through physical appearance, dress, gesture, and mannerisms, seeing a character from the point of view of another character, and most of all seeing the world through the character's eyes, experiencing their imagination and sometimes even sharing their fantasies, their memories and their dreams. It's this intimacy which enables us to identify with them. (Remember the beginning of *Midnight Cowboy*.)

We also learn about characterization through words, dialogue; the things the characters say and the things other characters say about them. Almost all major characters and many minor characters in films speak, unless they happen to be deaf and dumb in which case they would almost certainly find some equivalent of speaking to communicate their wants and needs. But dialogue writing is one of the great bugbears for many aspiring screenwriters. How often I have heard the refrain 'But I can't write dialogue', or 'I don't know how to write dialogue' or, 'Of course my dialogue isn't any good.' Why is this fear of writing dialogue so

215

common when we all use dialogue, we all talk to each other, in our daily lives?

I think there are two main reasons for this fear: the first reason isn't ostensibly to do with dialogue writing as such, it's more to do with the way we relate to the characters we create, and the second reason is to do with the craft of screenwriting and the lack of understanding many new writers have about the role the dialogue has to play in the overall scheme of things.

The Importance of Empathy

It's one thing to know a character from the outside, to know how they look, how they dress, how they move, what they do and the kind of things they say. But to create convincing characters, and to write convincing dialogue for your characters, you have to take a crucial step, and that step is from being outside of them, from seeing them in your imagination, to fully entering them, becoming them in your imagination.

Empathy literally means the power of understanding and imaginatively entering into another person's feelings. An empathic person is usually a caring person because they can imagine what it's like to be in another's shoes. And it's the same with your characters, it is only when you are inside of them, thinking their thoughts, feeling their feelings, experiencing the world through their eyes, that you really begin to understand who they are and know, not just the kind of things they would say, but what they do say and how and why they say it.

Inside every dramatist there is a secret actor trying to get out. When it comes to actually being an actor, on stage or in front of a camera, you might be the most appalling bag of nerves and entirely unconvincing. But when you are alone at your writing desk, inside your imagination, you come into your own, you become the most brilliant and versatile of actors, you have the ability to move in and out of all of your characters at will, you play all the parts, you become each of them and experience each of them from the other characters' point of view. You know what they are thinking, what they are feeling, what they want and what they don't want, what they do and what they would never do in a million years, and you know what they say, how and why they say it, what they wish they had said and what they regret having said.

This necessity to empathize with your characters applies equally to those who are bad or evil as well as to those who are good. And

216

the prospect will may well appal you. How can you possibly empathize with a torturer, a concentration camp commandant, a child molester, a psychopath. But empathize with them you must, because you will only be able to create a whole character for them, rather than a familiar stereotype, when you can see the world from their point of view, and not just know but feel their wants and needs. This is one of the most difficult tasks for any writer and could be what distinguishes the great writers from the good. Macbeth and Lady Macbeth are bad characters. The reason they have so fascinated mankind, and film-makers (Polanski and Kurosawa to name just two), since Shakespeare first created them is because, through Shakespeare's empathy with them, we not only understand their badness, we recognize in it ourselves. Empathy is the only route to insight, both for you and for your audience.

The question for us is how you can further train your ability to empathize so that creating characters and writing dialogue becomes a natural and organic part of your writing process.

Portraits

A good way to begin this exercise is to incorporate it into your free-writing programme. In other words to devote some of your hour-long writing sessions to focusing on specific character portraits.

Also, at first, it's best not to try and create fictional characters but to focus on portraits of people from your own past life. This is because people you have known have revealed themselves to you in special, unique and intimate ways through actions, words and gestures which are sometimes very direct and at other times full of complexity and contradictions. And it's these special characteristics, the small and intimate details of the ways characters manifest themselves, which bring them alive on the written page and on screen.

I suggest you begin writing about characters from your past, even though you may still know them in your present, because your memory will already have begun the process, first by deciding what to remember and what to forget, so the scenes that come into your mind are those that have some special meaning for you, and second by sifting out irrelevant details and retaining only those images, actions, feelings and words spoken which give special insight into the character in the scene or sequence remembered.

Another useful way of getting to know a character is to write a brief life history, writing down all you know about them in note form, where and when they were born, where they grew up, what their relationships with their parents and brothers and sisters were like, special friendships, important incidents that helped to form their personality, important adult relationships, important choices they made in their lives and why. Again begin with characters you know or have known well enough to piece together a network of connections which gives insight into who the character is.

Both these exercises will have a very important part to play when you begin to work with fictional characters, or even if you decide to research into an historical character. Through the little scenes and sequences you write, you will learn the kinds of particular details that illuminate character and event, as well as getting you used to focusing on the heart of the matter. And the brief life histories will tell you the kinds of things you need to know about a character's past in order for you to empathize fully with their present actions. It will also tell you if you are creating a fictional character who is acting or behaving in a totally implausible manner.

It is often the case that you, as the writer, know a great deal more about all of your characters, than ever appears in the text of your scripts. But this is no bad thing. In my experience many of the first conversations you will find yourself having with your director and the actors will be concerned with much of this background information because this is their way of getting into the script and so an important part of the beginning of their creative process.

When you are well used to empathizing with and writing about characters you know, their dialogue will begin to flow quite naturally because it is an intrinsic part of their self-expression. And a natural outcome of this approach is that you will find yourself writing, with the same degree of inner knowledge and complexity, about characters you have invented or researched, and their dialogue will also flow, as they express or pursue what they want or need, and cardboard characters and stereotypes will become a thing of your past.

The Craft of Writing Dialogue

Speech can tell you more about character than any other manifestation of personality. The way a person talks reflects their communality – their country, their region, their city (or even a specific district in a city, like the East End of London or the Bronx in New York), their education, their class. At the same time their speech is, like their fingerprints, unique. Their tone of voice, their speech rhythms and their use of language makes a person as easy to identify on the telephone as if we had met them in the street and tells us not only about the particular mood they happen to be in, but also about major aspects of their personality.

Apart from empathy, the single most important attribute for a writer is to be fascinated by the way people talk. Listening must be as important a part of your personal training programme as looking. And the best way to begin is to get into the habit of noting down what you hear, whether it's short snatches of dialogue overheard in the street, the philosophical or political debate you had over dinner last night, or the confused feelings your friend or lover confessed to you recently.

One of the first things you will notice, when you start recording dialogues in this way, is how difficult real communication is and how much of conversation is spent avoiding rather than striving for communication. Dialogue is all too frequently not so much listening and responding as watching eagerly for the next opportunity to grab a space in the conversation and continue with your own train of thought. This kind of conversation can best be described as interrupted monologues. You will also notice how rarely people talk directly about anything, instead their dialogue is full of sub-text, postponement of the question, avoidance of the question, manipulation, play, jokes, wit, sudden unexpected outbursts, contradictions, non-sequiturs.

One of the reasons for using memory when you do this 'listening exercise' is because your memory is a natural editor, it retains only those moments which have meaning for you and naturally provides you with an illusion, rather than an imitation, of real life. The same applies to most good film dialogue. If you compare a transcript of a taped conversation with a page of screenplay dialogue, even if the taped conversation is interesting, more often than not it will have a flat, rambling quality about it, whereas good screenplay dialogue will be performing so many different functions, in both the text and the subtext, that it apears more life-like than real life. This is because it is about life as it is subjectively experienced rather than objectively recorded. Even documentary film makers spend a great deal of time in the editing room cutting dialogue scenes in an attempt to communicate the essence of what was said, rather than what was actually said. But in fiction the dialogue is performing many more functions than just communicating the essence of what was said. The first of these functions lies in implying the psychological subtext.

Every screenwriter is also a psychologist, constantly questioning the complex inner workings of their characters' minds. To illustrate how this works we can take just one simple situation – a person wants somebody to do something for them – and consider just a few of the many possible permutations arising from the situation.

1. I want you to do something for me, so I ask you and you say yes.
2. I want you to do something for me but you might say no, so I remind you of something I did for you, so you will feel indebted to me.
3. I want you to do something for me but you might say no, so I try and persuade you with logic, reason, passionate argument, pleading for the cause, etc.
4. I want you to do something for me but you might say no, so I pull rank, reminding of you of my superior status, hinting that I can make your life difficult if you refuse.
5. I want you to do something for me so I threaten you physically.
6. I want you to do something for me but I'm so shy, or ashamed, that I can't find the courage to ask you.

Each of these propositions tells us, even in its abstract form, something about the character of the wanter, or the character of the recipient of the want, or both, and a little about the nature of their relationship. Each of them, that is, except for the first, 'I ask you for what I want and you say yes', which is also the least interesting because the transaction is perfectly straightforward, it contains no conflict. But characters in real life, and in films, are rarely that straightforward, unless what is wanted is relatively unimportant. If what is wanted really matters most of us are capable of behaving in the most extraordinary, contorted, creative, imaginative, misguided, funny, conniving, scheming, calculating, machiavellian, destructive or self-destructive ways to get it.

Just think of the implications of all this, and all the other possible life-situations and resulting permutations, on what we, and even more so, on what our characters say to each other.

Conveying the psychological subtext is just one of the many functions that fiction dialogue has to perform. Below I have listed some more functions and taken an extract from the original screenplay of *Midnight Cowboy* by Waldo Salt so that, by considering the effects of the text, you will be able to see how these functions actually manifest themselves.

Some More Functions of Dialogue

1. To reveal something about the character of the speaker.
2. To reveal something about the character of the recipient.
3. To reveal something about the nature of the relationship between the character and the recipient.
4. To give the audience information relevant to the developing story.
5. To connect with the previous scene and to set up the next scene.
6. To foreshadow what is to come, or to 'plant' some information which will have a part to play later in the story.
7. To carry exposition, or tell us something which has happened off-screen which we need to know to have insight into the developing story.
8. To make the scene believable or life-like.
9. To reflect the speaker's mood or emotional state.
10. To be economical, which means the dialogue is there for one of the above reasons and there's not too much of it.

Midnight Cowboy: Joe Buck's first meeting with Ratso

TEXT	EFFECT
INT. BAR. DAY	
JOE sits at the bar, staring morosely at his image in the mirror, oblivious to the assorted types hiding from daylight in the barn-like saloon, waiting for night to fall.	The set-up: Joe, upset after his first defeat, is vulnerable.

RATSO'S VOICE
  Excuse me, I'm just admiring
  that colossal shirt . . .
	Does Ratso really like Joe's shirt? Or is he after something?

RATSO studies Joe across the corner of the bar – a sickly, child-sized old man of 21 – hopefully nursing an empty beer glass, contemplating the money on the bar in front of JOE.	Sizing Joe up? An empty beer glass plus his interest in Joe's money on the bar – so he's after Joe's money

221

TEXT	*EFFECT*
RATSO That is one hell of a shirt. I bet you paid a pretty price for it. Am I right?	Beginning the con, flattery, trying to find out how wealthy Joe is.
JOE Oh, it ain't cheap. I mean, yeah, I'd say this was an all right shirt. Don't like to, uh, you know, have a lot of cheap stuff on my back.	Joe's falling for the bait! Ratso's touched his weak spot, his pride in his clothes. What's more, he's pretending to be wealthy!
RATSO spits as JACKIE leans on the bar next to Joe – a feminine young person, heavily made up, hair teased, wearing earrings and a lace-trimmed blouse over shocking pink levis.	So Ratso's not the only one who sees that Joe's easy bait.
JACKIE Got a cigarette, cowboy?	In this New York bar Joe's outfit stands out like a Christmas tree.
RATSO (*a stage whisper*) More goddam faggots in this town.	Fighting to get his pitch back.
Reaching for a cigarette, JOE glances at JACKIE, startled as JACKIE twitches his pink levis angrily and turns away.	Joe heeds Ratso's warning.
JOE Shee-it . . . (shakes his head) Kee-rist, you really know the ropes. Wish to hell I bumped into you before. I'm Joe Buck from Texas and I'm gonna buy you a drink, what do you say to that?	Further revealing his naivety and vulnerability. Realizing what he needs is to 'know the ropes'. What's more, he also needs a friend and thinks he's found one.

TEXT	EFFECT
RATSO Enrico Rizzo from the Bronx. Don't mind if I do.	Building up his own image to match Joe's.
JOE (*slaps the bar*) Same all around! For my friend, too!	Showing off, spending his meagre resources. We know he's in danger, but he's oblivious to it.
In a booth now. JOE is refilling RATSO's beer glass as he speaks.	Brief time-cut – their new position in the bar increases the intimacy.
JOE . . . you see what I'm getting at here? She got a penthouse up there with colour TV and more goddam diamonds than an archbishop and she bursts out bawling when I ask for money!	Joe's telling his new friend his problems – looking for advice. He certainly needs it but is Ratso the right man for the job?
RATSO For what?	
JOE For money.	Ratso plays innocent which heightens his villainy.
RATSO For money for what?	
JOE I'm a hustler, hell, didn't you know that?	Joe's aim confidently reasserted
RATSO How would I know? You gotta tell a person these things. (shakes his head) A hustler? Picking up trade on the street like that – baby, believe me – you need management.	A moment of hope, maybe the streetwise Ratso is not so bad, after all Joe does need help.

TEXT	EFFECT
JOE I think you just put your finger on it, I do.	Joe also sees the sense in what Ratso is telling him.
RATSO My friend O'Daniel. That's who you need. Operates the biggest stable in town. In the whole goddam metroplitan area. A stud like you – paying! – not that I blame you – a dame starts crying, I cut my heart out for her.	O'Daniel? a memorable name. Sounds very convincing although maybe a little over the top, is it real or part of the con?
JACKIE I'd call that a very minor operation . . .	Jackie gives us the answer.
RATSO grabs the neck of a bottle, sliding back in the booth. JOE scowls as JACKIE appears with the tall farm boy.	Ratso's vulnerable now.
JACKIE . . . in fact, you just sit comfy and I'll cut it out with my fingernail file, Ratso.	Increasing our awareness of Ratso's physical vulnerability.
RATSO The name is Rizzo.	So he's sensitive about his name.
JACKIE That's what I said, Ratso.	Now we see Ratso's vulnerabilities we begin to care about him.
JOE (*suddenly*) Hey now, you heard him.	So does Joe, he leaps to his defence.
RATSO That's okay, Joe. I'm used to these types that like to pick on cripples. Sewers're full of 'em.	Ratso is strengthened by Joe's trust and brawn. Also tells us his predicament – a cripple trying to survive in New York's 'sewers'.

TEXT	EFFECT
JACKIE May I ask one thing, cowboy? If you sit over there and he sits way over there, how's he gonna get his hand in your pocket? But I'm sure he has that all figured out . . . (to Ratso) Good night, sweets.	'Cowboy' – reminds us of Joe's predicament. Jackie shops Ratso in revenge for when Ratso shopped him earlier and we learn that Ratso's a pickpocket.
JACKIE swings his handbag over their heads and walks away.	Jackie's convinced his warning will pay off, but are we?
RATSO *(calls after him)* Faggot.	Ratso's trying to win Joe's confidence back by slurring Jackie.

Although all the functions I mentioned earlier are at work in this scene they don't, of course, all have to be operating in every scene. But it is a rule of thumb that if you come across a section of dialogue and you can't think of single good reason for it being there, although it might, in itself, be wonderful, the script will usually benefit from cutting it out. Another thing you have to take into account is the overall rhythm of the screenplay. A dialogue scene may be beautifully written, you feel proud of it and it performs all of the above functions as well, but at the same time the scene may be so long that it breaks the rhythm of the developing film. It is as if you have slipped into a theatre play by mistake. This is also a good, although sometimes painful, reason for cutting it, or failing that, for moving some of the important dialogue to another scene.

Another rule of thumb is to ask yourself if what is being said in the dialogue could possibly be communicated in a more filmic way through image or action. Your medium is, after all, film, not theatre, and what a character does often tells us more about them than what they say.

It's also worth remembering that silence, in films, can be as powerful, if not more powerful, than long speeches or explanations. Characters, like people in real life, are not only interesting because of what they reveal; their mystery, or what they choose to keep hidden, can be even more tantalizing. In real life, if someone tells us too much about themselves too early in a relationship they can rapidly become as boring as someone who refuses to open up at all, so we begin to wonder if there's really anybody in there worth knowing. The presence of an actor or actress can contribute enormously to this mystery. And in film the huge size of the cinema screen and the potential of the close-up means that a single look or gesture, or in Robert Mitchum's case a slight twitch of his eyebrow, can tell us as much as a speech, and in a far more captivating way.

The text-effect method I used for the *Midnight Cowboy* scene is a very good way of finding out about the craft of dialogue writing as a part of your personal training programme. If you apply the method to a variety of different screenplays (which are increasingly appearing in published form) you will soon learn, not only a variety of craft skills which will help your own work, but also how many widely differing approaches there are to writing dialogue, according to who the writer is and what the writer is trying to say.

If, for instance, you look at Harold Pinter's dialogue in *The Servant* you will see how his primary concern is to explore the complexity of his character's manipulative power struggles, whereas Marguerite Duras' dialogue in *Hiroshima Mon Amour* has a different mood, rhythm and emphasis altogether, as her two protagonists, motivated by their new-found love for each other and their need to exorcise past traumas (his in Hiroshima, hers in war-torn France), struggle to reach each other fully. For Duras there is conflict enough to be overcome in the mere fact of her characters' separateness.

I think this difference demonstrates how the most important function of dialogue is that it serves your characters and what you, as a new and highly individual writer, are trying to say through your characters. Which takes us back to the two aspects of your self-training as a writer, the conscious and the unconscious, and another warning: try not to get the two aspects of your training mixed up. When you are working on the first drafts of your 'portraits' or free-writing *don't* analyse the dialogue or test it for text-effect, or consciously apply structural principles to what you are writing, or you will inhibit your flow and never find your own voice as a writer.

The conscious analytical judge or critic in you should always be restrained until the time is right, which is when you decide you are ready to move from the unconscious free-flowing stage to the conscious crafting stage. It's always better to have a scene that is pages too long, but truly original and expressive, to mould and craft and make economical at a later stage, than to have a technically competent scene that fulfils all the functions of dialogue but is somehow dead on the page. In other words trust the process and what you are learning from the craft side of your training will automatically feed into your unconscious.

4 The First Draft and After

There is no 'right' way of writing a first draft. Some writers like an office hours routine, writing from nine to five with strict lunch and tea breaks; others will write an entire first draft in frenzied sittings, working day and night, with the minimum of breaks for food and sleep until the draft is finished; but most writers find a routine that best suits them somewhere between the two. The same variation of approaches can be found when it comes to writing methods. The two main approaches can be described as 'holistic', working over the whole story in outline form before beginning the first draft, and 'linear', after an intense period of gestation or research plunging in on page one and discovering where the story takes you. Again most writers find that the way that suits them best is somewhere between the two.

An outline is a precis of the entire story of the film. (My story breakdowns of *Midnight Cowboy* and *Viridiana* in Part Two will give you some idea of what an outline looks like, but these were, of course, based on finished stories rather than being a part of the process of bringing a story into being.) You are ready to write your story-outline when you have generated or researched your subject and the story is beginning to take shape in your mind. Take about ten pages of paper – each page to represent the major segments of your film; the beginning, the six or eight development sequences, and the ending – and write in precis form the location and contents of the major scenes and sequences that make up each film segment. Then stick the eight or ten pages up on the wall so you can see the protagonist's entire journey, the structural patterns and unity of the whole film in front of you.

The purpose of the story outline is to help you work out what your story is and to enable you to find and remedy any structural flaws before you begin writing the first draft. The outline should therefore be a malleable thing so that you can easily change the order of scenes and sequences, insert new ones, delete old ones, try out new beginnings or endings, thread in new characters or new story-lines and take out old ones. You may find that you are continually having to return to the drawing board because you can see that the story you had in mind is not yet pulling together as a whole. And the drafting and redrafting may take some time, but in the long run it will save you the time and unnecessary heartache of writing scenes and sequences which eventually have to be cut because they don't fit into the unity of the whole.

Some writers prefer to write their scene descriptions on index cards because of this need for plasticity. They can then pin the index cards to the wall to see the shape of the entire film and alter the order, insert or remove cards with ease. Other writers feel that the neat, orderly nature of index cards blocks their imagination and prefer to use the traditional cut and paste method. Other writers choose to write their story-outline in prose form, like a short story. And others prefer not to work from a story-outline at all. They feel that the energy and originality in their writing comes through the 'linear' method.

The 'linear' method is really free-writing in first draft form. The danger is that, as in life, if you don't know where you're going or why, you will probably get hopelessly lost. On the other hand, if you come to writing the first draft after a fruitful period of gestation, when you've got to know your story well in your imagination, you've got a clear idea of the conflict facing your protagonist – you know his or her aim, or where he or she is trying to get to, and why – and your creativity is stimulated by the challenge and the risk of plunging straight into the first draft to see whether you sink or swim, then this is clearly a way forward for you. An advantage of this method is that you may stumble on an extraordinary place which, because you never knew it existed, you would not have thought to include in your story-outline. This underlines the danger of attempting to use either method without incorporating free-writing (allowing your imagination to flow without constraint) into the process. If you go straight into making a story-outline with index cards without having had a period of free-writing beforehand the work will soon begin to feel calculated and formularized and lack that sparkle of surprise and spontaneity that characterizes good, original work. And if you attempt to go straight into a first draft without the energy generated by the imaginative flow of free-writing you will find your story soon dries up. But, as I said earlier, most writers use a mixture of both methods; if you get lost in a first draft you can always use the story-outline to help find your direction again and if you find that the story-outline is making your work too calculated you can revive your spontaneity by free-writing the draft.

One of the reasons some writers feel an ambivalence about the story-outline is that it has a dual purpose; as well as being an important stage in the creative process it is also a sales document – film producers decide whether or not to commission writers on the basis of these few pages. For this reason it is essential for professional writers to be able to write effective outlines. But, having a document that is a part of the early stages of a creative process, and as such being constantly revised according to the discoveries made as the work progresses, also being used as a sales pitch, can be dangerous, because of the tendency to assume that a story which has been sold, even if only in outline form, is somehow carved in stone.

It is this that has led to the fear many writers have that once sold the story-outline might 'die' on them. Once an idea becomes carved in stone creative energy can die: the story is no longer a question, instead it has become an answer, it has lost its mystery and so its hold over its creator. To avoid this happening it is important that both the writer and the producer treat the outline as work-in-progress and as such a malleable document which will continue to grow and may undergo quite radical change during the realization of the project.

Whether you've plunged straight in or you're working from a story-outline, once you've begun your first draft what matters most is that you keep your concentration, rhythm and flow of writing going until you've completed the screenplay. A routine and writing discipline are enormously helpful at this stage. It doesn't matter so much what your hours are, but that you have regular hours that you associate with writing the draft, and you treat that time as sacrosanct. Again this is a way of letting your unconscious know that you are working so it will contribute to the process, because the most important thing at this stage is that your concentration is focused in such a way that you are expressing fully your feelings, thoughts and ideas. The critical judge in you must still be kept at bay, or your writing flow may become blocked. At this stage it really doesn't matter if each individual scene is not perfectly crafted, if the dialogue scenes are too long or too short, or if some of your scenes seem to have gone 'over the top' in order to express your point. All these problems can easily be rectified when you come to write the second draft.

The first read through is an important event. This is the first time you will be able to get a real sense of how your story is working as a film. So you must beware of reading it too soon after finishing the draft. You may feel so euphoric – you've finally got the script down on paper – that you've no real sense of how it will affect an audience. Or conversely, you may find that you are in the grips of a kind of post-natal depression and, oblivious to what is working well, you are able only to focus on the problems or failings. This inability to be able to value or love your own work can be as damaging as over-estimating it. So make sure you read your work only when you feel distanced enough to be both appreciative and critical. Now is also the time to give the script to a few carefully chosen people for feedback.

The ability to give feedback is a highly developed skill in its own right and developing skills takes time and practice. Many people mistakenly think that feedback means either generalized praise of the 'I really loved it' variety, or negative criticism of the 'I didn't like it at all' kind, without being specific about what was or wasn't liked. The objective of feedback is for the writer to experience how what they have written affects an audience: what it is that holds your audience's attention, what moves them, what makes them laugh, what makes them sit up and take note, what confuses them, what bores them, what makes them lose their belief and interest in the story – in short what each scene and sequence makes them feel and think.

Only in the light of the answers to the above questions will writers be able to judge whether they are succeeding in communicating what they intended. Also, if the person giving the feedback 'didn't like the script at all' the writer will be able to make the very important distinction between whether the reader's dislike is based on a misunderstanding due to some confusion in the text, which can be rectified, or is an actual rejection of what the script is about at either a political, philosophical or emotional level. If this is the case you probably need to find a reader who shares your beliefs and values before you can evaluate the script.

To give the kind of detailed feedback that I have described above, for an entire screenplay, is obviously a big job and of the kind that only an experienced writer, script editor or writing teacher will be able to perform easily. You may not know such a person who is willing to spare you the time. If this is the case try finding a writing partner or forming a writing group. This will enable you to swap your work and to take turns giving and receiving feedback with people who have an interest and investment in doing so. This will also give you a chance to develop your critical skills in relation to your own work as well as that of your colleagues. You will find that it can take half an hour to read through and carefully analyse a single five or six-page sequence so I suggest that, in your first few sessions together, you swap single sequences, not entire screenplays. You will find that the learning gained from the in-depth feedback of a single sequence will quickly inform the rest of your writing. And when the time comes to swap your whole screenplays you can then focus mainly on questions of structure, character development and theme.

For all writers (new or old), receiving feedback on a new work is a complex experience. You are emotionally raw, this is the first time your work has been read and you desperately want it to be felt and understood. You feel naked, stripped of all your defences and so wholly identified with your script that each word of criticism can be felt as a personal attack. Yet you have to fight against these feelings and remain open to criticism if you are to develop as a writer, because feedback sessions can be as beneficial to your creative process as all the stages of learning you have been through so far. When the feedback process is working well it can generate highly stimulating and creative discussions about your script. A fresh mind on your work can help you probe more deeply into your subject and give you insights that might not have occurred to you while you were working alone. Also, as in any good therapy session, an apparently irresolvable problem, once shared, can throw up some possible solutions and give you the renewed energy you need for writing the next draft.

In the theatre, particularly in England and America, it's normal for the theatre writer to initiate and develop the play, working largely alone until, satisfied that the play is finished, he or she finds a director for the project. The theatre director's job is then quite clear; his task is to realize the writer's play. The writer is traditionally present at the first read through and main rehearsals of the first production of a new play and the final refinements to the text are made as a result of seeing how the play is working in performance – but each re-write can only be made at either the initiative of the writer or with the writer's permission. It is also usually clear to a theatre audience what should be credited to the writer, and what is to the director's credit.

Such clearly defined norms for the roles of writer and director don't exist in the film industry, which tends to give the director the major credit for the film, irrespective of whether or not he wrote the script. This is mainly due to the hybrid nature of the film medium. It is the director who draws together all the different artistic contributions: writing, directing, acting, art-direction, camera, sound, editing and music, which in combination, as we discovered in part one of this book, go to making up film language. So the final level of authorship clearly lies with the director.

But how much credit this final level of authorship should be given, to the exclusion of the earlier levels in the script development, is an ongoing debate in film history. The argument for writer's authorship says that the screenplay can exist without the film, but few films exist without the screenplay (although certain experimental directors choose to work without a script). The argument for director's authorship, or 'the auteur theory', says that the same screenplay if made by two directors would result in two quite different films because the meanings and the themes communicated through the film language would take predominance over those communicated through the script. Personally I'm not convinced by either argument. Making a film is always a team activity and so true credit for authorship will vary from project to project just as the roles of the writer and director, and their relationships with each other and the team, will also vary from project to project.

It is not difficult to see why the writer going on to direct his or her own screenplay is the ideal model – the self-expression that has gone into making the screenplay can be realized in film language without the discontinuity of handing the script over to another individual for interpretation. Ingmar Bergman, who began his career in films as a screenwriter, is one of the world's greatest writer-directors. And his published screenplays are far from merely being blueprints for his films, especially *Wild Strawberries* and *Fanny and Alexander*, which are both as complex and absorbing to read as any good novel. Indeed, if you read *Wild Strawberries* carefully you will find that the text indicates a greater complexity than Bergman was able to realize in the finished film, because film requires a certain simplicity so that it can put its point across without losing the audience. Pasolini was another great writer-director and was already an established novelist before he entered films as a screen-writer and later began to direct his own work. And Bertolucci, who believes that 'cinema is the true poetic language' began his artistic career as a poet.*

But being a writer-director is not necessarily the best solution. Anyone who has either written a screenplay or directed a film will know what a gruelling prospect combining both tasks can be. The writer-director must have an enormous amount of creative energy to sustain a project from the birth of the idea through both the writing and the directing processes. Also, having talent and skills in both writing and directing remains a relatively rare combination.

This is why some directors choose collaboration, which they also find more creatively stimulating than working alone. It enables them to be fully integrated into the writing process, so that they can realize their own vision, whilst benefiting from the talent and craft skills of their writer collaborator. Buñuel chose to work in this way. His films, whilst being inimitably his, also show the distinctly different inputs of his three major writing collaborators, as demon-strated by the difference and similarity in both style and theme in *The Exterminating Angel*, which he scripted with Luis Alcoriza, *Viridiana*, which he scripted with Julio Alejandro, and his later works – *Belle de Jour* and *The Discreet Charm of the Bourgeoisie* – which he scripted with Jean-Claude Carrière. We can see the same kind of change in Billy Wilder's films. His first major collaborator was Charles Brackett, with whom he wrote most of his early work including *Sunset Boulevard* and *Double Indemnity*, and his later work, which included *The Apartment* and *Some Like it Hot*, was written with I. A. L. Diamond.

Forming such collaborations, so that both parties can maximize their creative potential, demands a remarkable compatibility. If this is achieved, as in Buñuel's and Wilder's case, it can give stunning results. But such compatibility is not easy to achieve because many writers simply cannot work in this way. Their creativity is a more personal affair and, as we have seen, in the early stages demands a degree of isolation, quiet reflection and introspection to encourage the imagination to flow. Also such collaborations demand a degree of ego-sacrifice on the part of the writers. After all, who, outside of

*Ephraim Katz, *The International Film Encyclopedia* (Macmillan, 1980) p. 116

the film industry, has heard of the writing collaborators of Buñuel or Wilder or, for that matter, of the collaborators of numerous other of the world's foremost film directors? As a consequence those writers who want to make a name for themselves must choose to either direct their own work or to move to another medium like the theatre, literature or television, rather than be thought of as an adjunct to the director's writing arm.

So for many writers a better model is for them to write the screenplay in close consultation with the director, but for the boundaries between their two roles to remain clearly defined. In this model the initial idea may be the writer's or the director's, and there will be regular meetings between the two throughout the scripting process. (Sometimes the producer is included in this process.)

One director who has been successful using this model is Alain Resnais. His highly personal style is apparent in all of his films. This may be because many of the writers he has worked with (such as Robbe-Grillet on *Last Year at Marienbad* and Marguerite Duras on *Hiroshima Mon Amour*, both top French novelists, and David Mercer on *Providence*, a leading British television writer), have shared his preoccupation with the somewhat blurred boundaries between our experience of the present, the past and memory. Resnais minimizes the discontinuity between writer and director by realizing their work in true theatrical tradition, but with the additional benefit of having been a party to their creative process. On the writing of *Hiroshima Mon Amour* Duras writes: 'Their (Resnais and Jarlot's) advice was always precious, and I was never able to begin work on any episode without submitting the preceding one to them and listening to their comments, which were always lucid, demanding, and productive.'*

Finally, the most common model in the commercial sector of the film industry is for the writer to sell a story-outline and then to develop the screenplay in consultation with the producer. Or sometimes the producer will approach the writer with an idea of his or her own for development in close consultation with the producer. (As we have already seen, David Puttnam likes to work in this way.) The director is then found when the screenplay is ready to go into production and the final rewrites will be done in consultation with

---

* Marguerite Duras, *Hiroshima Mon Amour and Une Aussi Longue Absence* (Calder and Boyars Ltd, 1966) p. 7

the director. The system is then more similar to the theatre model, in the sense that the director works on the final rewrites of a screenplay rather than being a party to its conception and development, and his or her task is to interpret the text and translate it into film – although writers, unless they already happen to be well-known in another discipline, like Harold Pinter, are rarely given the status during the production process or get anything like the credit they would get in the theatre for their work.

There are obvious financial reasons for this approach. The producer, with the backing of a production company, can afford to pay the writer and, although it may make artistic sense, it is not often considered economically sensible to bring the director into the picture until the production company has finally decided to make the film. And most production companies commission a great many more projects than they actually make, on the basis that it is only when they have the finished screenplay that they can really judge whether it's worth making into a film. Although there are some producers who prefer to back the director's choice of project and who see the artistic responsibility for the script development as an intrinsic part of the director's role. This approach applies especially to those producers who adhere to the auteur theory. French producer Anatol Dauman is just such a producer. He has played an important part in enabling many of the world's top directors, such as Alain Resnais, Jean-Luc Godard, Robert Bresson, Walerian Borowczyk, Wim Wenders, Volker Schlöndorff, Andrei Tarkovsky and many more, to make the films of their choice according to their own artistic judgement.

If your screenplay survives the course and finally goes into production, the excitement of being a part of a team putting on a show for an audience is one of the reasons some writers choose the screenwriting profession. The process of making the film, like that of putting on a play, can give you the opportunity to get away from the isolation of being alone in a room day after day, creating an imaginary world which is entirely subject to your control but with only your imaginary characters for company. Whereas engaging with the film-making team, at first the producer and director and later the actors and crew, can, despite the power struggles and manipulation games, be great fun and can also bring fresh stimulation, new energy and new ideas to your development as a writer. Discussing your characters with the actors, and hearing your dialogue spoken aloud for the first time, is an invaluable learning experience and, for a writer, there is nothing more rewarding then seeing your work on screen, in front of an audience, for the first time.

The above, like much of what I have written in this book, is an ideal and somewhat rare scenario; an example of the best to be aspired to rather than the usual screenwriter's experience. But it would take whole book to do justice to the question of how best to maximize the creative potential in the relationships between the writer, director, producer and the film-making team – and at the same time to explore properly present industrial practice and the conflicts between cultural and commercial values.

5 'And they all lived . . .'

Since men first developed the power of speech, and spent long dark evenings huddled together around an open fire, stories have had a central part to play in the life of every individual and indeed, in the life of humanity itself. Story-telling connects us to our roots, our ancestors, the world around us and our destiny. And the best stories cause us to feel the awe of such connection.

Home, or the place where we sit round the fire and tell stories, is also the place where, as John Berger put it, 'the vertical line crossed with a horizontal one. The vertical line was a path leading upwards to the sky and downwards to the underworld. The horizontal line represented the traffic of the world, all the possible roads leading across the earth to other places.'* So home, the place where we tell stories, is not only the place of our connection with the archetypes, the Gods in the sky above and the ancestors in the ground below, it is the heart of the family romances where we act out the intimate dramas of our daily lives, and it is the place of intersection, where we reflect on what we discover about the world through travellers' tales told by returning voyagers.

If we hear the words 'Once upon a time', or 'Once in an old castle in the midst of a large and dense forest . . .' many of us still feel a familiar tingling of excitement – we are about to be transported into the strange and magical world of the fairy story. These stories, which have been handed down from generation to generation, first by word of mouth, then written down, and most recently through film and television, are instantly recognizable and at the same time most extraordinary: a wicked queen transforms herself into a witch in order to give her daughter a poisoned apple; a beautiful princess is imprisoned by her jealous father in a tiny room at the top of a tall

*John Berger, *And our faces, my heart, brief as photos* (Writers and Readers, 1984) p. 56

238

tower; a boy climbs to the top of the huge beanstalk, which he discovers growing outside his bedroom window, and finds himself in a strange and dangerous new world; in punishment for a sin a handsome prince is condemned to inhabit a beast's body – only the kiss of unconditional love can free him from the spell.

Fairy stories are always optimistic. Although lasting happiness is never gained without a long and difficult journey and many challenging incidents, the characters the child identifies with always live '. . . happily ever after' because they have learnt from the many moral dilemmas and tests of character they have encountered along the way. These are the rites of passage which assist children in those most difficult questions of childhood, which Bruno Bettelheim in *The Uses of Enchantment* defines as: 'Who am I? How ought I deal with life's problems? And what might I become?'* These are all questions which many of us remain bound up with for much of our adult lives, which is one of the reasons why fairy stories continue to be so compelling; not just because they are exciting and magical and remind us of our childhood but because they deal with the ageless and timeless archetypal conflicts at the root of all our hopes and fears and they tell us that as long as we are good people and act wisely all will be well in the end.

But optimism is not a characteristic of the grown-up's fairy story, the myth, which is more usually tragic. Myths are also archetypal stories and in their traditional form they also tell of fantastic events taking place in fantastic worlds. But, unlike fairy stories, the characters in myths are always larger than life, superhuman, and their conflicts, which represent the full range of human conflicts caused by the aspirations and frailties deep within our individual and collective psyche, also have a larger than life, timeless quality. This is why, for instance, the plights of Oedipus, or Orpheus and Eurydice, or Penelope are as relevant to us now as they were to the ancient Greeks and which is why we need to see the essence of the stories acted out, over and over again, in the guise of new characters and new periods in history.

Aristotle said that 'the friend of wisdom is the friend of myth'.† A mythic story is a story that has its roots in the universal experience, which is why all great stories are, almost by definition, mythic stories. But it is no good for a writer to set out with the primary

---

*Bruno Bettelheim, *The Uses of Enchantment* (Thames & Hudson, 1976) p. 47
†Quoted by Bruno Bettelheim, *The Uses of Enchantment* (Thames & Hudson, 1976) p. 35

intention of writing a mythic story. The writer's job is to delve into the truth, which, as we have seen, can only be found in the particular and, if Apollo looks kindly on you, the truth that you find might turn out to be mythic.

Ingmar Bergman,* in a speech from the opening scene of *Fanny and Alexander*, put it this way:

> OSCAR
>
> . . . My only talent, if you can call it talent in my case, is that I love this little world inside the thick walls of this playhouse. And I'm fond of the people who work in this little world. Outside is the big world, and sometimes the little world succeeds for a moment in reflecting the big world, so that we understand it better. Or is it perhaps that we give the people who come here the chance of forgetting for a while . . .

---

*Ingmar Bergman, *Fanny and Alexander* (Panthean Books , 1983) p. 26

Acknowledgements

First, I should like to express my thanks to those people in my life from whom I have learnt a lot: my parents, Mary and Peter Potter, to whom this book is dedicated; Rus Gandy,.who was an invaluable friend and adviser when I was formulating many of my teaching ideas; and my husband, Brian Clark, for our many stimulating discussions about every aspect of this book, and for his detailed feedback on the manuscript.

I should also like to thank: those of my students in Britain, Canada, Denmark and Greece who have participated in the writing workshops and so contributed to the growth of much of the material in this book; Professor Brian Huberman of Rice University Media Centre, for our many enjoyable conversations about mythology and the Western genre; and Norman Jewison, for inviting me to run the first workshop at the Canadian Center for Advanced Film Studies when it opened in 1988.

Finally, my gratitude to the British Film Institute, especially Jim Adams and Jackie Morris; U.I.P.; Contemporary; the Kobal Library; and John Schlesinger for use of his personal stills library.

Index

Aquirre, Wrath of God 208
aim, in classic narrative 86
Akerman, Chantal 162, 164, 165
Alcoriza, Luis 234
Alejandro, Julio 101, 150, 234
Alice in the Cities 208
Allen, Woody 154
aloneness and creativity 196
Andersson, Bibi 19
antagonists 113
Antonioni, Michelangelo 153, 154
Apartment, The 234
archetypes 67, 68, 75; feminine 165–6,
    167; *For a Few Dollars More* 69–75;
    masculine 165–6
Arieti, Silvano 196, 197, 198, 199
Aristotle 41, 85, 86, 88, 89, 90, 91, 154,
    160, 165, 239
audience: communication with 191–2;
    expectations of 21–2; effect of
    narrative departures on 151, 153, 154
Australian Aborigines, and archetypes
    68
auteur theory 233
authorship 233
autobiographical story-telling 198–9
Avventura, L' 153–4

beginnings: in classic narrative 88;
    Midnight Cowboy 93–101; *Viridiana*
    101–14
Bell, Alexander Graham 197
Belle de Jour 234
Berger, John 160, 238
Bergman, Ingmar: *Fanny and Alexander*
    198, 233, 240; film, ingredients 6, 82;
    film language 56, 64–5, 206; image,
    primacy of 6, 82, 206; interior

landscape 23; *Persona* 8, 9, 12, 17, 21,
    23, 170, 177; screenplays 233; *Wild
    Strawberries* 41, 42, 43, 49, 56, 64–5,
    233–4
Bertolucci, Bernardo 49, 56, 57, 234;
    film language 64, 65
Bettelheim, Bruno 192, 239
body language and gesture, use of 32
Bondarchuk, Sergei 156
Borowczyk, Walerian 236
Brackett, Charles 234
Bresson, Robert 236
Buñuel, Luis 101, 114, 145, 149,
    234–5

Cannes film festival 154
Carriere, Jean-Claude 234
catalysts 152, 153
catharsis 41, 88, 187
change, and narrative form 166
chaos, defined 39; science of 165
characterization 215; in classic
    narrative 87; dialogue in 215;
    empathy in 216–17; and story 215;
    training in 217–18, 226
Cimino, Michael 154, 155, 158, 159,
    160
classic narrative form: change and 166;
    departures from 151–69; feminine
    aspect and 166–7, 170; structure,
    basic principles 86–9; transformation
    and 166; economy, principle of 110;
    unity, principle of 110
Classical Literary Criticism (Aristotle)
    89n, 155n
climax in classic narrative 88–9,
    135
collective unconsciousness 165

Index

commercial and cultural values, conflict between 2
communication with audience 191–2
conceptual basis of film 1
conflict: and creativity 198–9, 214
Conformist, The (Il Conformista): film language 64, 65; memory sequence 49–57
connections, making 23
Connolly, Ray 198
Conversing with Mother 64
Costa-Gavras, Constantin 213
creative process 170; introduction to 191–5
creativity, preconditions for 196–9
Creativity: The Magic Synthesis (Arieti) 196
credits, opening 19
crisis in classic narrative 88, 135
cultural and commercial values, conflict between 2

Dauman, Anatol 236
Davis, Terence 198
daydreaming, and creativity 197
Dentellière, La, see *Lacemaker, The*
determinism, linear rational 165
development sequences in classic narrative 88, 89
dialogue: characterization and 215; editing 219; expositional 29–30; functions of 219–21, 226; and psychological subtext 220; recording 219; secondary importance 6; and silence 225–6; and text-effect method 222–6
dialogue writing: as craft 218–21; fear of 215–16
Diamond, I. A. L. 234
directors: collaboration with writers 234–5; individual life view 151; role in cinema 233; in theatre 232; and writers 233–5
discipline, and creativity 199
Discreet Charm of the Bourgeoisie, The 234
Distant Voices, Still Lives 198
Double Indemnity 234
dramatic irony, in classic narrative 88
dramatic narrative form 85

dramatic question, in classic narrative 87
dreams 39, 40; depiction of 56; language 39, 56; life experience in 65; *Wild Strawberries* 41–9
Dreamtime, The 68
Duras, Marguerite 226, 235

Eastwood, Clint 69
economy 89–90, 110
editing, importance of 219
Effie Briest 68
ego, role in transformation or change 166
empathy: importance of 216–17; training 217–18, 226
endings: in classic narrative 88; *Midnight Cowboy* 135–42; *Viridiana* 142–50
Enigma of Kaspar Hauser, The 209
eskimos, sculpture 209
expectations of audience 21–2
exposition in classic narrative 87
expositional dialogue 29–30
Exterminating Angel, The 234–5

fairy stories 151, 238–9; and rites of passage 239
Fanny and Alexander 198; opening 240; screenplay 233–4
fantasies 39–41; *Kaos* 57–64, 65
Fassbinder, Rainer Werner 68
Fast Fade (Yule) 198
fears and hopes in classic narrative 87
feature film see film
feedback, giving and receiving of 232
female types 160–1
feminine aspect and classic narrative form 166–7, 170
femininity, repression of 165–6
film: theme 23; conceptual basis 1; primary factor 6, 82, 206; on television 5; time, compressed 39–40, 56; as universal medium 2; as hybrid 85; inner structure 86; as microcosm 6; alternative structure 151
film industry: director's role 233; and writers 191; writer's role 233; as entertainment medium 2; relation to market 191

244

film language: constant change 41;
ingredients of 6, 7; use of 24, 38, 64,
65, 66
film noir 161
first draft screenplay 228
first read through 231
Fitzcarraldo 208
*For A Few Dollars More (Per Qualche
Dollari in più)* 68–75; archetypes in
70–1, 74–5; climax 68, 69–75
form as formula 92
free-association 197
free-thinking, and creativity 197
free-writing 201–6; first draft form
229–30
Freud, Sigmund 68, 74, 160

gathering material 212–14
generating material 200–12
genre 155; disruption of 155
gesture and body language, use of
32
Godard, Jean-Luc 236
gods, dramas of 90
Gone With the Wind (Mitchell) 161
Goretta, Claude 32, 33
Greeks, Ancient: archetypes 68; basic
structures 85
gullibility and creativity 197–8

Heaven's Gate 154–60; protagonist 156,
159
Herlihy, James Leo 93
Herzog, Werner 208–9
Heston, Charlton 27
Hiroshima Mon Amour 226, 235
holistic writing method 228–9
home, and story-telling 238
hopes and fears in classic narrative 87
Hurt, John 155

identification: in classic narrative 87;
intimacy and 215; and recognition
through metaphor 67–8; and
vulnerability 114
images: and action, dramatic build up
38; gathering 206–7; as metaphors
67; personal relationship with 206;
primacy of 6, 82, 206; sequences in
film 2; and sound, relationship 6;
subtext of 21

image-sound level, remoulding at 151,
154, 155
inactivity, and creativity 196
index cards, scene descriptions on
229
information, withholding 77
Interiors 154
interrupted monologues 219
intimacy, and identification 215
irony, dramatic, in classic narrative
88

Jacobs, Jolande 68n
Jane Eyre (Brontë) 161
judgement, untimely 197–8
Jung, C. G. 68, 165

Kaos: boundaries, blurred 65; fantasy
sequence 57–64, 65; metaphor in 67,
77, 81–2; opening 57–64; pre-credit
sequence 75–82
Kekule von Stradonitz, F. A. 197
Kings of the Road 208
Kristofferson, Kris 155
Kurosawa 153, 217

Lacemaker, The (La Dentellière) 32–8;
film language, use 38; gesture and
body language in 32, 33, 36–8
language, film, see film language
Last Year at Marienbad 235
Leigh, Janet 27
leitmotives, psychological 199
Leone, Sergio 68–9, 70, 155, 208
linear story 5, 21
linear structure 86
linear writing method 228, 229

Macbeth (Shakespeare) 154, 217
Magnificent Seven, The 153
market: audience as 191–2; writers and
191
material: gathering 212–14; generating
200–12
matriarchal epoch 165, 166
memory 39, 40; *Conformist, The* 47–57;
details of 40; editing, natural 219;
language 39; life experience in 65;
repressed 40; selective 40; traumatic
40–1, 198, 199; trigger 51–2; in
creativity 197, 202, 217, 219

Index

Mercer, David 235
metaphor 67; *Kaos* 77–82; recognition and identification through 67–8; in creativity 197
microcosm 5–6; feature films as 6
Midnight Cowboy: aim 100; beginning 93–101, 215; climax 135, 139, 142; cowboy motif 137, 138, 141; crisis 135, 138; dramatic question 96, 136; ending 135–42; episodic structure 92; hopes and fears, 99, 100–1; motifs 124; motivation 97, 100; obstacles 96, 100, 139; original screenplay 221–5; outline 115–25, 228; protagonist 100; resolution 140, 142
Mildred Pierce 161
Mirror 167–9
Missing 213–14
Mitcham, Robert 226
montage 8; opening of *Persona* 9–19, 21, 22
moral responsibility 90–1
moral stance 23
motivation in classic narrative 87
myths 68; as archetypal stories 239

narrative, basic principles 151
novelists, creative flow 201

obstacles, in classic narrative 87
Oedipus myth 68
opening, in classic narrative 88, 89
openness, vulnerability and 193
optimism in fairy stories 239
outline 228–9, 230; dual purpose 230; as sales document 230, 235

Pasolini, Pier-Paolo 152–3, 234
past traumatic conflicts, and creativity 198–9, 214
pastiche 192
patriarchal epoch 165, 166
patterns, seeing 23
Per Qualche Dollari in più, see *For A Few Dollars More*
Persona: crisis and climax 178–87; development sequence 170–7; feminine aspect in 170; interior landscape 23; opening credits 19;

opening montage 8–21, 177, 183, 187; subject of 8; subtext 177
Pinter, Harold 226, 236
Pirandello, Luigi 57
place, developing a sense of 209–12
'plants' in classic narrative 88, 104–5
Poetics, The (Aristotle) 90
poetry, similarity to film 22, 234
Polanski, Roman 217
portraits exercise 217–18, 226
predictability, drama and 38
premise, in classic narrative 86
process, definition of 194
producers, role 235–6
production company 236
protagonist: aggressively striving 160, 166; aim 160; in classic narrative 86, 152, 153; effective 160; multiple 153; passive 165; woman as 160–5
Providence 235
psychoanalysis 40, 68, 165
psychological leitmotives 199
psychological subtext, and dialogue 220
Puttnam, David 198, 235

readiness for recognizing similarities, and creativity 197
recognition: and identification through metaphor 67–8; of similarities 167
rejection, protection from 193
religion, archetypes in 68
remembrance of past traumatic conflicts and creativity 198–9, 214
Rendez-vous d'Anna, Les: female protagonist 162–5
repetition 22
research 212–14
Resnais, Alain 235, 236
resolution in classic narrative 89
responsibility, man's 90
Return of the Goddess (Whitmont) 165
rites of passage, fairy stories and 239
Robbe-Grillet, Alain 235
Rocky 198

Salt, Waldo 93, 220
Sartre, Jean-Paul 74
scene descriptions, outline 228–9, 230
Schlesinger, John 93

Schlöndorff, Volker 236
screenplay: authorship 233–5; first
    draft 200, 228; first read-through
    231; outline 228–9, 230; overall
    rhythm 225; producer's role 235–6;
    role 195; routine and writing
    discipline 230; text-effect method
    226; writer as director 233; writing
    methods 228
screenwriters, see writers
screenwriting, see writing
Sculpting in Time (Tarkovsky) 86
sculpture, eskimos 209
self, as stranger 201
self-discipline 199
self-discovery 192–3, 194, 200–1
self-expression, artistic 193
sense of place, developing 209–12
sensibility 5; raising 5
Servant, The 226
Seven Samurai 153
silence, importance of 225–6
similarities, recognizing, and creativity
    197
Simon, John 6n
Smultronstallet, see Wild Strawberries
Some Like It Hot 234
sound: to shift attention 25; and
    image, relationship between 6;
    secondary importance 6; uses 22
source material 212
Spaghetti Westerns 155
Stallone, Sylvester 198
Stamp, Terence 152
story 8; autobiographical 198–9; basic
    principles 151; characterization and
    215; expectations of 151; success,
    factors affecting 32
story-outline 228–9, 230; dual purpose
    230; as sales document 230, 235
story-telling 238
stranger, self as 201
structural analysis: dangers of 92;
    feature films 151
structure, inner 85; in classic narrative
    86–9; concepts of 93; dynamic
    energy of 85; linear 86; sense of 152;
    and unity 152
Sturges, John 153
subtext: of images 21; psychological,
    and dialogue 220

Sunset Boulevard 234
surprise 22

Taming of the Shrew, The (Shakespeare)
    161
Tarkovsky, Andrey 85–6, 167, 169, 236
Taviani, Paolo 57, 65, 75, 208
Taviani, Vittorio 57, 65, 75, 208
text-effect method, and dialogue 226
That'll Be the Day 198
theatre: director's role 232; writer's
    role in 232–3
theme, in classic narrative 89
Theorem 152–3; protagonists 152–3
time, compressed 39–40, 56
Touch of Evil: exposition in 29; film
    language, use 38; opening 23, 24–31
transformation and classic narrative
    form 166
truth 192
TV, film drama on 5

Ullmann, Liv 20
unconscious self 39, 194; generation of
    material 201–6, 212; importance 201
unity: in classic narrative 89, 110;
    sense of, striving for 89; structure
    and 152
untimely judgement 197–8
Uses of Enchantment, The (Bettelheim)
    192, 239

Van Cleef, Lee 69
Viridiana: aim 110; antagonist 110, 113;
    beginning 101–14; crisis 145; cross
    and crown of thorns motif 149;
    dramatic question 106; ending 142–
    50; exposition 102; hopes and fears
    114; Last Supper image 142–3, 145,
    150; motivation 113; obstacles 102,
    104, 113, 149; outline 125–34, 228;
    'plants' in 104, 109, 110; protagonist
    110; resolution 148; scapegoat,
    avoided 145, 150; screenplay 234;
    skipping motif 146, 147; structure 92;
    themes, intertwined 150; timing,
    and dramatic effect 112; woman
    protagonist in 161
Voight, Jon 93
Volonte, Serge 69

Index

vulnerability: identification and 114; and openness 193

War and Peace 156
Ways of Seeing (Berger) 160
Welles, Orson 23–4, 31
Wenders, Wim 208, 236
Western genre 155, 159; mythology of 155, 159
Whitmont, Edward 165–6
Wild Strawberries (Smultronstallet): dream sequence 42–9, 56; film language 64–5; metaphor in 67; pre-credit sequence 41–2, 49; screenplay 233–4
Wilder, Billy 234–5
Wings of Desire 208

woman: passive role 161–2; as protagonist 160–5; types 160–1
writer collaborators 234–5
writer-directors 233–4
writers 191; development 194, 200; directors and 233–5; film industry and 191; individual life view 151; openness 193; status 236; team spirit 236–7; in theatre 232–3; working methods 200
writing: discipline and routine 230; first read through 231; methods 228; as profession 236–7
writing group, feedback from 232
writing partner, feedback from 232

Yule, Andrew 198n